S0-AKK-504

Alaska Viking

©1992 Hal Gage

Alaska Viking
An Autobiography

Keith Austin Iverson

Keith Iverson
8/95
Off DA!

R & P Publishing
Homer, Alaska

R & P Publishing
Post Office Box 2265
Homer, AK 99603-2265

Copyright © 1992 by Keith Iverson

All rights reserved, including the right to reproduce this book or portions thereof in any form without written permission from the author.

Library of Congress Catalog Card Number 91-68483

ISBN 0-9631375-0-6

Lines from "The Road Not Taken" from *The Poetry of Robert Frost*, copyright © 1969, reprinted by permission of Henry Holt and Company, Inc., New York, N.Y.

First Edition

Cover art by Steve Herbert
Cover design by Chris Kent
Back cover photograph by Tom Walker

Printed in the United States of America

For Pearl and Julian, who created me out of love, guided my early years, and stood by me through good times and bad.

ACKNOWLEDGMENTS

Writing and self-publishing my autobiography was an adventure that I never could have completed without the help of Steve Levi, Tom Walker, Tom Bodett, Art Davidson, Kathy Hatch, Polly Hess, Chris Kent, Steve Herbert, Chris Lopez, Tony DeMichele, Scott Semans, Anne Gainey, Bob and Edie Gould, Billy Choate, Anne Marie Holensven, Peter Buser, Judith Brogan, Bill and Dolores Butler, Tom Choquette, Will File, Sam and Joyce Crawford, Linda Kerr, Don and Marcia Nattress, Rick Oldham, Sue Parker, Mac and Kimball McIlvain, Randy Brandon, Glen Bracale, Marina Schaum, Beth Graber, Steve Curtis, Gregg and Helen Parsley, Dan Poynter, and everyone else who contributed their suggestions and support.

Special thanks to my editor, Linda Gunnarson, for making the rewrites fun; Hal Gage and Shannon Weiss, for their help with self-publishing; my sister, Julie Norman, for her loving encouragement; and the book's sponsors.

A few names in the book have been changed, on request, to protect these people's privacy.

CONTENTS

PREFACE

It took nearly fifty years to live this book, with the last five of those years spent writing it. During the process of reliving my life and writing the story, I came to a better understanding of myself, the road that led me from the city to Alaska, and the challenges of a wilderness life. I also became more aware of the world outside my isolated home in Sadie Cove and made a commitment to help preserve the land that I love.

The story of the *Exxon Valdez* oil spill is more detailed than other episodes in this book because of the importance of this disaster to Alaska and the rest of the world. It was just one battle in the environmental struggle, but my experience on the front lines of the cleanup effort showed me that the survival of both nature and humankind depends upon a pledge from each and every person to preserve our home—planet Earth.

Early Adventures

The red-eyed dragon on the prow of our Viking longship stares ahead into the dense fog that hangs over the calm sea. My battle station is midships, and I join the other thirty-one oarsmen as we stroke our 72-foot warship through the frigid waters. Our long beards and the animal skins we wear protect us from the cold. Swords, spears, and battle axes as sharp as Odin's lightning lie at our feet, ready for instant action. Horned helmets and shields glisten in the damp silence.

This ship of stern men and I are joined in a common bond—a Viking adventure to raid a small coastal village somewhere ahead in the fog. Norse blood fuels our bulging muscles as they easily propel our ship through the sea, out of the fog, and into dazzling sunshine. The gods have been good to us, for dead ahead a mile away lies our objective—a cluster of weather-beaten buildings set back from a gravel beach.

Our valiant leader bellows the command to attack, and the longship surges ahead as every back bends to the oars. As the wooden keel touches bottom, we grab our weapons and charge up the beach toward a tall, ancient building that looks like a watchtower. The Berserkers—those Viking madmen who lead the attack—rush ahead, kick in the door, and disappear inside.

I approach the same entry with my battle axe held high, its razor-sharp edge thirsting for blood. A sign over the door reads "Salty Dawg Saloon, Homer, Alaska." I have the strange feeling I've been here before.

As we enter the dimly lit room, I and my Viking brothers are struck dumb by the scene before us. The saloon is filled with beautiful women drinking pale ale from golden goblets. We drop our weapons and give a lusty cheer, for we know we have entered Valhalla, Viking heaven, and these fair maids are the Valkyries welcoming us to an eternity of revelry.

Odin, my hundred-pound husky, jumps on the bed and starts licking my face. The dream lingers, and I smile, wishing I could return to my fantasy. Knowing it's impossible, I tell my dog Odin about my Norwegian ancestors. For three hundred years the Vikings were the world's greatest adventurers, warriors, and merchants, sailing their open wooden longships south to England, Ireland, Scotland, and mainland Europe. Exploring north and west, they settled in Iceland, Greenland, and for a short time in North America, which they discovered five hundred years before Columbus. The word "Viking" was originally a verb, even though today we use the term to signify the early Scandinavian peoples of Norway, Denmark, and Sweden. To them, to go viking was to go on a raid or an adventure.

Odin and I leap out of bed and start the day. With my first steaming cup of coffee, I walk out onto the deck, inhale the chilly fall air, notice the snow is lower on the mountain, and turn up the collar of my wool shirt. The calendar says it's October 1990—the day isn't important.

Looking out over the calm waters of Sadie Cove, Alaska, where I have built my home and a new life over the past seventeen years, I can't help comparing my wilderness world with that of my Viking forefathers. As they did, I live close to nature, but instead of sailing a longship and carrying a battle axe, I travel by motorized skiff and wield a hammer. We both made our homes in the deep blue fjords of the north, but they had new lands to explore and conquer, whereas I must be content to master myself and the disciplines of living in the wilderness. Vikings and Alaska are synonymous with adventure, and that is what brought me to this last frontier.

In looking back over my life, I can see the path that led me north. Instead of being born Keith the Blond of Norway in 900 A.D., I was born Keith the Iverson of America in 1942. My earliest memories are of my mother and father—Pearl and Julian—in Coeur d'Alene, Idaho, the town of my birth. Along with my sister, Julie, and brother, Jon, I was raised by loving parents and relatives.

Grandma and Grandpa Iverson often took me trout fishing. Grandpa, with his well-chewed cigar clenched in his teeth, would show me how to put a wiggling worm on a hook, and while Grandma spread out the picnic lunch, she would say in her lilting Norwegian accent, "By golly, Keith! I tink I yust heard a big one yump."

Aunt Mabel and Uncle Jake had a rustic cabin on a small lake where they helped me catch a whiskered old bullhead that lived under their dock. Aunt Irene and Uncle Carl were always good for an afternoon of swimming at Sander's Beach or fishing for sunfish off the rocky shores of Tubs Hill. Those hot summer evenings spent on the bank of a slow-moving river, fast-flowing stream, or quiet and calm lake began my love affair with nature.

Each summer, the family would spend two weeks vacationing at a rented cabin on Coeur d'Alene Lake. Fishing, swimming, boating, and hiking filled my days, and adventures beckoned from around every tree and down every trail. Getting into trouble was easy for a tow-headed, freckle-faced kid exploring the wonders of the woods.

I remember, as if it were yesterday, my first adventure. Everyone but me had gone inside the cabin. As the light faded and the air cooled, I started down to the beach—the bullfrogs were calling. I lowered myself to the ground and began slowly crawling through the tall grass toward one especially loud ree-beep. Looking back over my shoulder at the distant light from the cabin window, I became aware that I was alone in the dark. At first, I got so scared I almost peed in my pants and ran back screaming; but then a frog croaked, and I knew I had to catch one, even if the boogeyman caught me and I got warts.

I held my breath as I sprang forward and trapped a big croaker under my shirt. With my trophy struggling in my hands, I ran back to the cabin to show the family my prize. Upon entering the kitchen, I yelled, "Mom! Dad! Come see what I got."

From the living room, Dad called back, "Wash up first."

I couldn't wash my hands and hold the squirming frog, so I stuffed it into a big pot on the stove and slapped on the lid. Mom walked in as I was drying my hands and took the cover off the pot. The bullfrog sprang for freedom, Mom screamed and fainted, Dad ran in to help Mom, and I stood there knowing I was in big trouble— I'd just killed my mother.

To my relief, Mom recovered, but Dad sent my frog back to the lake and gave me a stern lecture. Later that night I heard a coyote howl and went to sleep wondering how hard it would be to catch one.

My second-grade year was a memorable one. Our family moved to Portland, Oregon, where I was put back a grade due to reading problems. With Mom and Dad's help, my studies became easier, and life in school started looking up.

At eleven years old I experienced my first summer camp, going with the other members of my Hi-Y Club to Spirit Lake at the base of

Mount St. Helens in Washington State. While we were loading our gear into the boat that would transport us to Camp Mehan at the far end of the lake, I met an older man who introduced himself as Harry Truman. I asked him how he had liked being the president and got a chuckle in reply as he pushed us off the shore.

Upon arriving at camp we met our counselor, Omar, who for the next three weeks would be our mother, father, and taskmaster. Omar wasted no time informing us he wanted to get in shape for his coming football season and challenged us to break the camp record for a four-day hike. I'm not sure if we had any choice, but we agreed anyway.

The morning we began, we were all eager to set a new camp record. When we got to the top of Goat Mountain, I felt like I was going to die. Though I was the smallest of our group, I carried one of the biggest loads. The rugged, rutted trail was steep, and my heavy pack felt like it wanted to suck me into the ground. I vowed to keep up with the others, and I found if I thought of other things, it took my mind off the pain.

When the hike ended, we had set a new record—sixty-four miles in four days. I felt proud of our achievement and relieved as I took off my pack for the last time. As I soaked my blistered feet in the lake, I realized my size didn't matter in the woods.

Later, while attending Madison High School in northeast Portland, I studied hard to get good grades, sang in the choir, wrestled varsity for four years, and worked a variety of jobs to save money for college.

The state of Oregon is blessed with a variety of natural wonders, and, with my high-school buddies Mike Reinhart and Vic Spainhower, I explored its outdoors. We swam at Rooster Rock, hiked on Mount Hood, and walked the long, white beaches of the coast, where the endless waves roll in from the Pacific Ocean.

Our favorite area was Eagle Creek, with its clear, cold, fast-moving water and good trout fishing. After driving up the Columbia Gorge, we would park our car at the end of the road and hike up a trail cut into the side of the cliff. We had a secret spot where we camped next to the creek and spent many evenings around a fire getting smoke in our eyes, eating the fish we caught, and talking about how we wished we could stay there forever.

The University of Oregon accepted me after my graduation from high school in 1961. To earn the money to begin classes in the fall, I worked in the woods for the U.S. Forest Service at Zig Zag Ranger Station on Mount Hood. My crew fought fires and built trails that would eventually become logging roads. We worked in the Bull Run area, where the virgin forests of fir, hemlock, and cedar had never heard the roar of a chainsaw or the lumberjack's call of "Timber."

When the summer ended, I took the $600 I'd saved; put away my caulk boots, double-bit axe, and hard hat; packed my city clothes, slide rule, and expectations; and headed off to college.

I was eighteen years old when I registered as a pre-med student at the University of Oregon in Eugene. Studying, intramural sports, dorm life, and falling in love every other day kept me busy. On pledging Sigma Phi Epsilon fraternity, I added more activities to my schedule and started making lists to keep everything organized. With my new friends, we held all-night bull sessions where we discussed, argued, and theorized on everything from women to war, money to medicine, and politics to philosophy.

After my first term, I returned home to Portland for the Christmas holidays with average grades and the need to get some outdoor exercise. I went skiing on Mount Hood with my buddy Jack and on the last downhill run broke my leg.

The next day, my sour mood changed to one of hopeful anticipation after making a date with an old high-school girlfriend. That night we drove to our favorite parking place on Rocky Butte, and I "became a man" in the front seat of a 1950 Plymouth. As the windows fogged over and our heavy breathing rose to a frantic pitch, my cast got tangled in the steering wheel and started the horn honking. The magic moment I'd so often dreamed about didn't exactly live up to my expectations, but I no longer needed to lie about my virginity.

In spring my fraternity held its big annual dance, called Odin's Orgy. Since Odin was a Viking god, we dressed ourselves in animal skins, wore horned helmets, and hung wooden swords on our rope belts. The party started when we took our dates to a secluded park, where we emptied several kegs of beer and ate barbecued steaks and corn-on-the-cob with our hands. After creating general mayhem in the woods, we returned to the fraternity house, where we danced, tried to convince our dates that free love was okay at an orgy, and generally made fools of ourselves before getting sick. For one night the Viking spirit lived on at the University of Oregon.

During my sophomore year, I began organizing a trip to Europe with four fraternity brothers. When my parents learned of my plans, they were against it. If I dropped out of school, they argued, I would never return to finish college. I told them the trip was just another part of my education.

After finishing my sophomore year, I worked in the woods to earn the money for my travels. While surveying in big-timber country, I became sick, and to my surprise my doctor told me I had two ulcers. A special diet cured my illness, and the draft board changed my classification from 1-S (student status) to 1-Y (draftable only in a national emergency).

The trip to Europe was planned for January 1964, but as the hot summer months passed into a rainy fall, one by one my friends decided not to go. Unlike me, they would be drafted if they dropped out of college. Now I had to make a decision. Do I go alone, or do I forget my urge to travel, take the conservative road, and go back to school? I decided to go to Europe.

My viking began the first week of 1964 as I drove from Oregon to New York City. As an inexperienced twenty-one-year-old from Portland, I wasn't prepared for what I found in that crowded city of 8 million impersonal, noisy, intriguing people. It was exactly what I needed to further my development.

At the end of January I boarded the Holland America ship *Ryndam* and sailed for Europe. Those eleven days at sea were filled with delicious meals, drinking, dancing, and staying up most of the night singing folk songs to guitar music. A shipboard romance complete with champagne and moonlit nights advanced my worldly education.

Upon disembarking at Rotterdam, in the Netherlands, I and a group of friends from the ship drove to the Winter Olympics in Innsbruck, Austria. In this charming town nestled in the Alps, I met people from all over the world, learned how to yodel, and cheered the American athletes. Two weeks later I took a train south to the warm beaches of Spain.

As winter warmed to spring, I rode my thumb and hitch-hiked along the French Riviera to Rome. During my three-week stay, I slept in a youth hostel, ate local workers' food, and tried learning a few words of Italian. The language barrier seemed to relax after I bought a classical guitar in a shop near the Coliseum and started learning to play it among the ancient ruins. Music became my ambassador in the cities and on the road.

In the next three months I traveled through Italy, France, Belgium, and Germany, enjoying the food, art, and history and meeting many friendly, open, and caring people.

After passing through Denmark and Sweden, I arrived in Oslo on May 17, Norway's Independence Day. Fortunately, the Scandinavians spoke better English than I did Norwegian, because all I could remember from my childhood was "Ya, sure, ya betcha," and "*Drit te buxa*" (a baby pooping in its pants).

At a party I met blonde-haired, blue-eyed Synnøve. We spent the next week touring Oslo, and Synnøve taught me a great deal about my Norwegian and Viking ancestry. The more I learned, the prouder I became, and I vowed to do something exciting with my life.

Reluctantly, I left the land of *lutefisk* (fish) and *lefsa* (flat bread) and boarded a ship for northeast England, where I continued my hitch-hiking tour. In London I met Al, a young Californian, who like myself was burnt out on museums, statues, and ancient ruins. We were homesick, and it was time to go home.

It was June when Al and I booked passage on a ship back to New York City. At the end of our seven-day voyage across the Atlantic, we joined others on deck and celebrated as the Statue of Liberty welcomed us home. There wasn't a dry eye in the group.

Al and I zipped through the New York World's Fair and then drove Route 66 straight through to California, where I headed north to Portland and the end of my travels. As I pulled up in front of my parents' home, Dad was working out in the yard. When I got out of the car, he didn't recognize me. Maybe it was my longer hair and European clothes, or perhaps I walked a little differently from when I left. He was surprised when I said, "Hi, Dad, your wandering son has returned."

He shook my hand and said, "Welcome home." After looking me over he added, "You've changed!"

As we walked into the house to find Mom, I smiled—I thought so too.

I settled into familiar surroundings and thought back over my travels. My six-month viking had cost $1,500. It had been an education not offered on a college campus, and I was a little older and a lot wiser. Most important, I learned to believe in myself and knew I could make it on my own.

I needed a job to make money for my return to the university in the fall. Finding employment in the middle of the summer was so hard I finally took a job selling Collier encyclopedias door-to-door. While I bruised my knuckles canvassing the neighborhoods in Portland, Dad became the first salesman in the United States to sell $1 million worth of cowboy boots in one year, and we didn't even live in Texas! To my surprise, I made enough money to get back in school and wondered if salesmanship was hereditary.

As a junior at the University of Oregon, I completed my first term of organic chemistry and dropped out of pre-med—six more years in school was not what I wanted to do. But I did want a degree, so I switched my major to the business school.

My senior year, I took advantage of our campus placement service and, through many job interviews with prospective employers, learned how to sell myself. The whole family attended my graduation in August of 1966. At twenty-three years old, I walked down the aisle to receive my diploma—a bachelor of science degree in marketing. Mom and Dad beamed with pride, brother Jon smiled, knowing he'd inherit the Hudson Hornet we'd shared the past year, and sister Julie gave me a big hug and said, "Welcome to the real world."

I'd accepted a sales job with Owens Corning Fiberglass Corporation, and they wanted me to begin work in Los Angeles the week after I graduated. While packing for my move south, I thought about my future. Would I climb the corporate ladder, get married, raise a family, and take early retirement? Or become a playboy with a flashy sports car, date beauty queens, and discover a cure for hangovers? Whatever my road, I was ready to answer the call of the big city.

Breakaway

The job in Los Angeles lasted only six months. When my employer wanted to transfer me to Chicago, I made the decision not to leave the West Coast and quit. After interviewing with Kaiser Industries in the San Francisco Bay Area, I was again working as a salesman in the building industry.

As I drove into the city that would be my new home, the radio was playing, "If you're going to San Francisco, be sure to wear a flower in your hair ... " It was 1967, the "Summer of Love," and the so-called hippie movement had begun. Revolution and marijuana were in the air. The sixties generation defied laws and challenged the establishment with their long hair, colorful clothes, free-spirit philosophy, and drugs. I was coming from a different perspective. I had a crew cut, wore a business suit, believed in the money ethic, and drank martinis. They read *Soul On Ice* and studied Gestalt therapy, while I read *Playboy* and studied how to make a million in a month. They were into awareness; I was into looking good. They gathered at coffee houses, concerts, and around the Cal-Berkeley campus, while I mingled at cocktail parties and attended business meetings in skyscrapers. We all believed in peace, but I supported the war in Vietnam in hopes that it would stop the spread of communism. I was a product of the establishment; they were trying to start a new age of enlightenment.

After two months of apartment living, I bought an unfinished houseboat and moved it to a marina in Alameda. For six months I lived in sawdust, but finally finished my bachelor pad with its black marble bar, Swedish fireplace, spiral staircase, plush upstairs master bedroom, wall-to-wall stereo, thick white-shag carpeting, and electric drapes. To complete the image, I leased a new Porsche and began enjoying the single life.

Living in a marina full of sailboats allowed me to fulfill a long-time interest in sailing. I began crewing on any wind-powered craft that would allow me on board. An afternoon of relaxed sailing was always enjoyable, but the competition of racing gave me the biggest thrill. As my skill grew, so did the size of the boats I helped sail. Eventually, I did most of my sailing on a 36-foot Erickson. The Friday night yacht-club races were more social events than contests, but on weekends we joined hundreds of other boats to race the wind on San Francisco Bay.

The sea was in my blood, but I also had another love—the mountains. Luckily, I met Bill, who introduced me to the high Sierra. We often escaped to the Carson Pass area, where we worked up a good sweat hiking over 9,000-foot passes to fly fish for trout in the clear, cold streams and lakes scattered among the grey, granite peaks.

City life began losing its luster. I'd worked for Kaiser for two years and knew it wasn't what I wanted to do for the rest of my life. So I quit, got my California real-estate license, and began selling recreational property. It took less than a year to see that my life wasn't headed where I wanted it to go. When I got a new job with Kirsch Company as an architectural consultant for the eleven western states and Hawaii, I thought I was back on the right road. However, six months later, I saw that my job wasn't the problem—I was. City life hadn't changed, but I had. I was bored with the social scene and business games and needed help finding a way out of my unhappiness.

The helping hand came from my long-time friend Neil Steinberg when he told me about his experience with encounter groups. The weekly meetings had helped him overcome many of his problems, and he suggested they might help me too. I was willing to give it a try.

At my first encounter-group meeting on the Berkeley campus, I felt as out of place as I would wearing a three-piece suit in the mountains. I walked into the room wearing the newest casual fashion from a vogue men's clothing store and for a moment considered leaving with a remark about being in the wrong building. The dozen young men and women who watched me enter looked like they all shopped at the Salvation Army, and the smell of musky incense totally overshadowed the Old Spice I wore. They were shaggy but clean, and I needed help; so instead of running off, I took a deep breath and joined them.

Our leader introduced himself and then asked each of us to talk about our reasons for joining the group. During the rest of the four-hour session we played a variety of games to help us relax and become more aware of ourselves and those around us. Some exercises involved hugging and making eye contact. This made me very uncomfortable and I shared my feelings with those in the room. After the session, I walked out feeling more relaxed and looked forward to our next meeting.

After eleven meetings and a weekend retreat, I became a strong believer in the merits of encounter groups. Not all my questions were answered, but I made a good start. I saw that we all shared the same problems, insecurities, and guilt. The only thing that made us different was our outward appearance. Feeling good was now more important than looking good, so I let my hair grow a little longer, started reading books on Gestalt therapy, and tried living for the moment.

One fall I had a party on my houseboat to watch the movie *The Vikings* on television. Among my guests were my sister, Julie, and her boyfriend, Hugh. While mixing drinks and talking to Hugh, I learned he'd lived in Norway for three years and spoke fluent Norwegian. Like me he was very interested in Viking culture.

The movie began as I refilled everyone's glasses. When Ragnar (Ernest Borgnine) jumped into the wolf pit, I told my date I wanted a horned helmet and sword for my birthday. By the time Inar (Kirk Douglas) and Eric (Tony Curtis) started throwing battle axes at the castle doors, I was trying to talk Hugh into starting a club called Berserkers International.

When the movie ended, my guests voted to go dancing in San Francisco, but not me—I had already started rowing a small dinghy to the city. Maybe I was getting bored as a city Viking.

I needed to think about my future and wanted a break from the fast lane, so when I met Sandi MacCalla at my twenty-eighth birthday party, I asked her if she would like to spend the Thanksgiving holiday camping in the high Sierra. Sandi had little camping experience and had never been around snow, but she agreed to go.

We drove up to Carson Pass, then strapped on snowshoes, shouldered heavy packs, and hiked into mountains covered with six feet of snow. It took all day to struggle over the steep, icy, 9,000-foot pass that led to a high valley where we planned to spend our relaxing holiday weekend. As darkness descended, we arrived at an abandoned, one-room cabin that would be our home for the next couple of days. Exhausted, we ate a light dinner, zipped our down sleeping bags together, blew out the candle, and fell asleep, surrounded by cold silence.

The next day we woke up with sore, stiff muscles, but we felt good because we'd earned the pain. We spent most of the day gathering firewood to cook and stay warm. I wanted to be alone to do some thinking, so as Sandi relaxed with a book, I took off into the woods. It was time to confront myself and my discontent with the city.

I had nothing to distract me but the cold, so I sat under a gnarled, old tree and pondered my problems. By other people's standards I had a good life, but I wasn't happy. Lately, I'd been in a very bitchy mood—my Porsche had a new dent, and I didn't have enough money to buy more toys. Was happiness based on money and status symbols? It scared me to think I might be in the same rut when I turned sixty-five years old. I didn't like most parts of my city life, yet I stayed. So, what was I going to do about it?

After several hours I saw the solution—I'd quit complaining, stop living by other people's standards, take control of my life, and get out of the city. I'd never know what I was searching for unless I took a chance and began the search.

Snowshoeing back to the warm cabin, I felt like a great weight had been lifted off my shoulders. Later that night my thoughts turned from satisfaction to survival when the worst blizzard in fifteen years hit the Sierra. We woke up when it started snowing inside the cabin. The wailing wind was driving snow through cracks in the walls, and each gust felt like it would destroy our shelter.

At first light, Sandi and I packed our gear and started snowshoeing the six miles to our car. We trudged through deep snow and whiteout conditions, and although the wind had died down, it took us all day to cover two miles. After setting up our tent next to a frozen lake, we spent several hours fixing a meal and melting snow to drink.

As we crawled into our sleeping bags, I heard a jet pass overhead and chuckled at our different situations. The jet's passengers traveled in the luxury of a warm cabin while eating steak, drinking cocktails, and watching a movie as they covered 600 miles in an hour. Sandi and I snuggled in the snow after feasting on freeze-dried French onion soup and Tang and had gained two miles while sweating all day through winter weather. They were warm and secure while we were chilled and surviving; but, I realized, I'd rather be where I was—living an adventure.

The next day seemed to go on forever. It began with a traverse along the base of a cliff to find a route to the top. In the process we triggered an avalanche and narrowly escaped joining the snow as it thundered down the steep slope. Worn out, we reached the top only to face more energy-draining conditions. On level ground, we plowed through snow up to our waists, and even with a compass and topographical map I wasn't sure of our location until we ended our ordeal. Through the whole experience, I admired Sandi's endurance and level-headed persistence.

As darkness arrived, we finally came to the road. We didn't care that our car was completely buried in snow or that we couldn't keep our teeth from chattering—we had made it, and were still hugging when a car stopped and took us into Tahoe.

Both our lives changed because of our wilderness adventure. Sandi decided never to go camping again, and I vowed to leave the city to look for a lifestyle closer to nature.

It took more than a year to break away from the city. To visualize my progress and help cure an occasional case of the doubts, I made a two-part "retirement" chart. The first section showed what equipment I needed: VW camper, 35mm camera, skis, tent, sleeping bag, climbing gear, and fishing supplies. By selling my city belongings, I weakened the chains binding me to my old life and helped buy what I wanted for my travels.

The second part of my chart looked like a barometer showing the $15,000 I wanted for my quest. I'd settled on this amount after many hours of thought. I knew the economics of city living, and my trip to Europe gave me an idea of traveling costs; but there were still many unknowns regarding my future life on the road. If I set the figure too low and then my money ran out, I'd have to return to the city to make more. If I set the figure too high, I might never meet my goal and begin my quest.

The day finally arrived when I had checked off everything on my chart, and I cut the main chain binding me to the city by quitting my job. My last weekend in town, I gave myself a going-away party so that I could say good-bye to my friends.

On May 1, 1972, I left big-city life. I was twenty-nine years old with no obligations except to myself. My first destination was Alaska, where I wanted to spend the summer and fall. Then I planned to return to one of the western states to downhill ski all winter. If my money held out, I would next travel to New Zealand and Australia to see what they had to offer. Would I find what I was looking for? Hell, I didn't know, but I'd have fun trying.

The Search
Chapter 3

Free at last. I'd broken away from the city and given myself two things people rarely have together in their youth—time and money. Now I could go play and at the same time look for that special place to call home.

My destination was Alaska, but I wasn't in a hurry. My quest started when I drove north across the Golden Gate Bridge. The old redwood forests and endless white surf took over my senses and slowed me down. As I drove along the coast in my VW camper, I was singing Joan Baez's "I Live One Day at a Time."

When I putted into Portland, Oregon, I wasn't sure how my Mom and Dad would react to my plans. I valued their opinion but had to do what was right for me. It didn't take long to learn they thought:
I was wasting my education, dropping out of society, running away from my responsibilities, and going through a rebellious phase. I believed I was continuing my education, looking at a different side of society, running toward my responsibilities to myself, and going through a rebellious phase. We didn't change each other's minds, but I still enjoyed the visit.

Most of my time in Portland was spent preparing for my trip to Alaska. To get there I would drive the 1,800-mile Alaska-Canada (Al-Can) Highway, which was mostly unpaved. I bought a copy of the *Milepost* (a guide to services and attractions along the road), purchased containers for extra gasoline, put wire screen over the camper's windshield and headlights to protect them from flying gravel, and collected supplies for flat tires. I hoped my precautions would keep the road mishaps to a minimum.

During my last-minute preparations I met Mindy, and after getting to know each other, she asked to join me. I liked the idea of sharing the road.

It was time to begin our trip, so after saying good-bye we drove out of Portland, through the state of Washington, and crossed the border into Canada. The next several days were spent driving the 600 miles through British Columbia to Dawson Creek, the official beginning of the Al-Can. Along the way we met many others driving north. At night we gathered in campgrounds like gypsies—getting there was half the fun.

The first milestone along the Al-Can was at mile 83.6, where the pavement ended. Ahead lay 1,100 miles of gravel road where the weather dictated the driving conditions. Dry weather meant dust that seemed to work its way into everything. A downpour quickly turned the road into a muddy soup. Regardless, on we went, enjoying the friendly Canadians at roadside facilities and the uninhabited wilderness in between.

Mindy and I took turns at the wheel, and because of the long daylight hours, we usually kept going well into the evening. As we drove, I thought about the road's beginning. The U.S. Army Corps of Engineers built the Al-Can during World War II, shortly after the Japanese invaded and occupied two Aleutian Islands in southwest Alaska. The military believed it would be a vital supply line to help defend the north country, and the road was carved out of the wilderness in an amazing eight months and completed in November of 1942. At mile 496.5 we came to Liard Hot Springs in the Yukon Territory, where we stopped for two days to rest our road-weary rumps. Sitting in a clear, steaming pool with only my head above water, I toasted the road builders of thirty years before.

Rested, relaxed, and water-wrinkled, we continued our trip north to mile 919.4 and Whitehorse, the biggest city in the Yukon Territory. At this thriving town on the bank of the Yukon River, we enjoyed the paved streets, visited the paddle-wheel boats, replenished our supplies, cringed at the cost of gasoline, and were soon back on the road.

To break up the seemingly endless miles, Mindy and I took many rest stops to hike and fish. Around every bend a new mountain beckoned, and we stopped counting the lakes, rivers, and streams we saw. We tried our luck fishing for grayling, mackinaw, and northern pike and were seldom disappointed, even when we cast into waters right next to the road. The vastness and beauty of this northern wilderness made up for the many hours spent driving.

At mile 1,221.8 we reached our goal—Alaska. Before going through the U.S. Customs office, I stopped the camper, got out, dropped to my knees, and kissed the pavement. I couldn't have been happier to get off the gravel road unless Alaska's Governor Bill Egan had been there to welcome us personally. Instead, we were greeted by a friendly Customs official, who asked if we had any drugs as he looked through the camper. I answered, "We don't do drugs, but we have been known to take a snort of whiskey."

He smiled and said, "Enjoy your stay." Then he waved us on.

It was pure pleasure to drive on pavement again, and I automatically increased our speed. A few miles down the road I learned of my dangerous mistake when I saw the first "Bump" sign just as the camper went airborne. A little further on was a sign that read "Dip," and as the road dropped out from under us, I slowed down—we weren't in any hurry anyway.

As we drove to Fairbanks, Mindy read aloud from a history book we'd bought about the Frontier State. The name Alaska comes from the Aleut word *Alaxsxaq*, meaning the place where the sea breaks on itself—the Aleuts' way of saying mainland. Europeans "discovered" Alaska in 1741, when Vitus Bering, a Dane exploring for Russia, sighted the mainland and claimed it for his employer. At that point, the Eskimos, Indians, and Aleuts had lived there for at least 11,000 years. The United States bought Alaska from Russia in 1867 for $7.2 million, or just two cents an acre. The purchase was called Seward's Icebox or Seward's Folly, since Secretary of State William Seward negotiated the sale for what most Americans considered nothing but worthless ice and snow.

When we visited in 1972, the forty-ninth state had a population of 324,000 people sharing 586,000 square miles of land. To put its size into perspective, if Alaska were cut in half, Texas would be the third-largest state.

Mindy and I drove into Fairbanks, the state's second-biggest city and end of the Al-Can Highway, at mile 1,523. I'd driven almost 3,000 miles since leaving San Francisco, almost all due north. It felt good knowing so much untouched wilderness remained on our planet. The trip had already exceeded my expectations and we still had Alaska to explore.

Fairbanks, located in the state's interior, was having a heat wave. Although this city is very close to the Arctic Circle, we were stripped down to shorts and T-shirts in the 90° F heat. Talking to local folks, we learned that winter temperatures regularly dropped below -40° F. I began to realize this was a land of extremes.

The people were friendly, helpful, proud of their state, and often outspoken. On a side trip out of town, I pulled off the road to take a picture of a moose, and before we could get going again, two drivers of cars with Alaska license plates stopped to see if we needed help. A bumper sticker on the second good Samaritan's car read "We don't give a damn how they do it Outside." I couldn't help liking these rugged individualists called Alaskans.

While in Fairbanks, I developed the plan I'd follow for the rest of the summer. I'd come to Alaska to experience the wilderness, but I realized that the cities also were a big part of the state's personality. Mindy and I would drive the roads and visit the towns, but still spend most of our time in the wilds, or what Alaskans called the Bush. With my general plan formulated, we headed south for Valdez, a small town on the coast.

Driving to Valdez, we crossed long stretches of rolling hills, drove through lush green valleys, and maneuvered over stark mountain passes. I was constantly awed by the vast beauty of the ever-changing scenery and the abundance of wildlife. The reflection of a snowcapped peak in a clear, blue lake or fields of yellow and red wildflowers appeared with such frequency we quit pointing them out to each other. However, we made a contest out of seeing who could spot wildlife first. Our feeble attempts to capture the essence of this wild land on film were only an excuse to linger a moment longer and overload our senses with its wonders.

I felt free knowing I was living with no time frame other than the seasons. It was good waking up in the morning not knowing what surprise the day would bring.

In the middle of heavily forested wilderness we suddenly came upon cars parked bumper to bumper on both sides of the road. They lined the highway on each end of a bridge, and as we slowed to look at the river, I got a glimpse of people standing shoulder to shoulder along the bank. As I searched for a parking place, I wondered if someone had drowned and they were dragging for the body.

Mindy and I walked back to the bridge for a closer look and found the people were fishing for salmon. This was a form of fishing I'd never seen before. As we watched, I began to laugh at the humor of the situation.

Hundreds of bright red salmon crowded the river, but they seemed outnumbered by the fishermen along the shore. The salmon were frantically trying to work their way upstream to spawn while the people were in a fishing frenzy as they jerked their rods back and forth in hopes of snagging a fish. Red, yellow, green, and gold lures flew through the air, landing in the water, bushes, and occasionally on other fishermen. When an angler hooked a salmon, a shout of "Fish on" rang out, followed shortly by cussing as the fisherman ran along the bank fouling the lines of others in his attempt to land his catch. To add to the excitement, dogs were barking, kids yelling, and several spectators like myself stood back laughing at the action.

I wanted to catch a salmon for dinner, but it looked too dangerous by the bridge, so I got my rod, hiked downriver, and found a quiet hole occupied by one other fisherman. On my third cast I hooked a feisty fish with my light gear. The 10-pound salmon jumped twice and took off downriver as I adjusted the drag on my reel and tried to slow it down. Ten minutes later our evening meal lay on the bank. Now I could catch and release several more, just for the fun of it.

As I leisurely cast into the fast-moving water, I started talking to the fisherman upstream from me. After exchanging a few pleasantries, we both stopped and looked at each other. He said, "Keith, is that you?" It was Jerry, a fraternity brother from college whom I hadn't seen in seven years.

We both forgot about fishing, sat on the bank, and caught up on what we'd been doing since leaving school. Jerry was in the Air Force and stationed at Fairbanks and would soon return to civilian life in Oregon. I was on the road looking for the meaning of life. We were both amazed to meet on a remote river in Alaska. After talking for a while we wished each other good luck and parted. As I walked back to the highway with my fish, I thought, "This sure is a small world!"

The next morning Mindy and I drove into Valdez. Besides the beauty of the mountains and water, we couldn't miss the row upon row of 48-inch pipe stacked in fields next to the highway. Local folks told us the state and federal governments were negotiating with a group of giant oil companies to build a trans-Alaska pipeline from the huge oil fields in Prudhoe Bay to their small town on the shores of Prince William Sound. The 800-mile pipeline would be the world's biggest private-construction project, and the building would soon begin. Mindy and I talked about returning to Valdez to work, but I wasn't really interested. The oil industry held no appeal for me, and I knew it would be just another job where the only incentive would be the money.

We left Valdez and drove the 300 miles to Anchorage, Alaska's largest city. Its 48,000 people lived at the north end of Cook Inlet, hunkered up against the Chugach Mountains. This "All-American City" was beautiful but bustling, and I knew it wouldn't be long before I'd leave for the quiet of the country.

While exploring the main part of town, Mindy and I bought postcards to send to our friends and family in the Lower 48. Every store had pictures of the destruction created by the Good Friday earthquake that devastated Anchorage on March 27, 1964. The 8.4 temblor caused 114 deaths and $750 million in damage. The city had rebuilt, but a walk through eerie Earthquake Park—where slabs of earth tilted at odd angles—served as a grim reminder of nature's powerful forces.

One afternoon Mindy and I found ourselves in a Fourth Avenue bar, quenching our thirst and talking with an old, grizzled sourdough. His name was Jake, and each time he took a drink, the beer bottle disappeared into his bushy white beard. I asked him where he was from, and he replied, "Well, I live out in the Bush, which means there aren't any roads to take me home. I only come to Anchorage once a year for supplies. You two cheechakos couldn't make it where I live."

It sounded like a challenge, but instead of arguing the point, I said, "Guess I wouldn't know until I gave it a try."

We'd read that a cheechako was any newcomer to the state, and a sourdough was a long-time resident; but we weren't sure how to make the transition, so we asked Jake.

He killed another beer, then answered, "To be a sourdough, you have to do three things: piss in the Yukon River, kiss an Alaskan, and kill a polar bear. And don't get the last two mixed up."

We all laughed, but I thought the way he looked, maybe he'd learned the hard way. As we started to leave, Jake put his arm around Mindy and said, "You could be on your way to becoming a sourdough by giving this old Alaskan a kiss."

Mindy smiled and gave him a peck on the cheek. I don't think it was the type of kiss Jake had in mind, but he was a gentleman. After saying good-bye, he added, "I wish you both good luck. To see the real Alaska you have to get out of the city, and out there you'll find what it means to be a sourdough."

Mindy had been a good friend and companion on our month-long trip north, but the time had come for her to fly back to Portland.

In early June, after one last hug at the airport, I drove out of Anchorage and headed south to the Kenai Peninsula.

Everyone I'd talked to—old-timers and cheechakos alike—said the Kenai Peninsula was the outdoors mecca of the state. After fishing her rivers, lakes, and streams, I had to agree. Near Kenai Lake, in a stream with no name, I caught my limit of grayling on spinners. Fly fishing on the Russian River, I caught and released several 10-pound rainbow trout. I wore myself out landing kings and red salmon with light gear and egg clusters on the Kenai River. Most of the fish I caught I returned to the water, keeping only enough for my meals. After two weeks I was getting pretty tired of eating fish. I needed a shower, clean clothes, and some conversation, so I drove south to the town of Homer.

On a warm, cloudless summer day, I parked my camper in a viewing area perched on the top of a high bluff and looked out over the diverse and striking landscape. Homer is nestled along the northern shore of Kachemak Bay and was home to about a thousand people who shared the land with a dark green spruce forest. A finger of land called the Homer Spit juts out from where the road ends to more than four miles into the blue waters of the bay.

From where I stood, the spit seemed to be pointing south across the bay, as if to emphasize the special beauty of that wild, roadless region where the mountains meet the sea. The tree-lined bays and coves rise steeply to the snowy peaks, and squeezing out from the high ice fields were glaciers, their ancient blue ice glowing from centuries past.

As I drove down the bluff road, through town, and out onto the spit, it was love at first sight. This was truly spectacular scenery, and I thought, "Maybe this is the place I've been searching for."

I parked the camper near the end of the spit, walked across the road to a three-story building that looked like a lighthouse, and entered a door under a sign that read "Salty Dawg Saloon, Homer, Alaska." I crossed the sawdust-covered floor and found a seat at the crowded old bar, where customers had carved their names to let others know they'd been there. From their clothes and conversations, I recognized fishermen, local business people, tourists, and a few folks in from the Bush. I knew I'd come to the right place to meet the people of the area.

I saw a guitar resting on the wall, and after a couple of drinks I picked it up and strummed a few chords. Next thing I knew, several folks bought me whiskey in return for requested songs. After a few more cocktails, my shyness took a hike, and as I banged out familiar tunes the whole bar joined the singing. I don't remember all their names, but that night I talked and sang with what seemed like everyone in town.

For the next several days I fished off the long gravel beaches, explored the town, and walked the docks at the boat harbor. While admiring the design of one sturdy wooden fishing boat I met Billy Choate. He sat on deck mending gear as I played tourist and asked him about Homer, the sea, and commercial fishing. That night at the Salty Dawg we told each other our life stories, and I learned a lot about my new friend.

I saw in Billy those things that made it easy to admire the people of Alaska. He had a quiet strength that came from confidence in himself, pride in his work, and a deep love for the land and sea. Having been raised in Homer, he'd seen the town grow, and was sensitive to the changes and protective of the quality of life he enjoyed. Billy, like many other Alaskans, was a breed apart: he was a survivor and lived life to the fullest.

The Salty Dawg Saloon proved to be a popular watering hole and social club for many local characters. It was there that I met Lynn Danaher, a good-looking, spirited lady new to the Last Frontier. She worked as the day bartender at the Dawg while her man, Joe Bennett, was out commercial fishing. I got in the habit of visiting with her during the slow hours, and one afternoon Lynn told me of a horseback trip she and her friend Danny were taking to Caribou Lake at the head of Kachemak Bay. When she asked me to join them, I immediately agreed and left to pack my gear.

The next day we began our trip by driving the bumpy, graveled, twenty-six miles of East End Road to the Rainwater Ranch. When we arrived, I got my first glimpse of homestead life in Alaska. Charlie Rainwater and his young sons, Chris and Mike, were harvesting hay, so Danny and I helped load the heavy, sweet-smelling bales on the horse-drawn wagon. Once we got into the rhythm of the work, the only sounds that broke the silence were the singing of the birds and the creaking of the horse's harness. It felt good to work under the hot sun, and we all were sweating freely when the dinner bell rang from the ranch house.

Lynn had helped Janice Rainwater prepare a hearty meal of moose meat, potatoes with gravy, fresh garden vegetables, and homemade bread. We ate and talked and talked and ate while enjoying a spectacular view of the mountains and glaciers across the bay. Besides harvesting everything on the table, the Rainwaters had homesteaded the land, built their home, and raised a family in the wilds. When it was time to say good night, I went to bed filled with good food and conversation.

Everyone got up early, and after a big breakfast Danny, Lynn, and I went off to catch the horses we'd ride to Caribou Lake. I'd been on a horse only once in my life, and it was tied to a corral fence, so the anxiety attack I experienced when I first saw the big, snorting beasts was only natural. They looked damn near wild. I thought of asking if there was an old, sway-backed nag in the back pasture for me to ride, but my pride kept me quiet. After considerable effort, we were saddled up and ready to go.

We waved good-bye to the Rainwaters and headed down a trail that led to the beach a thousand feet below the ranch. My horse, Sandy, liked to walk close to the edge of the steep drop-offs, so as we descended, I kept only the toes of my boots in the stirrups, ready for an instant bail-out. We reached the beach without any mishaps, leisurely followed the shimmering coastline for a mile, and then turned inland. As we continued over the little-used trail, Lynn described the swamps we would be crossing once we got to the top of the bluffs in front of us. Visualizing what that would be like didn't excite me much, but I was sure glad to know there weren't any snakes in Alaska.

The trail led through grass as high as the horses' heads, and they became very skittish. Suddenly, something big went crashing through the brush ahead of us, and the horses went crazy. They reared up and tried to go back the way we'd come, which I thought was a damn good idea. Luckily, whatever spooked them went the other way. We finally got the horses quieted down, only to find the trail was too overgrown with alder to continue. This adventure would be a great learning experience, if I lived through it.

Instead of turning back, we dismounted and led the horses up a steep, open slope toward the top of the bluffs. When we were halfway up, Danny's horse stepped on his foot, and as he hopped around in pain we heard a shout from Lynn. I turned just in time to see her horse, Canyon, rear up, lose its footing, and roll all the way to the bottom of the hill. Danny and I hurriedly tied off our horses, and all three of us slid down the incline to where Canyon lay. We found him dead with a broken neck.

We stood there silently trying to comprehend what had happened. The realization that death is so close in this wild land affected us all. We were just thankful Lynn hadn't been riding the horse when it fell.

It was a slow, sad trip back to the Rainwater Ranch. When we arrived, Lynn tearfully explained the tragedy. Charlie and Janice were saddened but understood it wasn't our fault. They went on to explain that the horse had gotten its name when, as a colt, it fell down a canyon and almost died.

As we drove the dusty road back to Homer, I reflected on the fact that not all treks have happy endings. Sometimes accidents happen, no matter how careful you are. Maybe that's what adds the thrill and excitement to venturing into the unknown. I knew I'd take the risk again, only next time I'd walk.

My stay in the Homer area was near an end. I knew the image of its wild beauty would be with me for a long time, but what impressed me even more were the people I'd met. These adventurous, proud folks had become my friends, and I would not soon forget them. As I had a farewell drink with Billy in the Salty Dawg, he shook my hand and said, "You'll be back."

My next stop was Talkeetna, Alaska, about eight hours' drive from Homer and two hours north of Anchorage. When I pulled into this small, quiet town of 180 people, I met Karl Donner, a German doctor preparing to climb Mount McKinley, or Denali—the original Indian name, meaning "The Great One." Luckily, Karl's English was much better than my German, and we spent several enjoyable hours each night sitting around a campfire on the bank of the Susitna River, talking about life in general and his ascent of the mountain in particular.

The bush pilot Don Sheldon would fly Karl's expedition into the base camp at 7,000 feet elevation on the Kahiltna Glacier. Once on the mountain, Ray "Pirate" Genet would lead the team to the 20,320-foot summit. I was somewhat familiar with what climbing Mount McKinley entailed, having read Art Davidson's book *Minus 148°*, about the first winter ascent of the highest mountain in North America. In fact, the main reason for coming to Talkeetna was to explore the possibility of climbing it myself.

While living in California, I'd done some rock climbing and winter mountaineering in the Sierra, and my desire to climb Mount McKinley was a natural extension of those experiences. On arriving in Talkeetna, I learned the only way to climb The Great One was to pay a guide or be a member of a climbing team. Nobody had attempted a solo ascent, but I knew that was way beyond my ability. My choice not to climb didn't stop me from enjoying the company of the hardy men of the mountain.

The night before Karl began his climb, we were watching the dying embers of our campfire when he asked me a question that sent my blood racing. "Keith, we have become friends, and I would like it that we share some adventure together. After I climb the mountain, I will go kayak the Yukon River. Would you like to come with me?"

I was honored and said, "Yes, Karl, I'll share the river with you."

That night I hardly got any sleep with plans for our future trip splashing around in my head.

The next day Karl flew off to conquer Denali and I drove north to experience the wonders of Mount McKinley National Park. Each morning I took the free shuttle bus into a different area, hiked into the back country to photograph and observe the wildlife, and returned with the last bus to my camp for the night. The Forest Service brochure listed 130 varieties of birds and 31 kinds of mammals that made the park their home. During the week I explored McKinley Park I saw Dall sheep, red fox, wolf, lynx, black bear, caribou, moose, and several grizzlies. It was a thrill to roam free with the wild ones and learn their ways.

I had more good weather than bad, and whenever I got a glimpse of Denali's icy peaks, I thought of my friend Karl up there experiencing The Great One on a more personal level. On returning to camp late one afternoon, I leaned of trouble on the mountain. Three members of an all-woman Japanese climbing team were missing, and the search had begun. Mount McKinley had a reputation for spawning some of the worst weather in the world. Not all return who challenge its storm-blasted heights.

I met Karl when he flew back to Talkeetna after his successful ascent. He felt good about reaching the top but sad over the fate of the missing Japanese climbers. His rescue team found the bodies roped together high on the mountain they tried to conquer.

Karl and I left Talkeetna and drove north to Fairbanks to buy the equipment we'd need for the Yukon River. There we met Clem and Pat Rawert, the Klepper kayak dealers for the area. They invited us to join them for lunch and afterward suggested that we stay at their home while planning our expedition. We bought two one-person, folding Aerius kayaks with extra paddles, acquired topographical maps of the Yukon River, and stocked up on freeze-dried food. After crossing off everything on our list, we said good-bye to our helpful hosts, packed our gear in the VW camper, and headed south to Skagway in southeast Alaska.

On arriving in Skagway, we decided to climb the Chilkoot Pass and follow the famous route taken by the 1898 gold seekers to the Klondike. After arranging to have our kayaks and provisions sent to Lake Bennett via the White Pass and Yukon Railway, we taxied out to the trailhead, shouldered our heavy packs, and disappeared into the mist-shrouded forest. It felt good to feel a weight on my back, listen to the sounds of the woods, see the bright colors of fall, and taste the sweat dripping off my nose.

The day we climbed the steepest section of the Chilkoot Pass (where the Ninety-eighters had cut 1,500 steps in the ice) wasn't a good one. It started with Karl and me getting sick on the freeze-dried dumplings we ate for breakfast and got worse as we struggled up through the constant, wind-whipped downpours. When we reached the top of the 3,500-foot pass, we were soaked with sweat and rain. To add to our misery, the snow that began falling hid the trail. Just before dark we made camp among a thicket of scrubby trees, ate a cold dinner, and crawled into damp sleeping bags. My last thoughts before sleep took me were of those gold-crazed prospectors who broke the trail seventy-five years before me.

Two days later we walked into Lake Bennett Station just as the narrow-gauge train pulled in full of tourists and our equipment. While we unloaded our kayaks, the sightseers walked their poodles and bombarded us with questions about our river trip. It was a relief when the train departed and left us alone to assemble the boats and pack for our journey.

I had had very little experience in a kayak and thought it wise to test one before starting our paddle down the Yukon River. After putting the empty boat into the cold, blue water of Lake Bennett, I gingerly wiggled into the cockpit and paddled away from shore. Karl shouted, "If you flip over, use the Eskimo roll to get back up!" Being a novice, I'd never heard of the technique. If I was to get wet, better now than later, I thought. So I dug hard into the water, and the blue canvas boat shot forward. After testing its speed, I turned circles, backpaddled, and saw how far over I could lean. I was amazed. The kayak was very stable; it just felt tippy.

The first day of September, Karl and I slid our loaded boats into the water, saluted the old log church built by the Klondike gold rushers, and started paddling the ninety miles of lakes that formed the headwaters of the Yukon River. The lonely call of a loon sounded the perfect note for the beginning of our voyage.

One day and twenty-six miles later, we beached our boats at the small town of Carcross. Karl and I treated ourselves to a meal and a beer at the Caribou Hotel, which had been in continuous operation since 1898. While enjoying someone else's cooking, we met an old-timer who had crossed the Chilkoot Pass with the gold prospectors. He sat in a corner of the bar cussing at anybody who would listen. That parrot had one hell of a vocabulary.

As we got up to leave, we noticed an Olympic broadcast on kayaking on the hotel's television. We watched as the world's best maneuvered their boats through the foaming rapids of the manmade course. I didn't know it then, but my parents in Oregon were watching the same show. When they saw what they believed I was going through on the Yukon River, they knew they'd never see their oldest son again.

Karl and I had started too late in the season to kayak the entire length of the 1,900-mile river to the Bering Sea. When winter arrives in northern Canada and Alaska, it does so suddenly. Its cold, white hand grabs the land and doesn't let go until spring. We planned to keep paddling as long as we could, pulling out just in time to escape winter's icy grasp.

We established a daily rhythm, and the constant dipping of our paddles carried us through Tagish Lake, fifty miles from our starting point. The only changes were in the weather and our moods. On our sixth day out, it began snowing giant flakes as we set up camp for the night. This wasn't a good sign, and we both grumbled through our chores.

After dinner I sat next to the roaring campfire washing the dishes. Karl rummaged in his pack, removed several bags, and with a smile smeared across his face, said, "Keith, my friend, it is time for my surprise to you. Tonight we drink *Nickoloshkas.*"

As he laid out the ingredients and started preparing the concoction, Karl told me our drinks originated in his homeland. On top of a thin, round slice of lemon, he put a spoonful of instant coffee and one of sugar. After popping the mountain-shaped morsel into his mouth and chewing a bit, he took a big swig from the brandy bottle that magically appeared in his hand. I noted the smile of satisfaction on his whiskered face as I tried one myself. After four or five *Nickoloshkas* we started singing German drinking songs and didn't care how hard it snowed.

Breaking camp the next morning was slower than usual because of the foot of snow on the ground, but we were both in a good mood. This was the day we'd finish kayaking Marsh Lake and enter the Yukon River. The lakes gave me much needed practice, but now I wanted to experience the excitement of fast water.

The Yukon River begins wide and slow, but after a sharp bend it sweeps down the narrow, steep-cliffed Miles Canyon. We couldn't see very far into its dark interior, so we had no idea of what awaited us. The river's speed accelerated, sucking us into the sunless canyon. Karl and I both yodeled as our kayaks surged down the long tunnel of boiling water. It took all my concentration and strength to control my boat. As I shot through a whirlpool, I glanced up and saw a footbridge across the river. People were looking down and taking pictures, but I was moving so fast I didn't have time to wave.

The roller-coaster ride through Miles Canyon ended as suddenly as it began when we shot out onto a small lake. The dam that created the lake had buried the famed Whitehorse Rapids, where many Klondike-bound gold rushers died trying to maneuver their crude boats through its foaming channels. For those nineteenth-century prospectors the rapids had meant danger and death. For Karl and I it wasn't the white water but the dam that created a problem. It would take a full day to portage our heavily loaded kayaks around the manmade barrier.

We beached the boats next to the spillway and were unloading our equipment when two men drove up in a pickup truck. First they asked questions about our trip, and then both began helping with our gear. Finally, the driver suggested we put the kayaks in the back of his truck and drive around the dam. Thirty minutes later we were back on the river, paddling downstream. An hour later we pulled into shore and started making camp in Whitehorse, Yukon Territory. We were still setting up the tent when two suspicious Canadian officials paid us a visit.

The Customs officers said they knew when we entered their country and asked what took us so long to report our presence. I explained there wasn't any Customs office where we crossed into Canada on the Chilkoot Pass, and our trip to Whitehorse couldn't have taken any less time with our means of transportation. On hearing our story they became quite friendly and invited us to their office to fill out the required forms and join them for tea. After we became legal visitors to Canada, Karl and I went to the post office to see if we'd received any mail.

To my surprise, I got a letter from California that took only six weeks to catch up with me. Friends from the Carson Pass area of the Sierra offered me a job at their ski resort, and they wanted me there as soon as possible. Karl and I talked late into the night about my options. The offer of a job in the mountains would fit perfectly into my goal of skiing all winter. Freezing weather could end our kayak trip at any time, and Karl pointed out that he'd originally planned to do the expedition alone. After considering all the choices, I made my decision. I'd return to California and a winter of skiing.

The next morning Karl and I parted. He would continue down the Yukon to Dawson City, weather permitting, and I would take the White Pass Railroad from Whitehorse back to Skagway and then head south. We shook hands, bear-hugged, and wished each other good luck, but there were no good-byes. My friend would meet me later, on the ski slopes in the Sierra.

I looked out the frosty window of my railroad car as I enjoyed the warm glow of its woodburning stove. Gone were the red, yellow, and orange colors of fall. What took Karl and I two weeks to hike and paddle would take me less than a day of rested travel. As the train descended into Skagway, I saw the cold, white hand of winter throwing snowballs at the caboose.

My VW camper was parked where I'd left it, and that night I drove it aboard the M.V. Malaspina. The ferry would cruise south through the 670-mile Inside Passage of southeast Alaska. Along the way it stopped at the coastal towns of Haines, Juneau, Petersburg, Wrangell, and Ketchikan. I wanted to see this part of Alaska, so closely linked with the sea.

I hadn't been on the sea since leaving the San Francisco Bay Area and realized I'd missed it. As we powered through the protected waters I was awed by the silent mountains that rose up from the sea and ringed the deserted bays and coves. It was like going back to a primitive time; the misty green forests hadn't changed in thousands of years.

Adding to the setting were the variety of birds and animals that scarcely noticed our passing. Bald eagles rode the winds; porpoise, seal, and sea otter occasionally broke the waves, and I could only guess at what kinds of critters swam below us. One morning a pod of ten orcas—killer whales—swam by our boat blowing mist into the frosty air.

Along hundreds of miles of beach the only settlements were the isolated coastal towns we visited on our way south. I liked them all, but my favorite was Petersburg, also known as Little Norway of Alaska. As I walked through town, it reminded me of villages I'd visited in big Norway—all freshly painted, neat, and tidy.

During my wandering in Petersburg I met an old fisherman named Ole down by the docks. After talking for a while he invited me to join him for a drink at a nearby bar. As he ordered two beers, he asked, "Well now, Keith, how do you spell Iverson?"

I answered, "With a son."

He replied, "Then you must be of Swedish ancestry."

Before I could protest that I was from Norwegian roots, he started reciting the rhyme, "Ten thousand Swedes chased through the weeds by one crazy Norwegian."

We talked for more than an hour, and Ole kept me laughing at his square-head jokes up to the time I reboarded the ferry. We shook hands in parting, and the last thing he said was, "Iverson, you're okay for a Swede."

My Alaska journey ended when I drove off the ferry in Prince Rupert, British Columbia. As I drove south to California I had plenty of time to think back on the best summer of my life.

I'd traveled to Alaska in search of adventure and a place to call home. What I'd found was a rugged country of indescribable beauty and a proud, spirited people who were its true wealth. My search wasn't over. I still had much to learn, see, and explore, but Alaska had touched me deeply and someday I would return.

Continuing Quest

It seemed like years since I'd left San Francisco. The city hadn't changed, but I had. The frantic freeways, crowds, and hectic lifestyle seemed more threatening than any of my adventures in Alaska. I spent one day visiting friends before driving into the mountains.

The first snow of the season began falling as I entered Carson Pass in the Sierra. I still had $14,000 in my savings account, so I wasn't too disappointed about arriving too late to get a job at the new ski resort at Kirkwood Meadows. I'd survived a blizzard and caught many trout in these mountains, so it felt right to spend the winter even if I didn't have a job.

One of the lessons of the road I'd learned was don't get disappointed when plans fall through. If I stayed flexible, more times than not, something even better would present itself, and that's what happened. While visiting my friends the Berglunds, they asked if I wanted to caretake their summer resort at Cables Lake. With Kirkwood Meadows only five miles away, I could live in a quiet, comfortable cabin while fulfilling my plan to be a ski bum for the winter.

It was late October, too early in the season for good skiing, so I spent my time winterizing my cabin and meeting the local folks. While driving down the highway I visited Silver Lake Resort. I'd always admired its peaceful setting, rustic cabins, and friendly service and often fantasized about owning the property. Pulling into their parking lot, I saw a "For Sale" sign—maybe my search had ended.

During the next three weeks, I met with the owners, inspected the buildings, analyzed the business records, and tried raising money to buy the resort. The asking price was $150,000, which meant I only needed to raise $136,000. While making a list of potential partners, I came out of my elated mood long enough to see the reality of the situation. I wanted to be my own boss, and if I did raise the needed cash, I'd be only a minor owner. If I wanted to get into the resort business, it would be better to build my own. As I put away my notes on the postponed project, I looked out the window at four feet of fresh snow—it was time to go skiing.

Kirkwood Meadows was in its first season as a ski resort, so we locals had the mountain to ourselves during the week. Every morning we met at the lodge for coffee and conversation before testing the slopes. The weather dictated snow conditions, and we skied everything from ice to powder. Sharing a wind-blown chairlift, the speed and challenge of an icy downhill run, or a hot-buttered-rum after a day of skiing built strong bonds between the men and women who worked and played on the mountain.

Saturdays brought an avalanche of traffic, fancy ski outfits, and snow bunnies up from the flatlands. Living through a hectic weekend of socializing on the slopes, bragging in the bars, and all-night parties was hell, but somehow we survived.

One morning in mid-December I was getting ready to leave my cabin for another day on the slopes when someone knocked on the door. To my surprise, there stood my kayaking partner Karl, looking like he'd snowshoed all the way from Alaska. Our happy reunion lasted the rest of the day as we talked about what we'd done since parting on the Yukon River.

Karl made it to Dawson City before winter forced him to quit paddling. He related how the highlight of his trip took place on Lake Labarge after strong head winds blew him back across the long lake. He made camp in a raging blizzard and built a large fire to dry out and keep warm. While sitting next to the bonfire, he read the Robert Service poem "The Cremation of Sam McGee." After a few *Nickoloshkas*, he looked into the flames and saw old Sam sitting there, begging him to put more wood on the fire.

My friend skied with me for a week before leaving to climb mountains in Mexico and South America. On his last day, we were finishing breakfast when a broadcaster on the radio said something that attracted our attention. An old sourdough, who had crossed the Chilkoot Pass in the 1898 Klondike gold rush, had died. At 120 years old, he was the last survivor of the famous stampede north. Karl and I knew they were talking about the parrot we had met in the Carcross Hotel on Lake Bennett. It saddened us to hear of the end of an era.

In January, the Nordic ski shop had a party to introduce the local downhill skiers to the latest California trend in winter sports: cross-country skiing. With a full moon shining down and free barbecued steaks, beer, and ski equipment, quite a crowd gathered. Few of us had ever been on a pair of Nordic "skinny skis." After a few unsuccessful runs we quit trying to learn how to turn, built a ski jump up the hill from the barbecue, and had a contest to see who could jump the farthest and stay up the longest. The totally out of control winner didn't fall until he skied through the party, scattering people and sending sparks flying.

The party was near an end, but several of us stood around the dying embers of the fire. I began talking with a young woman named Liza Kroeber, and the longer we spoke the more she attracted me with her easy smile, sparkling brown eyes, and zest for life. When we said good night, we agreed to meet the next week to continue the conversation.

We did meet the next week, then every other day, and soon we were constant companions. Liza was many years younger than me, but very aware of the world around her. Music was one of the real joys of our relationship, and we'd spend hours playing our guitars and singing folk music. Our friendship grew until we were more than friends—we were in love.

Winter was melting into spring. Skiing would soon be over, and I started thinking about my planned trip to New Zealand and Australia. An uneasy feeling about what to do next kept me on edge. I was getting tired of saying good-bye to friends and didn't want to think about leaving Liza. I needed to be alone to think things out. So, on a clear, crisp day in March, I grabbed my ice ax and headed up the nearest mountain. Several hours later I stood alone on top, looking out over the dazzling white peaks of the Sierra. After talking to myself for more than an hour, I knew what I wanted to do.

Once I made the decision my inner struggles disappeared. I felt light and free glissading down the steep slopes. As the cabin came into sight, I couldn't wait to tell Liza and started running. Out of breath, I burst through the door and said, "I'm going back to Alaska to start a new life in the wilds. Will you come with me?"

Smiling, she said, "Yes, I'll come with you."

As we hugged, she added, "I knew that would be your decision."

Surprised, I asked, "How did you know when I didn't know myself?"

Liza answered, "All you've done all winter is talk about Alaska."

We waved good-bye to California as we headed north. As I drove, Liza read aloud from J. R. R. Tolkien's *The Lord of the Rings*. The miles passed, the pages turned, and as she finished the trilogy we pulled up to the Salty Dawg Saloon on the Homer Spit. At the bar, as if he'd never left his stool, sat Billy Choate, my fisherman friend from the summer before. He looked up from his beer and said, smiling, "I said you'd be back."

I was back, but now what? I'd chosen the Homer area because it had fine folks, combined the mountains and the sea, and had the best coastal weather in the state. However, Liza and I wanted to go a little farther, cross the bay, and build our home where the only road was the water.

To look for land we needed a boat, but I had only my kayak from the Yukon River. Our Homer friends told me I was nuts; nobody in his right mind used a kayak to cross Kachemak Bay. They weren't far off in their estimate of my sanity, but ocean kayaking intrigued me. Besides, Alaska natives had kayaked in northern waters for thousands of years.

At nine o'clock on the morning of the summer solstice, June 21, I slid my kayak into the calm, blue waters of Kachemak Bay, waved to Liza, and started paddling. I'd only traveled a hundred yards from shore when the huge, black body of a whale surfaced twenty feet in front of me. I could smell its salty breath as it blew a fine mist into the air. As it disappeared below the surface, I took a deep breath and yodeled to release the energy that surged through my body. Taking the noble creature's appearance as a good omen, I continued paddling.

It took an hour to kayak the five miles across the bay. Small sandy beaches, long stretches of gravel, and craggy cliffs divided the clear water from the heavily wooded spruce forests. A few rustic cabins stood as silent reminders of others' dreams. All day I paddled the coasts of Neptune, China Poot, and Peterson bays, Halibut Cove, Rusty's Lagoon, and Ismalof Island. The more I saw, the more I knew this was the place for me.

I stopped to rest on Glacier Spit. After pulling my boat up the gravel beach, I stretched out under the warm sun and let the small waves sing me to sleep. The splash from a jumping salmon woke me up, and as I looked at my kayak, I thought how it had proven to be the most natural way to see the other side of the bay. Its silent passing didn't disturb the critters, and I wasn't reliant on a motor to get me where I wanted to go. Sitting alone on the beach, I felt like a modern-day Viking. This wasn't unexplored land, but it was new to me.

I'd stopped and talked to several people about buying land, and although what I learned didn't sound good, I was anxious to discuss it with Liza. At midnight I started my long paddle back to Homer. The lights of the spit twinkled in the distance, but they didn't seem to be getting any closer, so I started counting my strokes to pass the time. Like a long-distance runner, my body continued to work, but my mind escaped the monotony by taking a vacation to fantasyland.

The 6-foot dorsal fin of a killer whale breaking the surface of the water a hundred feet in front of my bow brought my body and mind back to reality. Halfway across Kachemak Bay, in the middle of the night, alone in a kayak, I met a whale with a name that leaves no doubt about the result of any close encounter. I held my breath, put down my paddle, and glided forward. I could hear my heart pounding as I waited for it to resurface. After several minutes I got mad at myself and continued paddling. What kind of a Viking was I? There wasn't anything else to do but keep going. If I was going to Valhalla, at least I'd go with a paddle in my hands. The whale vanished, but my mind played with him all the way back to shore.

I arrived back on the Homer Spit at 2:00 A.M. after kayaking thirty miles and found Liza sitting next to a beach fire awaiting my return. The excitement of the day kept me wide awake, and I began telling her about my trip. Like many newcomers to Alaska, we thought because of its size and remoteness, we could buy land for maybe $100 an acre. What I found across the bay blew that hunch out of the water. We didn't know that the state or federal governments and the Alaska natives owned 98 percent of the land, and it wasn't for sale. On a local level I learned that most of the property across the bay was designated as Kachemak Bay State Park in 1971. The few private pieces that were for sale had a selling price of $5,000 an acre. I still had $12,000 in my savings account, but it wasn't enough to buy a few acres, get an adequate boat, and purchase the necessary building materials, tools, food, and other supplies to begin a wilderness lifestyle.

After analyzing the situation, Liza and I agreed to spend all summer looking for land across Kachemak Bay. If we didn't find any acreage, we'd continue the search the next year in a more remote coastal area. At the very least, we'd have a great summer searching.

The next morning we discussed alternatives to buying land. We could build a houseboat and live on the water in some protected cove. Maybe we could become prospectors, discover gold, and stake a claim. As we laughed about that idea, I remembered that in Anchorage we'd met a man named Pettyjohn who had a mining company. When I called him, he offered Liza and me a job staking claims. So off to Anchorage we went with the early symptoms of gold fever.

Pettyjohn put us to work when we got to town. He gave us a stack of mining-law books and told us to read them—not once, but twice. He then explained the basic points of staking a mining claim. He encouraged us to study hard because he planned to fly us by helicopter to the headwaters of the Kahiltna River to stake gold claims while floating downstream in an inflatable boat. It wasn't Kachemak Bay, but after this trip we'd have the know-how to stake claims for ourselves.

In my reading I learned there are two ways to acquire a mine. The first was a discovery claim, whereby the person who finds the mineral can file for the rights to mine it. The second method was a relocation, which meant anyone could file on an existing mine where annual assessment work had lapsed. Liza and I would be staking discovery claims on the Kahiltna River.

After ten days in Anchorage we called for a meeting with Pettyjohn. We hadn't come to Alaska to be stuck in the city, and if he couldn't get us out soon, we were going back to Kachemak Bay to continue looking for our own land. He admitted it could take several more weeks to get out on his job. He understood our situation and brought out several maps to see if there were any mines in the Homer area. To our surprise and delight, we found the history of several old gold-mining operations across the bay. As we left, Pettyjohn wished us luck in staking our claims.

While searching the records in Homer, we learned that the old mines' assessment work wasn't up-to-date—they were open to relocation. So we packed our gold pan, flagging tape, and mining books, borrowed a two-person kayak, and started paddling across Kachemak Bay. On our way to the mines, Liza and I planned to visit a few folks who lived in the remote bays and coves.

Our trip across was uneventful until we entered China Poot Bay. As we approached the narrow entrance, a large wave caught us, and we surfed the last hundred yards into the shallow, calm waters. In this bay of gravel bars and blue-mussel beds we met Mike and Diane

McBride. They gave us a tour of their home and wilderness lodge while describing their future construction goals. Their enthusiasm was infectious, and I started thinking of our building plans. My desire to find land burned brighter than ever.

We left the McBrides and, after an hour of easy paddling, glided up to Ismalof Island in Halibut Cove, where we met the Tillions. Clem was an Alaska state senator, and his wife, Diana, was an artist who painted with octopus ink. They came to the island as newlyweds and raised their family on its isolated shore. We sat in their cozy home and drank coffee as Clem talked for several hours about the history of the area. Two stories caught my interest.

At the turn of the century Halibut Cove had the largest population in Kachemak Bay. It was home to a thousand Norwegians who had started a large fishing and cannery operation to catch and process the rare 6-pound herring that spawned in the area. The community prospered for many years until the herring disappeared because of overfishing and the dumping of cannery waste on the spawning beds. When the herring died out, the Norwegians left. Only a few stayed to call Halibut Cove home.

I was saddened by the story. Because of the mismanagement of my ancestors, future generations would never get to see a 6-pound herring.

The second of Clem's stories that particularly interested me concerned the old Aurora Gold Mines, which Liza and I were going to relocate. In the early 1900s, all of Alaska had gold fever. A group of miners came to Kachemak Bay and, while prospecting, found a small amount of gold in the stream that flows out of Portlock Glacier. They established a camp at Aurora Lagoon, formed a company, and got investors from the Lower 48. For several years the prospectors made a good living—not from the gold taken out of the ground, but from the investors they'd found.

Now Liza and I were anxious to get to the claims and do our own prospecting. We said good-bye to the Tillions, kayaked up the bay, and made camp on the Portlock Glacier stream that flowed between Aurora Lagoon and Mallard Bay. Exploring the land, finding an old mining tunnel, discovering specks of gold by panning the stream, walking on the glacier, and camping out was fun. Gaining title to the old mines required two weeks of hard work in the steep, buggy, coastal forest. Mining laws and the method of staking claims had changed little since the turn of the century. After using a machete to cut trails through thick tangles of alder and prickly patches of devil's club, we measured the boundaries of our claim with a hundred-foot rope and used a hand-held compass to establish direction. At each of the four corners we built a high rock mound to protect the filing information we buried in a sealed jar. When we finished, Liza and I broke camp and headed for Homer to register our three claims, take a shower, and get something to eat other than our daily diet of seafood.

It was good to be back in Homer. We cleaned up, legally recorded our mines, had a beer at the Dawg, and went looking for a good meal. After devouring two giant T-bone steaks, we picked up our mail. Liza started laughing while reading of news from home and handed me the letter. Her mom and stepdad were coming to visit us in Alaska.

When Joan and Ken came a week later, Liza and I guided them through the Homer area. The best way to show anyone the other side of the bay was on Clem Tillion's boat tour to Halibut Cove, so we boarded the 42-foot *Danny J* and motored out of the harbor on the end of the spit. Our first stop was Gull Island, a marine rookery where hundreds of sea gulls, murres, cormorants, and puffins return each summer to hatch their young. After leaving the squawking birds behind, we tied up at Clem's dock on Ismalof Island for a tour of Diana's art gallery. With coffee and cookies, Clem and Diana served us entertaining stories about their world of Kachemak Bay.

On the way back to Homer a stiff breeze whipped up from the west, and while the others stayed in the cabin I went forward to be alone and feel the wind in my hair. Silently, Liza's mother joined me, and together we stood watching the sea. After several minutes Joan asked, "Is this the life you want, Keith?"

"Yes, it is," I answered. "You know, I've met other good people like Clem and Diana who have made this side of the bay their home. I admire their hard work, independence, and resourcefulness. Their lives aren't easy, but they're rewarding. Most of all, they've chosen to be free and live their own dreams."

Joan looked out over the whitecapped bay and said, "You and Liza have your gold mines. Is that where you plan to build your home?"

I'd given that question much thought and answered, "I don't think so. We do own the mineral rights, and we'll maintain the yearly assessment work, but we won't build on them. I don't want to build our future on land that we don't own free and clear."

I paused before adding, "We'll keep looking for land the rest of this summer and fall, but if we don't find it in Kachemak Bay we'll try another area next year. If it's meant to be, we'll find it."

As we walked back into the cabin to get out of the wind and spray, I put my arm around Joan and gave her a hug. I liked this woman, for in her I recognized much of what I loved in Liza.

Joan, Ken, and Liza all returned to California for a family reunion. She'd be Outside for a month, and in her absence I'd continue the search for our land. Before she left we'd explored the middle and upper bay, but now I wanted to look farther south toward the small fishing village of Seldovia. A friend told me of a man named Bruce Covault who lived in Sadie Cove, a fjord with walls so steep he used a rope to get to his cabin. I wanted to see this rugged cove whose only resident was half mountain goat.

It was fall, and the days became shorter and colder. The winds blew harder and the waves grew bigger—bad conditions for kayaking open water. Winter was on its way, and I still hadn't found any land to buy. I figured there was time for one more trip across the bay before hanging up my paddle for the year.

On one particularly blustery day I took refuge in the Salty Dawg Saloon. While drinking beer and talking to friends I met Bruce for the first time. I was introduced as "the mad Viking who kayaked the bay," and he was presented as "that wild man living on a cliff in Sadie Cove." We two crazies hit it off immediately and proceeded to buy each other drinks while Bruce told stories about where he lived. The more I heard, the more excited I became to see this new area.

When he left, Bruce shook my hand and said, "I haven't told anyone, but there's a piece of land for sale on the beach below my cabin. I'd like to have you as a neighbor, so take a look and see what you think."

Joe Bennett was among our small group of friends sitting at the bar. When he saw how eager I was to see Sadie Cove, he volunteered to take me in his boat.

Early the next morning Joe and I left Homer, zipped across the bay in his skiff, and entered Sadie Cove. It was steep, deep, long, and narrow—a true fjord. The clear, blue water cut back into the land six miles, but was less than a mile wide. The mountain rising from the north shore towered 4,300 feet above the sea, and the south shore rose 3,000 feet. As we admired the raw, wild beauty, Joe said, "I'll bet this place blows like a bitch in the winter."

Two miles inside the entrance we came to the south-facing property, beached the skiff, and started walking around. The first thing I noticed was the gravel beach, steep slope of the land, and big trees. It was just three acres, but it went from sea level to a 400-foot elevation and was heavily timbered with hundred-foot Sitka spruce. I wanted the land even before I found the fresh water.

A small, clear stream flowed out of the woods and down the beach, where it joined the sea. One taste made me shiver and smile at the same time. The water splashing over the rocks sounded like a song of welcome. There weren't any buildings on the property, so I picked a site for our first cabin and started making plans to generate electricity from the fast-flowing stream.

Joe and I got back in the skiff and started for Homer. Looking out of Sadie Cove we could see Mount Augustine, an island volcano smoking on the horizon, eighty miles away. I'd found what we were looking for and said almost like a prayer, "God, I hope they don't want too much for the land!"

Back in Homer I wasted no time finding the owner of the Sadie Cove property. The records showed that John Cooper staked the site in 1969 but sold it to Ed Clop in 1970. I was in luck—Ed lived in town and was at home when I knocked on his door. After an hour of haggling we agreed on a selling price, and I bought the three acres for $2,250.

Liza would soon be back from her trip Outside, and I couldn't wait to tell her the good news. I'd already started making plans for a camping trip to our land in January. If we were going to be year-round residents, I wanted to see what it was like in winter. Wherever we spent the long, dark, cold months, we had much to do in preparation for our return to Sadie Cove in the spring. I eagerly awaited my first winter in Alaska with Liza. My search was over—this Viking had found his woman and a fjord to call home.

First Winter in Alaska

Freezing to death wasn't a good way to begin a new life. Could we survive our first winter in Alaska living in a tent in Sadie Cove? A shiver ran through my body and brought me back from my daydreaming into the reality of the Anchorage airport, where I awaited Liza's return from California. I put the chilling thoughts aside as I saw Liza walk toward me, tanned, smiling, and so full of life.

I didn't realize how much I'd missed her until we hugged. As we embraced, I knew my life had been less without her. The spell broke when we started laughing and speaking at the same time. We had so many stories to catch up on since parting a month earlier and didn't stop talking until we drove out of the city and into the mountains of the Kenai Peninsula.

I told Liza about meeting Bruce at the Salty Dawg, seeing Sadie Cove for the first time with Joe, and the joy of buying the land. As we pulled off the road to stretch our legs, I said, "We have our land, Liza, and it's there waiting for us. We could set up a tent camp and live next to the stream for the winter, but I think we need more experience, planning, and equipment before moving to the Bush. What do you think?"

"I'll be with you wherever we live," she answered, "but maybe we should take one of the cabins people offered us for the winter and move to Sadie Cove in the spring."

I smiled and said, "My thoughts exactly. Let's take another look at that old cabin on the Seward end of Kenai Lake that we visited this summer."

While we drove, Liza and I discussed our options. None of the cabin owners wanted rent, so money wasn't a factor in making a choice. They just wanted us to take care of their property for the winter. Now we had to choose which one would best meet our needs. We crossed off two cabins in Homer and one in Hope because they meant living in town. We eliminated Pearl Island, located in the storm-blown Gulf of Alaska, as too isolated. When we turned off the highway onto the gravel road leading to a small cluster of buildings on Kenai Lake, we knew we'd found our winter home.

The old, weathered sign nailed to a tree told us we were in Lawing. During our summer visit we'd learned that Nellie Lawing— "Alaska Nellie"—had settled in the area when the only transportation was the railroad connecting Seward to Anchorage. This pioneer woman built her home and wilderness museum out of logs on the shore of the lake. After feeding a trainload of travelers when they became stranded by an avalanche, the railroad rewarded Nellie by having every passenger train stop at her museum and gift shop until the day she died.

Looking out from the porch I could see why she'd picked this spot for her cabin. The steel tracks running parallel to the grey, gravel beach were the only sign of civilization. Beyond the icy, blue-green water of the glacier-fed lake rose dark-green timbered mountains with the season's first snow blanketing the peaks. Cottonwoods and birch surrounded the cottage, their red and gold leaves fluttering in the afternoon breeze.

The cabin blended old and new. It had electricity, both oil and wood stoves, no water, and an outhouse. To us it seemed the perfect place to spend our first winter on the last frontier. The few neighbors sharing the area would not disturb our privacy, and it was only twenty-three miles into Seward for supplies and an occasional night on the town. Lawing, though much less isolated than Sadie Cove, gave us time to plan, learn, acquire supplies, and buy the boat and tools we'd need for our passage into Bush living.

We moved into the cabin before making our first trip into Seward. After buying supplies, we spent several days looking at boats. Since the only way to get to Sadie Cove was by water, we needed a seaworthy craft for transportation. Liza and I finally found a 31-foot, well-used fishing boat named *Skilak*. Powered by a rusty gas engine, she had a small, dingy cabin in the bow. Dirty but sound, I thought, as I paid the owner $1,800. We now had a good winter project getting her ready for spring. *Skilak* wasn't a Viking longship, but she suited our current needs.

Liza and I had accomplished much since arriving in Alaska five months earlier. We owned a gold mine, found our land, bought a boat, and were living in a cozy cabin for the winter. However, with money going out but none coming in, I started getting a little nervous about our financial situation. Building our home in Sadie Cove would cost more than the $6,000 I still had in my savings account, but I felt confident something would happen to put a few more dollars in our jeans.

In early November, our closest neighbor, Crazy Peter—we weren't sure we wanted to know why he was called crazy—had a party to welcome us to the neighborhood. While Liza baked bread and rhubarb pie, I went hunting for the main course. Fog had drifted in from the lake and crept around the bare trees. I took my rifle off the wall, grabbed a warm coat, and quietly walked into the woods.

A short distance from the cabin I noticed two furry ears sticking up from behind a low bush, and I dispatched the critter with one shot. Bending down to pick up the Arctic hare, I saw a 3-pound chocolate boletus mushroom that would make a delicious addition to the meal; so I added it to my game bag. The hunt was over so soon that I sat down on a thick bed of moss to enjoy my success and the woods. In front of me I spotted a mound of dung, which made me focus on one of the great mysteries of the north—moose manure. How could such a large animal produce such small droppings? "Must be another of those moosteries of life," I chuckled out loud as I carried my trophies back to the cabin.

The party started with Crazy Peter and his flute welcoming us to his home. Liza and I played our guitars, and as other guests arrived they joined the singing. Before dinner, Jacque and Diana told hilarious stories about the play they were producing in Anchorage. Scott, an architect, contributed equally funny sketches on dealing with building codes in the big city. Ernie added wit and wisdom about surviving in the Bush. Friendly faces, a warm cabin lit with kerosene lamps, delicious food, and interesting conversation all contributed to the evening's success. As the wine and stories flowed, somehow we got on the subject of moose manure.

The brown, odorless, inch-long, oval scat is deposited in piles of 30 to 300 nuggets all over Alaska. After drying it, creative residents have been transforming it into a variety of gag gifts ever since the first tourist came north. We began talking about moose manure jewelry, Christmas tree ornaments, and swizzle sticks and then started creating our own ideas. After an hour of inventing play-on-word products, the only one I remembered was "Mooseltoe."

The next morning the word was still floating around in my head. While trying to wake up with a steaming cup of black coffee, Liza asked, "What's Mooseltoe?" as if she were reading my mind.

"I don't know," I replied, "but it should be fun putting some together."

We modeled our Mooseltoe after the traditional Christmas holiday plant. First, we cut green spruce sprigs and collected moose nuggets from the woods. Next, we dried the manure in our oven and found some red and white yarn in the back room of the cabin. With all the ingredients laid out on the kitchen table, we were finally ready to assemble our brainchild.

I tied the yarn in a bow around the sprig and stapled the moose nuggets onto the dangling ends of the yarn. With an impish grin, Liza said, "Let's try it out!"

That kiss definitely primed my primitive instincts, but I think Liza contributed more than the moose poop hanging over our heads.

Getting back to work, my next concern was packaging. A plastic sandwich bag might work just fine; it was inexpensive, you could see the product, and we had a supply in the kitchen. Next, I designed a label that read "Genuine Alaskan Mooseltoe," added our Homer address, and stamped on a $2 retail price tag.

To this point we'd just been having fun inventing the wacky idea, but why not try to peddle the poop? The worst a buyer could say was no. I changed into a clean wool shirt and walked into Rogue's Gallery Gifts on the highway. I knew the owner, Cece Clark, so my sales pitch was short and to the point: "Cece, do you want to buy some moose shit?"

She examined my package of Mooseltoe, laughed, and said, "I'll take a gross."

I just stood there in shock as she paid me the wholesale cost of $144. Not only did Cece like our idea, she suggested we take our product to Anchorage and sell it to the big city stores for the coming holiday season. As I ran back to the cabin to tell Liza, I started laughing. Maybe this would be our avenue to financial independence. I could picture my business card: "Keith Iverson, Entremanure."

To fill Cece's order and make enough for the Anchorage market, we planned to make 10,000 packages. Liza and I gathered 20,000 moose nuggets and stayed up all night drying them in our oven. We collected spruce sprigs in the woods, then bought yarn, staples, and sandwich bags, and had the labels printed in Seward. What we needed was an assembly line.

A party seemed the best way to mass-produce the finished product, so we sent out invitations to our friends and bought refreshments. We had a good time putting the Mooseltoe together and joking about our bizarre project. When we finally completed the job, Liza and I prepared to take our new gag gift to Anchorage.

I chose Carr's markets for my opening sales pitch. Thoughts of rejection and humiliation entered my mind as I walked into the central buying office of Alaska's largest grocery chain. After taking a deep breath, I told the receptionist I'd like to see the buyer for Alaskan gifts. She said that would be the owner, Larry Carr, and asked if I wanted to make an appointment. I almost ran out the door rather than explain that I wanted to sell him some moose manure, but before I could answer, a friendly voice behind me asked, "What have you got there, young man?"

It was Mr. Carr, so I introduced myself and my product. He chuckled and showed it to several people in the office to get their opinions. Some laughed, a few made no comment, and one woman wrinkled her nose. I stood in the middle of the room with the red glow of embarrassment on my face, waiting for the inevitable rejection. To my surprise, Mr. Carr invited me into his office and said, "I like your Alaskan spirit and your Mooseltoe. We'll take 1,000 packages."

After breaking the ice, we went on to sell "Genuine Alaskan Mooseltoe" to Sears, J. C. Penney, Elmendorf Air Force Base, Pay-N-Save, and most of the smaller gift stores in Anchorage.

Later that week we experienced the reality of operating a business. We learned that the spruce sprigs had dried out in the warm gift shops and all the needles were lying in the bottom of the plastic bags. Liza and I returned to all the stores we'd sold to and collected our faulty merchandise. We cut new sprigs, sprayed each one with a product the local florists recommended to hold the needles in place, and reassembled the products. Inhaling the spray probably shortened our lives by ten years, but we solved the problem and went on to sell 5,000 packages of Mooseltoe during the 1973 Christmas season.

The low cost of materials, labor, and overhead allowed us a tidy profit. We'd taken our crazy idea from its conception to the bank and knew it would provide a winter income for as long as we wanted to go out and collect moose poop.

We returned to Lawing in time to enjoy a relaxed, old-fashioned holiday with our friends. After the hectic promotion in Anchorage, the peace and quiet of our cozy cabin on Kenai Lake was just what we needed. The twinkling Christmas tree filled half the cabin, and of course we hung Mooseltoe over the door for New Year's Eve.

The short days of January gave us an excuse to put off working on our boat in Seward, but we still had plenty to do. In good weather we skied on the frozen lake, explored the woods, and visited neighbors. On blustery, blizzard days, we stayed inside and made love, music, and plans for the summer.

In late January we left Lawing to visit Sadie Cove. After packing our winter camping gear, Liza and I drove to Homer and met a shrimp fisherman named George in the harbor. As we bought some of his freshly caught shrimp for dinner, George said he'd be glad to take us across the bay when he went to check his pots early the next morning.

It was still dark when we met George and his deckhand on their fishing boat. After handing out coffee, they entertained us with stories about living and surviving across the bay. What we absorbed from these knowledgeable men could help us start our new life and possibly save our lives. We had much to learn, and we knew it.

As the boat turned into Sadie Cove, Liza and I went forward to get a better view. The fjord was the same, yet different from when I'd seen it in the fall. The steep, forested mountains rising out of the sea were still inspiring, but with a covering of winter white, the cove looked even wilder. I saw that the land had many moods, altered by weather and the changing seasons. When we lived in Sadie year-round, I looked forward to learning about all of those moods.

George dropped us off on the beach and said he'd pick us up in five days, weather permitting. After drinking from the ice-cold stream, I showed Liza the property. When I asked her what she thought, she answered me with a smile and a hug.

Our neighbor Bruce had offered to let us stay in his log sauna, so we shouldered our packs and started up the mountain. The stories about his land were true—we did need a rope to get to his cabin. We found the sauna, cleared the entrance of snow, built a fire, and made lunch. The tiny cabin was small but cozy, and sturdy enough to protect us from the worst weather.

Liza and I spent most of our time exploring the woods and beaches. We were up at first light and went to bed at sundown. Without tools we couldn't work on the property, but we did plan projects for when we returned in the spring. One cloudless night we stayed up late to watch the stars and made wishes whenever we saw one fall out of the sky. Our stay was like a preview of what life might be like when we lived in Sadie Cove year-round.

Like Sadie, Liza had a wild, free spirit, and I knew better than to try to tame either one. We did not talk of the future—either my dream of living in the cove would become her dream, or she would leave to live her own. At that moment, sharing an adventure in Alaska was enough for both of us.

George picked us up on schedule, but as we climbed aboard he said we wouldn't be able to cross back to town until the weather calmed. After leaving the protected waters of Sadie, I looked west and saw what he meant—white-crested rollers were marching down the bay, making a crossing to Homer impossible.

For two days we waited out the storm in a cabin in Little Jakolof Bay and learned much about our neighbors and life in the Bush. When we did cross to town it was a rough ride, and we were glad to see the harbor. Surviving across the bay meant living with the unpredictable extremes of nature, and I loved it.

Back in Lawing, life seemed to stand still. The days were getting longer, but not fast enough. Winter still held the land, and the blowing snow made it hard to work on our boat in Seward. Too much reading, planning, and sleeping made me restless and bored. February felt like it would go on forever.

Liza and I did get a break from the winter blahs whenever the train rattled over the frozen tracks in front of our cabin. The engineer got in the habit of blowing his whistle a mile before chugging through our front yard, so when Liza and I heard it, we'd drop what we were doing, step out on the porch, and wave. We both enjoyed the ritual and thought the passengers did too, since they always waved back.

With no television or radio, our only connection to the outside world was *Time* magazine. From it we learned of the latest fad—"streaking"—thrill-seeking eccentrics who ran naked through public places. Being a little nuts ourselves, we came up with our own version.

One quiet Sunday morning, Liza and I were relaxing in our loft bedroom reading a week-old funny paper when the train whistle blew. We stripped off what few clothes we wore, jumped out on the porch, and stood there waving to the train at -20°F as two of our women friends, who had walked in to visit, stepped around the corner of the cabin. Our version of streaking didn't seem to bother them a bit, but it sure got a response from the conductor, who leaned out the caboose window to get a better look and almost fell off the train. As we ran back into the cabin to keep from freezing, I heard one of our friends say to the other, "Worst case of cabin fever I've ever seen!"

Although traditionally March comes in like a lion and goes out like a lamb, that year in Alaska the lion was still roaring as we flipped the calendar to April. We'd been working on the boat in Seward, but this day we'd stayed home. As Liza read about gardening and I struggled through a manual on gasoline engines, someone knocked on our cabin door. Two men stood on the porch in Arctic survival gear looking like they'd just walked off a page from the L. L. Bean catalog. I invited them in for coffee, figuring that they must be lost after having taken a wrong turn in Chicago.

It turned out they were a producer and a director from a large advertising company in New York City, and they wanted to make a national Pizza Hut commercial in our front yard. After coffee I gave them a tour, and they agreed the location was perfect. Upon leaving, they said their crew would be back in one week to do the filming. Liza and I waved good-bye as they trudged through knee-deep snow back to their car on the highway. We looked at each other and broke out laughing. "They must be joking," I said.

True to their word, they all arrived the next week with a large caravan of vehicles, most of which got stuck in the snow when they left the highway. A giant Winnebago carried the men we'd met and the camera crew. Next, came a pickup truck with eight huskies and a dogsled. An Eskimo family dressed in furs came in a car, and a large truck carried the camera equipment, a papier-mâché igloo, and two dozen pizzas.

Liza and I served coffee and watched in wonder as the scene unfolded. The director of the commercial inquired about our wilderness lifestyle while we asked him about the ad. The sequence started with the Eskimo family sitting around the hearth in their igloo. After agreeing on pizza for dinner, they all jumped into their dogsled and mushed to the nearest telephone (a crank phone they'd hung on the outer wall of our log cabin). The father Eskimo called in their order to Pizza Hut (to go, of course), and then the family sledded into town. Later, in Anchorage, he was filmed running into a Pizza Hut restaurant, picking up his order, and returning to his waiting family in the dogsled parked on the street. Finally, their barking dogs pulled them back to the igloo, where they ate their pizza around a crackling fire. Liza cooked the pizzas in our oven, and I ran them out to the igloo propped up on the frozen lake. It took ten takes to satisfy the director with the final scene, but Liza and I had a great time. This was better than going to a movie.

When they finished shooting, the company packed up and left as quickly as they'd arrived. In one day they'd completed the commercial, popping in and out of our lives so fast it seemed like a dream. When they left us fourteen pizzas and a papier-mâché igloo, we knew what to do. The next night we had a pizza party around the burning igloo.

As April thawed into May, we started spending our time in Seward working on *Skilak*. After the cabin became livable, we moved aboard to cut down on travel time. The boat was stored on land, so Liza and I repaired several planks in her hull. By working long hours, we felt confident about getting the old gas motor running before returning to Sadie Cove at the end of the month.

As we played mechanic, Joe Bennett and the rest of the herring fleet motored into Seward. After laboring on *Skilak* all day, Liza and I would visit our Homer friend on his boat and talk fishing over a few beers. The fishermen were growing impatient as they waited for the herring to mature so they could be harvested. Cosmo, one of Joe's deckhands, had urgent business in Anchorage, but the call to start fishing could come at any moment. Joe was reluctant to let him go until I volunteered to fill in while he made a quick trip to the city.

As Liza and I started back to our boat, Joe said, "Keith, have your gear ready. If the call comes we'll be out of here fast, and it could be at night." His big hand shook mine, and he added, "We might make a fisherman out of you yet."

As I crawled into my bunk, his last words got me thinking. My new home was on the sea, and I had a boat. Maybe I should become a fisherman!

In the middle of the night someone woke me up by banging on our boat. I was ready to do some banging of my own until I recognized Joe's voice. "Time to go fishing, ol' buddy!"

I grabbed my gear, mumbled good-bye to Liza, and stumbled onto Joe's boat. As the 36-foot seiner motored out of the harbor and down Resurrection Bay, Joe stuck a steaming cup of black coffee in my hand and gave me a verbal crash course in herring fishing. Two hours later, as the first light of day silhouetted the surrounding mountains, he asked, "Any questions?"

"It would help if we could practice what you've been telling me, but I do have a question," I said. "Why are we in such a hurry?"

Joe explained that each fishery is regulated by the Alaska Department of Fish and Game to control how many fish escape so they can reproduce and allow the fishermen a harvest year after year. The system is governed by setting catch quotas and closing the season when they are filled. With so many fishermen after herring, it might take only an hour to fill the quota. If a crew or boat isn't ready for the opening, they may end the season empty-handed. Joe paused, then added, "Salmon fishing openings are longer and more relaxed, but with herring, if you snooze, you lose."

Joe decided to make a few practice sets. The skiff man fired up his outboard and towed one end of the deck-loaded net away from the bigger boat. We on the seiner powered off in the opposite direction. When all the net was out, both boats turned back toward each other, forming a big circle. The top of the net stayed on the surface with the help of small floats. The bottom of the net was weighted down with a lead line. After the two boats met, we used a power block to make the floating net smaller and close up the bottom. This method of fishing is called purse-seining. Once the fish were trapped, we would call a bigger boat—a tender—on the radio to come alongside and use its pumps to vacuum the herring into its hold. If everything went right, we could catch as much as 200 tons of herring in one set. At $600 per ton, even the 10 percent deckhand share sounded great.

We finished our practice set and tried it again. This time we caught a hundred pounds of herring and bettered our time. Joe was pleased with our work but not with what he heard on the radio. Fish and Game had tested some herring and found they still weren't mature enough to harvest, so back to port we went.

That night, Cosmo returned from Anchorage and I was out of a job, but not out of work. I still had plenty to do to finish our boat. Later in the week Liza and I finished overhauling *Skilak*, and the herring season finally opened. Joe's boat did well, and we were ready to return to Sadie Cove.

Instead of risking the Gulf of Alaska and spring storms with an inexperienced captain and crew, we had made plans to haul our boat by trailer to Kachemak Bay. While Liza stayed at the cabin to pack, I drove the 150 miles to Homer to meet our friend Ken, who had volunteered to help us move. I arrived late in the day, so Ken invited me to stay at his cabin. We drove out of town, parked the truck off the road, and strapped on our headlamps and cross-country skis for the mile-long trek to his cabin.

I noticed Ken slinging a rifle over his shoulder and jokingly asked, "Are we going to shoot dinner on the way in?"

His answer wasn't a joke. "Yesterday, a homesteader shot and wounded a big brown bear that was after his cattle. They last spotted him near here, so the gun is for our protection."

If I'd followed Ken any closer, we'd have been skiing piggyback. We got to the cabin safely, but several times I could have sworn I heard the wounded bear right behind me.

We got on the road early the next morning. Ken towed the trailer behind his pickup, and I followed in my VW camper. We picked up Liza and our gear in Lawing and then proceeded to Seward to load *Skilak*. With Ken and me towing the boat and Liza following in the camper, we took our time driving the icy roads.

We were only twenty miles from Homer when we met the moose. Ken and I saw him at the same time. The big, shaggy bull bolted out of an alder thicket a short distance ahead of us. Ken started pumping the brakes to slow down our 50-foot rig, and I braced myself for a crash. Miraculously, the bull crossed the road just before we passed. As we were recovering, I turned to Ken and said, "Good thing that moose wasn't a little slower, or we weren't a little faster." Just then a second moose came barreling out of the brush!

Ken started pumping the brakes again, and I knew this would be an even closer call. The cow moose ran out onto the highway directly into our path. We could see the look of fear in her eyes as she tried to stop, slipped, and fell. Now all we could see were four legs sticking straight up in the air as the moose slid down the road on her back just ahead of our truck. Ken finally pumped us to a stop, and the panicked moose regained her footing and disappeared into the woods.

As Ken and I got out of the truck, Liza walked up laughing and said, "That was one of the funniest things I've seen in a long time."

"It wasn't quite as funny from where we sat," I replied.

We all knew the comedy could have turned to tragedy if we'd totaled the truck or been killed by hitting a thousand-pound moose.

Before continuing, we looked around to make sure there wasn't a herd of the critters getting ready to charge out of the woods.

On boat-launching day, we thought we were ready to splash *Skilak* into Homer's small boat harbor at the end of the spit. I had the pumps primed, knowing the old wooden boat would leak a bit before the planks swelled up enough to seal the hull. As we slid the boat into the water, the people who came to witness the occasion uncorked the champagne I'd bought to celebrate the launching.

To my shock, *Skilak* didn't leak—she damn near sank! Several 2-foot geysers gushed up as I jumped aboard to start the engine and get the main pump going. Liza stuffed rags into the biggest leaks as the motor roared to life. The pump was solving the problem until the fan belt broke. Spectators grabbed hand pumps, and after a hectic hour we'd saved *Skilak* from going to the bottom.

As we stood on the dock sipping champagne, I heard a nearby fisherman say, "Just like my first boat."

It took three days for *Skilak's* planks to swell enough for the boat to stop leaking, but finally we got under way. Liza and I motored out of the harbor loaded with supplies on our maiden voyage to Sadie Cove. Crossing Kachemak Bay, I was excited yet concerned about facing the unknown challenges of building our home in the wilds of Alaska.

Building a Home

Liza and I beached *Skilak* at our new land on the first day of June 1974. Humankind had traveled in space and walked on the moon, but we planned to carve our home out of the wilderness and in some ways walk back in time. Society was seeking its answers to a better life through science and technology. I thought my questions could best be answered by living closer to nature. Neither way was wrong. We all must follow our hearts and instincts, and my path led to Sadie Cove.

We unloaded the boat and were setting up camp when Liza asked, "What do we build first?"

All our plans had concentrated on getting to the land and not on what to do after we arrived, so I didn't have an answer until I felt the need to relieve myself. After answering nature's call behind a bush, I replied, "We'll start by building an outhouse."

I made two rules for any project in Sadie Cove: do it right the first time and make do with what we had. So, after choosing a site up from the beach, we dug a hole that took three days to complete. Next, we built a deck over the huge pit, framed the outhouse walls, and nailed up log slabs we found along the shore. In town we found an old roof laying half buried in a field that looked about the right size for our new structure. On our return to Sadie, we stopped to beachcomb and uncovered a sun-bleached door with antique glass handles that would also fit our needs. Both fit perfectly.

To make our one-holer more comfortable, I started our library by building a rack and stocking it with *Alaska* magazine, *The Whole Earth Catalog*, *National Geographic*, and *Mother Earth News*. Liza hung white, frilly curtains around the window looking out over the cove, and I padded the seat with Styrofoam for chilly morning meditations. We added a touch of class with a 3-foot imitation-white-marble Greek wall mural we'd found in the Moose Pass dump. The outhouse took two weeks to complete, and every morning Liza and I took some time to sit back and admire our work.

We completed our first building project just in time for a family visit. When Mom and Dad arrived, we gave them a tour of our property and proudly showed off our progress. I'm sure they had their doubts about my sanity, but they were kind enough to say it was the nicest outhouse they'd seen in a long, long time.

As I took the folks to Homer on *Skilak*, Dad looked back at the untamed land we called home, and said, "I can see what you've written us about Alaska is true, but how can you survive living there in the winter? How can you fight nature?"

My answer was a lesson I'd already learned, "Dad, you don't fight nature, you learn to live with her."

Liza and I needed a place to live for the winter, so we started digging the foundation for the big house. Progress was slow because we spent most of our time working on our boat. After every trip to town we'd spend days maintaining the motor, repairing new leaks in the hull, or fixing a multitude of things that could and usually did go wrong. During the summer of '74, I learned to appreciate the saying "A boat is just a hole in the water you pour money and time into."

We were isolated but not alone. Bruce Covault returned to rebuild his cabin, which had burned down the previous fall. Our other neighbor, Slim Sidnal, also worked long hours trying to get a structure built before the first snow fell. When a project was too big for one person, we called on our neighbors to give us a hand and in the process became good friends. We had a common goal—to become the first year-round residents of Sadie Cove.

All summer, Liza was restless and seemed to be fighting an internal battle only she could resolve. At the end of August I was shocked when she told me she wanted to return to California and become a nurse. We'd lived together for almost two years and still loved each other, but now we each had to follow our own path. Her decision to leave caused me much pain, but I knew Alaska was right for me even if it meant building a new life by myself. We took our last trip across the bay together, and as I started back home alone, Liza stood on the end of the spit waving good-bye. The sea was calm, but it was the worst crossing to Sadie I'd ever made.

With winter coming I had little time to mourn losing Liza. Building a large cabin was out of the question, so I designed a 10 x 14-foot cottage that I could build myself out of beach logs. When I had time to build a bigger cabin, the cottage next to the stream would become my sauna, but for my first winter in Sadie it would be home.

The biggest job was finding enough logs for the walls. Every day *Skilak* and I searched the beaches for strays, and during my outings I met several other people who lived on my side of the bay. On Hesketh Island I pulled up on the beach in front of a weathered cabin and met an older man who introduced himself as John Dalgleish. I shook his hand and said, "I'm your new neighbor in Sadie Cove."

John looked at my full beard and shoulder-length hair and answered, "Someone told me there were a bunch of beatniks living there."

I almost started laughing—the last time I'd heard the word "beatnik" was in high school. I guess it just took a while for world events to reach John on his island.

He invited me in for coffee and proceeded to talk for the next three hours. John had been in the Merchant Marine during World War II and still wore clothes from the 1940s. He bought the 170-acre island with its two-bedroom home from fox farmers shortly after the war and had lived there alone ever since. I liked this spirited, patriotic sourdough and realized I could be looking at myself thirty years in the future. In parting, John gave me permission to take logs off his beach; now I'd have enough to start building my cabin.

The days were getting shorter, so it wasn't hard working from sunup to sundown. After Bruce and Slim moved to Anchorage for the winter, I worked mostly by myself. However, there were friends like Gary Gray who dropped in to visit and stay a few days to help me out.

Gary was a jovial bull of a man. The morning before he came to visit me, he loaded a full-size refrigerator by himself into his small skiff, crossed the bay to Halibut Cove, and carried it to his cabin. In Sadie, he threw hundred-pound bundles of roofing around with ease, and I appreciated his help and companionship. After we finished the roof, he skiffed out of Sadie to help someone else complete his house before it started snowing.

It took six weeks of hard work to finish the cabin. Compared to the tent I'd been living in, my new home felt like a mansion. The woodburning stove kept me warm and allowed me to cook standing up. The shelves and table I built gave me plenty of room to store my gear and eat my meals. I even had room for a few dinner guests if we sat really close. An old, overstuffed chair I hauled in from Homer gave me a comfortable place to read, and Coleman lanterns and kerosene lamps supplied the light. A window in my loft bedroom let me look out on the cove while the stream sang me to sleep every night. Now all I needed to be ready for winter was my food supply, which I'd buy in Homer and harvest from the woods and sea.

I wanted to explore the high valley behind my property, so on a clear, frosty morning I shouldered my day pack and started up the mountain. An hour later I was struggling through a thick patch of alder when I heard something big coming toward me. The thick brush limited my sight to fifty feet, so I climbed a small spruce tree to get a better view. From my pitchy perch I spied a huge bull moose, its impressive antlers whacking the branches as it waded through the underbrush. As I watched my winter meat supply disappear into the trees, I began planning my first moose hunt.

I'd never been much of a hunter; the biggest critters I'd ever shot were pheasant and rabbit. The bull in the valley must have weighed close to a thousand pounds. I wanted this hunt to be a success, from the stalking and shooting to the butchering and eating, so I went to my books to learn how to do it right. In my limited library I found a pamphlet on moose hunting from the University of Alaska Extension Service. The Coleman lantern burned late that night as I studied the informative booklet.

The next day I cleaned my .30-'06 rifle, packed my gear, and got ready to go early the following morning. Just before dark I went down to the stream for a bucket of water. I was concentrating on not slipping on the icy rocks when a male voice behind me said, "Howdy."

I was so surprised I dropped the bucket, lost my footing, and fell into the stream. As I scrambled out of the cold water, the stranger laughed. Standing there, dripping wet, I saw the humor of the situation and started laughing myself. With a big smile, Ray introduced himself and apologized for startling me. I invited him to put his bulky pack and rifle on the porch and come inside for coffee.

Ray explained that he and his buddy Tony, who was still up in the valley, had been dropped off by skiff in Eldred Passage, and they had hiked up the mountain ridge to camp out and shoot ptarmigan. Moose hunting wasn't in their plans; but when a big bull stepped out of the brush a hundred feet away, the opportunity was too good to let pass, and Ray dropped it with one shot.

When I heard what he said, I blurted out, "You shot my moose?"

The small upper valley offered limited habitat for big animals, and I felt certain the bull I'd seen was the same one Ray had shot. After explaining how I planned to hunt the same moose for my winter meat supply, Ray said, "Keith, we don't have transportation back to Homer, so if you help us pack the moose off the mountain and give us a ride to town, we'll share the meat."

I accepted his offer, and that night we feasted on moose steaks he'd carried out in his pack.

The next morning, I battled bugs and heavy brush while struggling down the mountain with an 80-pound pack on my back. When it started raining during my third trip, I remembered buying meat from a butcher shop in the city. Hunting wild game didn't cost much money, but you pay for it in time, sweat, and aching muscles. It took us four full days to pack the moose meat to my cabin, haul it to Homer, and store it in a freezer. It would have taken me two weeks if I'd hunted alone.

I didn't want to keep *Skilak* in Sadie for the winter with only a 100-pound anchor, so after hauling over the last of my supplies I beached her in Homer and caught a ride home with a shrimp fisherman who was working in my cove.

While building the cabin and getting ready for winter I'd been too busy to feel alone, but now I started questioning my life in Sadie. I had no boat to get to town, no radio for communications, my neighbors Bruce and Slim were in Anchorage for the winter, and Liza had moved to California. Nobody was in the cove but me, and I wasn't enjoying my own company.

One morning while walking on the beach, the 6-foot fin of a killer whale broke the water 100 feet from where I stood. Excited and not thinking, I turned around to share the thrill with Liza, but no one was there. At that moment a flood of loneliness almost drowned me in despair. I slumped to the beach and screamed out my frustration, "This isn't what I planned!"

As my words echoed off the cliffs, I realized I hadn't spoken for more than two weeks. Instead of giving myself a silent pep talk, I started talking out loud. "You're alone, but look at the positive side. You have an exciting life, a cozy cabin, a full pantry, lots of good books, and a list of interesting projects that will take two winters to complete. Go play your guitar—maybe the music will cheer you up."

I went to the cabin, sat down with my guitar, and started strumming. It didn't help; the music wasn't the same without Liza.

While trying to think myself out of the blahs, I verbalized my thoughts: "Nobody said this life would be easy. You chose your path, and maybe you're not supposed to be with anyone right now."

After thinking about what I had said, I continued talking. "You're still free to make choices. You can go back to town knowing you really didn't give this life a chance, or stay in Sadie and learn to live alone by getting to know yourself. It was a hard search finding a land to call home, do you think finding a woman to love will be any easier?"

I felt much better. One thing about talking to yourself—you can't lie or hide behind your own excuses.

On November 14, 1974, I was thirty-two years old. Kevin and Cindy Sidelinger, who lived on China Poot Bay, had promised to come visit on my birthday, and I was more than ready for some company. However, nature wasn't cooperating. Gale-force winds howled around my cabin, and I doubted that my friends would chance death just to make it to my birthday party.

All day I tried to keep busy with chores and hoped the weather would die down. Finally, I went inside, stretched out on my bed, and tried to get lost in a book. It didn't work; every ten minutes I'd look out over the whitecapped water. It was rough in Sadie, so I knew the outer bay would be stormy and dangerous. An hour before dark I accepted the fact that I'd be spending my birthday alone.

Just as I gave up hope, a skiff entered the cove, and I almost broke my neck getting out of the loft to greet my visitors. Waves were crashing on the beach, and we had a hell of a time getting my friends ashore and anchoring their 16-foot boat. When we got back to the protection of my cabin, they sang "Happy Birthday" and handed me a carrot cake Cindy had baked. It tasted delicious even though it was squashed flat from the rough ride. We sang folk songs, toasted each other, feasted on moose meat, and they even let me talk as much as I wanted. Late that night we had a pillow fight in the loft and went to sleep among the feathers. When we hugged good-bye the next day, I realized I wasn't living my life alone—I had my friends.

After my birthday bash, I waved down a ride to town and made a trip to Anchorage to sell Mooseltoe for the holiday season. Christmas and New Year were spent in Homer with friends, and my best present was one I gave myself—a CB radio and battery for my cabin in Sadie. In early January I hitched a ride back to the cove with my shrimp-fishing friend, who said he'd be back in two weeks. I was alone again, but now I looked forward to some quiet time after the hectic visit to the city.

I spent the first week settling into a daily routine. With only six hours of daylight, it was easy to get up before the sun. While waking up with my first cup of coffee, I'd play solitaire with a deck of cards so old I had to dust them with flour to keep them from sticking. After a couple of rousing games and a pot of coffee I was ready to plan my day. Being a list person, I'd write down what I wanted to achieve, then later get pleasure out of crossing off what I'd completed. The daily chores of cooking, carrying water, filling the lanterns, chopping wood, washing dishes, and cleaning the cabin seemed more enjoyable in my slow-paced winter world.

My big project of the week was designing and developing a materials list for the 100-foot wharf and house I planned to construct the next summer. I spent a lot of time drawing, calculating, and smiling as the project took shape on paper. I'll never know how many hours it took to complete; I'd thrown my watch away when I left San Francisco.

Taking a bath was always a chilling event. I tried washing in the stream, but while standing there naked and shivering on the icy bank, it didn't take long to realize that to harden my body to the elements was one thing, to freeze it was another. So I took my bath in an old galvanized tub in the cabin. I'd read that early Alaskans wouldn't bathe all winter, but for me a week was about all I could tolerate. I chuckled remembering how in my city life I often showered twice a day.

Each day ended with my nose stuck in a book. I might travel to Russia as a spy, sweat through a mechanics manual, or drool over an Alaskan cookbook. After a couple of hours I'd turn off the lantern, snuggle under the covers, and let the sound of waves and wind soothe me to sleep.

I kept a daily record of the weather, and the second week all I recorded were storms. Even on those days I tried to spend most of the daylight hours outside, and a walk on the beach became part of my daily routine. Sadie is a true fjord—narrow and steep—and when the big winds blow from the southeast out of the Gulf of Alaska, they accelerate when they enter the cove. Scientists call it the Venturi effect; we call them the Sadie Eighties.

On one particularly nasty day, I bundled up and went out for my walk as williwaws screamed down the side of the mountain. These sudden gusts created 200-foot-high water spouts that were blown out of the cove by the constant 60-knot winds. I could see the big gusts coming across the water, and just before they hit me, I'd turn my back and lean into them. It was exciting to feel such raw power so directly and still be fairly safe on the shore.

After an hour of playing on the beach, I saw a giant gust approaching from the head of Sadie. The wind extended across the entire cove and was blowing salty spray several hundred feet into the air. I watched the white wall of wind charge forward and heard a roar as it surrounded me. I turned my back and leaned hard. It slammed into my body, picked me up, and threw me twenty feet. When I landed in a heap, my legs were already churning, and I was off the beach before I could say "*Uff da!*"—a Scandinavian term meaning either really good or really bad. That gust must have been over a hundred miles an hour, and as I stood there with my heart in my throat, I suddenly remembered the old saying "Don't mess with Mother Nature."

The third week no one visited, but I wasn't alone. A mated pair of bald eagles screamed at each other from their perches high in the trees, six shaggy, white mountain goats grazed along the cliffs rising off the beach, and fifty noisy sea lions made the cove their winter home. Every morning on the way to the outhouse I could see a variety of new tracks in the fresh snow. It was like living in a zoo, but there were no fences separating me from the animals.

Unfortunately, a few of the critters became pests. One night while reading I heard the sharp snap of one of the traps I'd set to stop the nightly raids on my food supply. I investigated and found I'd caught a mouse. The book I'd put down was on curing animal skins, so I skinned the fluffy, little rodent, tacked the hide to a small board, and sprinkled it with table salt. As I put my trophy away, I tried to calculate how many mice it would take to make a blanket.

The following day I was out gathering blue-shell mussels for my evening meal when I was surprised to see a salmon jump out of the water. What's a salmon doing in these waters in the winter? I wondered. I didn't know, but my mouth watered at the thought of fresh fish for dinner. I grabbed a fishing rod, put the kayak in the water, and paddled out to where I'd seen the fish surface. After several hours I gave up on the salmon, but I did catch two cod. While enjoying a fresh seafood dinner, I read that what I'd seen was a white, or winter king, salmon. It wasn't in Sadie to spawn but instead was feeding on the abundant sea life of the cove. These fish can weigh twenty-five pounds, which would be enough to give my kayak a tow. If I caught one, maybe it could provide my transportation to Homer!

The fourth week I started getting a little concerned about my fisherman friend—he was overdue. However, I had plenty of food and postponed getting worried for another week.

One night after dinner I sat listening to my CB radio and heard a woman's voice say, "Mayday! Mayday! This is an emergency call. Does anyone in Homer read me?"

I recognized the caller. It was Diane McBride in China Poot Bay. Before I could reply, a man's voice came over the radio. "This is Homer. Read you loud and clear. How can I help? Over."

In a calm voice Diane explained the crisis. "I've received an emergency call from Josie Brown at the head of Kachemak Bay. Her husband, John, is choking on a salmon bone stuck in his throat. I'm the only one she can reach on the radio. Josie has pounded on John's back and tried reaching the blockage from the mouth. Neither helped. John is barely conscious and is starting to turn blue. Call the hospital in Homer and get instructions. Please hurry! Over and standing by."

I sat in silence, unable to help. I knew the Browns and whispered a prayer for John.

It didn't take long for the reply. "This is Homer back to the Mayday call. I have the hospital on the telephone, and here are the instructions for the Heimlich maneuver to clear the air passage. Put your arms around the choking victim from the back, join your hands at the bottom of the ribs in the center of the lower chest, and squeeze as hard as you can in one quick movement. This will cause any air still left in the lungs to forcibly eject the food stuck in the throat. Repeat several times if it doesn't work on the first try. Good Luck! Over."

Diane relayed the life-saving message to Josie on her isolated homestead thirty miles up the bay from where I paced the floor in Sadie Cove.

Several minutes passed before Diane was back on the radio. "This is China Poot calling Homer. Josie just told me the method did not work. What else can she do? Over."

Seconds counted, and time seemed to stand still until the answer came. "The hospital has given me instructions on how to give an emergency tracheotomy. Locate the Adam's apple on the front of the throat. Feel just below the cartilage where it sticks out the most, and with a sharp-pointed knife make a vertical cut into the air passage big enough to insert a small, hollow tube, such as a straw. This will allow air to get into the lungs and can keep the victim alive until help arrives. However, only use this method as a last resort. Tell her to try the Heimlich method again. Over and standing by."

After Diane relayed the message, I yelled, "Come on, Josie, you can do it!"

It seemed like a long time before Diane came back. "China Poot to Homer. Josie and John want to thank you and the hospital. She forced the bone out on her last try, and John can breathe now. He probably has some cracked ribs, but he'll live. I want to thank you too. This is China Poot, over and out."

The crisis was over, but after listening to the life-and-death drama, I started thinking about my own isolation in Sadie Cove. What would happen if I needed help? I had the CB, but what if I couldn't reach it? Too damn many ifs. This was the life I'd chosen to live, and if I started to think about all the things that could go wrong, I should move back to the city and rent a closet with maid service. The possibility of getting squashed flat while crossing the street was much greater than being killed by a bear in the Bush. As I climbed the ladder to my bed, I thought, I'll take my chances in Sadie.

Five weeks alone, my CB radio had a dead battery, and I was getting tired of talking to myself. My wanting to talk to someone had turned into a need. Maybe I could wave down a boat for a ride to Homer, but I hadn't seen anything on the water in a long time. As I thought about what to do next, I poured myself two fingers of whiskey. Sitting there sipping my after-dinner cocktail, I chuckled at remembering some old-timer warning me about living in Sadie Cove year-round. He'd said no one lived there because it was too steep, had no winter sun, didn't have a protected moorage, the wind blew like hell, and it was haunted. What he said gave me an idea—why not have a party?

I lit every lantern and candle in the cabin, laid out cheese and crackers, and went out into the dark to shout an invitation to anyone or anything in the neighborhood. I proceeded to promise a night of stimulating conversation, and since I was so desperate for company, even the topics of politics and religion were open for discussion. I dashed back to my well-lit cabin, where I poured myself another two fingers of liquid courage. Had I gone too far? What would I do if something did knock on my door?

After several more fingers of whiskey, I didn't care if Godzilla showed up. Nothing accepted my invitation, which might have been a good thing, but I thought I had a good time. The conversation was spirited, hors d'oeuvres delicious, and I went to bed thinking I should do this more often. In the morning I knew I should worry less about a ride to town and more about my acute case of cabin fever.

By the end of the sixth week I had finished my moose meat and my food supply consisted of some moldy cheese, stale crackers, and a can of unappetizing garbanzo beans. It was time to take control of the situation and kayak to Homer. If I could paddle the bay in summer, why not in winter? So, on a calm, cold day in mid-February, I cautiously kayaked the ten miles to town. The trip took three hours, and as I hit the beach in front of the Salty Dawg Saloon, I looked back and said, "I knew I could do it."

After storing my gear in the VW camper, I went in search of some companionship. The first person I met made the mistake of asking how I was doing—an hour later I was still telling him. At first, I had a little trouble with my mouth getting ahead of my mind, so I tried to talk slower and let my thoughts catch up with the words. I hadn't spoken to anyone in so long that the experience of conversation felt like an oral orgasm. I talked for two days to anyone who would listen, and Homer being a friendly town, I had no problem finding listeners.

Before kayaking home, I learned my fisherman friend hadn't come back to Sadie because of a bad auto accident. (I took back all the nasty things I'd said about him.) He recovered, and I learned two good lessons: first, living in the Bush meant relying on yourself, and, second, I could kayak the bay in winter.

The vernal equinox, March 20, brought twelve hours of daylight to Sadie, and all the critters in the cove had spring fever. Red squirrels chased each other around the woods while bald eagles tended their nests and screamed their love songs from the tallest trees. I knew how they felt; I was hornier than a four-peckered billy goat.

On a blustery day in April, Mike McBride pulled up to my beach with two other men in his skiff. It had been a cold, wet ride from China Poot Bay, and I invited them in for coffee and conversation. After Mike introduced the German hunters he was guiding, he asked if I'd seen any sign of black bears. While refilling their coffee cups, I said I'd seen more than fresh tracks.

Two days before, I felt the need to get some exercise and had gone out jogging. With the tide out, I huffed and puffed my way to the head of the cove. It was difficult picking my way over swollen streams and avoiding the large chunks of ice that littered the beach from spring avalanches. Scampering around a beached log I damn near tripped over a big black bear feeding on seaweed. Luckily, we sprinted in opposite directions, and I scooted back to my cabin much faster than I'd jogged out.

We told hunting stories until they got ready to leave, and then in broken English the German hunters asked if I had any trophies. I thought for a moment before remembering my indoor trapline. When I handed them the mouse skin thumb-tacked to a board, they laughed so hard I'm not sure they heard the clever tale I told about capturing the critter.

A week later, I got a ten-day job with South Central Timber Company to help pay for my summer projects. They hired men from my side of the bay to load log ships in Kasitsna Bay, five miles from Sadie. A neighbor from Tutka Bay picked me up in his skiff, and when we reported for work they gave us a choice of working in one of the four ship holds or out on the log rafts tied up next to the hull. I thought it would be safer outside, so after strapping spikes to the bottoms of my rubber boots, I joined the other workers on the floating forest.

Two of us attached heavy cables called chokers around the banded bundles of logs. After moving back a safe distance, we signaled the crane operator on the ship and he lifted the load into the hold. On board, the logs were secured for their journey to Japan.

The company provided our ten-man crew with room and board at the logging camp in Jakalof Bay and gave us sack lunches to eat on board the ship. This should have given us a chance to get to know the ship's Filipino crew, except for one small problem—none of them spoke English. The only word of their language I knew was *balute*, a fertilized egg delicacy that is eaten after being buried in the ground for several years.

During one of our lunch breaks, I tried striking up a conversation with a member of the Filipino crew. I used simple words and some sign language, but all he did was shrug his shoulders. We were getting nowhere until I made an egg-shaped snowball, pointed at my sculpture, and said, "*Balute.*"

A big smile crossed his face and in an excited voice he asked, "You eat *balute*?"

I laughed, wrinkled my nose, and answered, "No! No!" as I shook my head.

From then on, the whole Filipino crew called me Balute. As I worked on the log raft I'd hear a hearty "Hey, Balute!" and look up to see one of them waving. At lunch they'd bring me fresh fruit and show me pictures of their homeland. It amazed me how that one word broke the language barrier.

The day before our loading job ended, a combination of events occurred that made our jobs even more dangerous. The new snow and broken bundles of logs made walking on the raft slippery and unstable. My partner and I had just finished setting a choker and were running in opposite directions when the crane picked the bundle out of the water. The single logs started shifting, and before I could reach the safety of a stable bundle, the bark broke loose under my spiked boot. I lost my balance and came down hard on the back of my head. I felt myself blacking out but was able to grab a log before going underwater. I gritted my teeth and fought the blackness that was trying to take me. Just before losing consciousness I felt several strong arms pull me from the sea.

I only vaguely remember what happened next. A landing craft took me to shore, where an airplane waited to fly me to Homer. At the hospital they took off my wet clothes and wrapped me in warm blankets before taking X-rays. Dr. Eneboe came into my room with good news; I didn't have a skull fracture, only a concussion. After a good night's sleep, I was well enough to go home. As I checked out, a nurse handed me a note from across the bay. On a wrinkled scrap of paper I read the scribbled message: "Get good quick, Balute."

The logging company paid the hospital bill and sent me a check for my wages. I didn't want to spend another summer working on *Skilak*, so I traded her for a 22-foot skiff with an outboard motor and $2,000. Now I had a boat and enough money to start my next building project.

It was time to start construction on the 100 x 16-foot wharf I'd designed in the winter. My plans called for forty 14-foot-long pilings, and it took a week to locate and tow the beach logs to Sadie with my skiff. While scouring the beaches for piling logs, I inspected several old wharfs and talked to the men who had built them. What I learned made me adjust my own design, but increased my confidence that the structure could withstand the big storms of winter.

I chose to hand-dig the pilings instead of paying somebody to do it with heavy equipment. Each hole was five feet deep, but to get down that far in gravel I had to dig a pit six feet square. By working during low tides and shoveling at a steady pace, I could complete five holes a day. However, I needed help levering the piling logs into a standing position in the pits.

My neighbors Bruce and Slim were back in the cove, so they gave me a hand, although they had their own projects. Occasionally a boatload of visitors would stop at my beach, and more than once they stayed a while to help with the pilings. With half the work completed, I skiffed to town for supplies and to recruit some help.

I made signs with a Homer phone contact and tacked them up all over town. The message read:

HELP WANTED

BUILDING A WILDERNESS HOME IN SADIE COVE

ROOM/BOARD/TRANSPORTATION ACROSS THE BAY

CONTACT: KEITH IVERSON

Jeff and Cloud, two young men from upstate New York, came north looking for adventure and were eager to help me in exchange for the experience of living in the Bush. The work went so well that we finished the piling job in one week. We were out of building materials, so we agreed to continue the project in two weeks. My helpers hiked into the mountains behind my land to do some exploring, and I headed for town for more supplies.

Bartering and serious shopping were the only ways to get more building materials with a skinny bank account. My first success required little cash but a lot of work. I bought a fifteen-year-old barn twenty miles from Homer for $200. The catch was I had to tear it down and get the lumber to Sadie. My friend Robert volunteered to give me a hand and said, "People have barn-raising parties—why not have a barn-demolition party?"

I slapped him on the back and said, "Great idea! We'll do it."

We picked the day, invited the people, borrowed extra tools, bought five cases of beer, and were ready for the barn bash. Fifteen folks showed up, and six hours later we had a giant pile of boards stacked by the road ready to haul to Homer. If I had worked alone, the job would have taken me weeks to complete, and it definitely wouldn't have been as much fun.

Thanks to my friends' help, I was ahead of schedule, so I took a trip to the Moose Pass area. Besides fly fishing for grayling, I bought seventy-five oak beams for $1 apiece and twenty-five used windows for $2 each. To top off the successful trip, I met someone driving to the spit with an empty flatbed truck and talked him into hauling my load. Back in Homer I bought insulation, nails, and roll roofing from the local lumber yard. No deals there, but now I had all the supplies to complete my project.

Bruce and I had the same problem: a mountain of building materials on the spit and only small skiffs to haul it home to Sadie. Rather than spend all summer making freight runs across the bay, we each chipped in $100 and I went to town in search of a cheap miracle.

I tied up my skiff in the Homer harbor and heard a foghorn voice hail me from the bridge of a 120-foot landing craft. It was old Stan Lee from Kodiak; I hadn't seen him since he'd helped me with engine problems on *Skilak* the previous summer. Over coffee in his galley he asked, "What are you working on now, more engine trouble?"

I laughed and answered, "Not this time. I'm in town looking for a boat to get a big stack of lumber to Sadie."

He scratched the white stubble on his chin and said, "I'm going to Jakalof Bay tomorrow to pick up fuel barrels at high tide. I'll take your load over if you get it on board before I sail."

I appreciated the offer, but replied, "Thanks, but I can't afford your $1,200 daily fee."

"Who the hell said anything about money?" Stan snorted. "If you're in the Salty Dawg tonight, you can buy me a beer and we'll call it even."

As we shook hands, I said, "Thanks, you old sea dog. And don't worry, I won't ruin your reputation by telling anyone how much you're helping me out."

That night we drank more than a few beers, and in the process I recruited four young men to experience the joys of hauling lumber. Early the next morning we started loading the boat. After sweating all day, we dropped the last board on deck, cast off the lines, and headed across the bay.

Bruce saw us enter the cove and met me on the beach when we dropped the bow ramp of the landing craft. With the help of Stan's crew we finished unloading in two hours. As we watched the boat leave, Bruce turned to me and said, "I'm afraid to ask what that cost."

"Stan did it for free," I replied. "But I spent the $200 on the loading crew and a few beers for the captain."

As we looked at the mass of boards scattered along the beach, I said, "You know, half the work of building in Sadie is getting the supplies over here."

The next morning Jeff and Cloud returned thinner, but smiling, from their camping trip. Now it was time to have some fun pounding nails. After taking four days to deck the wharf, we were ready to build my new house.

Life on the ocean can be a blessing or a curse. As elsewhere, there are two high tides and two low tides every day, but in Kachemak Bay we can get a 30-foot vertical drop or rise of water in six hours, a +24-foot high tide to a -6-foot low tide. In Sadie, during a series of big tides, the water comes halfway up my pilings, but when it goes out, I have 200 feet of beach.

The day we began framing the wharfhouse, I stood on the deck looking at the tide chart to see if the water would be low enough to dig clams for dinner. Turning to the page for June, I read a -3-foot low, just right for steamers, and automatically checked the high. It read a +30. A chill ran through my body as I yelled, "A 30-foot high tide! How the hell could I make such a mistake?"

"What's the matter?" Jeff asked as he looked up from his work.

I was so mad at myself it took a minute to calm down and reply, "I designed the wharf six feet too low. The house will be an aquarium, not a cabin. How could I be so dumb?"

Cloud took a look at the tide book and said, "Keith, you were reading the tides for Anchorage."

I grabbed the book and laughed in relief when I saw he was right. Damn, for once it felt good to be wrong.

The skeleton of the wharfhouse went up faster than I figured, and when we finished framing, I walked through the airy rooms imagining them done. The 10 x 30-foot first floor included a pantry, kitchen, living room, and an enclosed porch. Upstairs would be a bedroom with plenty of space to read and shelve my library. It wasn't a big building at 500 square feet, but it would be more comfortable than the sauna with its 140 square feet.

With the framing completed, Jeff and Cloud moved on with my thanks to Kodiak, where they had commercial fishing jobs. After they left, I put on the roof, installed the windows, built doors, and nailed up the siding. The wharfhouse was finished on the outside with the old, bleached barn wood, so it looked like it had been on the beach for twenty years. I didn't care that the finish work wouldn't be done by winter. With the building enclosed, it would be a good cold-weather project.

In the fall, I worked for two weeks salvaging a capsized cargo barge in Halibut Cove. It paid good wages, but while on the job a storm destroyed my skiff. I didn't want to spend another winter in Sadie without transportation, so I went to Homer to buy a boat.

I was amazed at how much money people wanted for anything afloat. I'd almost given up when I ran into Roy in the harbor. After hearing my problem, he told me of an old, beat-up boat in his yard he'd sell for $200. The price was right, so I went to take a look. The 14-foot plywood skiff looked pretty bad painted in several different shades of green. However, it had a sound hull and could haul more than my kayak, so I bought it. The skiff would fill my needs until I could afford something more seaworthy. Its name just popped into my head—*Green Death*.

I loaded the boat with supplies, attached the 25-horsepower outboard from my destroyed skiff, and headed home. It leaked, but bailing solved the problem. After my first crossing, I saw that the boat would work out fine if I picked good weather. I liked this skiff—*Green Death* had character.

After selling Mooseltoe in Anchorage, I returned to Sadie knowing my second winter in the cove would be better than the first: I had transportation, Bruce and Slim would be home, and I looked forward to finishing the wharfhouse. I felt fulfilled with my life in the Bush, although I still needed to find a way to earn a living.

National Mooseltoe Campaign

My neighbor Bruce and I sat in the finished wharfhouse one night in mid-January of 1976 talking about life in Sadie Cove. "We've been here long enough to realize the hardest part of surviving in the Bush is finding a way to make a living," I said.

He agreed and added, "I've bounced back and forth between the cove and Anchorage to make the money I need. Sure wish I could find an easier way."

"Maybe there is no easy way," I suggested. "A couple of one-week jobs and the $4,000 worth of Mooseltoe I sell each year is barely enough to make it through the winter."

Bruce chuckled and remarked, "Last Christmas a man from California made millions of dollars selling Pet Rocks."

"People will buy anything if you put it in a pretty package," I replied. "But as a man who sells moose manure, I sure can't criticize the public's buying habits."

"Hell, Keith, if people Outside will buy plain rocks, I'll bet they'd buy your fancy shit," my friend pointed out.

We laughed, but he had a good point. "Great idea!" I said. "If I thought I could make a million dollars selling Mooseltoe nationally, I'd leave Sadie for a year and try it."

The idea lit a fire under my imagination and started the creative juices boiling. "I know it's easier said than done," I said, "but let's have some fun and plan it out."

I got us each a beer, pulled out a pad of paper, and for three hours wrote down ideas on how to sell Mooseltoe in the Lower 48. We discussed collecting the moose manure and went on to analyze manufacturing, labor, logistics, supplies, sales, profits, packaging, publicity, pricing, taxes, transportation, capital, and costs. When Bruce walked up the mountain to his cabin, I was still jotting down notes.

The next morning, over my first cup of coffee, I reread what I'd written to see if the plan had any merit. After finishing my fourth cup of caffeine, I made up my mind and ran up the steep path to share my decision with Bruce. When I told him I wanted to give the wacky idea a try, he asked, "How will you start?"

He seemed a little surprised when I answered, "I'm going over to Homer tomorrow to raise the money."

The bank proved less than receptive when I outlined my plan and asked for a loan. But what had I expected with only *Green Death* and a remote cabin for collateral and a bizarre idea to pay back their investment. I needed to find someone with money who had faith in me and my abilities. The letter read: "Dear Mom and Dad, I've decided to go national with Mooseltoe. Enclosed is an outline of my strategy. Will you please loan me $30,000? Your hopeful son, Keith."

Two weeks later my answer came in the mail. My folks weren't wealthy, but they had enough faith in me and my plan to lend me the money. Now I had capital to make my project work. To accomplish my goal I had to return to the city, but now I'd be working for myself. I had no doubt that producing and promoting a product as perverse as moose poop for praise and profit would be a city adventure.

In February I winterized my home in Sadie Cove, packed my plans, and started driving to the Lower 48. Before leaving Alaska I stopped in Anchorage to begin the paperwork that would protect the name Mooseltoe with a trademark. My lawyer, Bill, wrote down the facts, took some samples, accepted a check for $500, and sent the information to another attorney in Washington, D.C., to begin the long legal process. If my product sold as well as the Pet Rock, I didn't want another company cornering the market on moose manure. Making Mooseltoe a success required the same procedures and protections as less eccentric products.

I'd driven the Al-Can Highway five times, but never in winter. At the Canadian border the thermometer read a numbing -40°F! The VW camper handled like a cold, stiff tank, and although the woodburning stove I'd installed glowed red, I still wore my winter survival gear. Knowing if I turned off the engine it wouldn't start again till spring, I picked up a frozen hitch-hiker near Whitehorse in the Yukon Territory, and together we drove straight through in four days.

Upon arriving in Oregon, I traded my wilderness wools for a suit and entered the business world. I needed a base of operations other than my parents' home, so I rented an office with a warehouse in Tigard, a small town on the outskirts of Portland.

If Mooseltoe made a million dollars, I wanted to protect my profits by becoming a corporation. So my high school and college buddy Jack, who had his own law practice, prepared the papers, explained their meaning, collected the fees, and Alaskan Mooseltoe Co., Inc., was born.

I needed to connect with the big markets of San Francisco and Los Angeles, so I headed south to California. Driving through Eugene, Oregon, I chuckled at what my marketing professors at the university there would think of my project. Funnier yet, what would I have thought of my present life when I was a college student twenty years earlier?

As I crossed the California border the radio broadcast, "A volcano has erupted near the small town of Homer, Alaska. Mount St. Augustine blasted ash and smoke 40,000 feet into the air. There is no word on damage or casualties."

I damn near had a wreck getting off the freeway to find a telephone. The lines were jammed by concerned people like myself trying to find out about family and friends, so it took half a day to get through and find out there were no injuries or devastation. After hearing the good news, I reflected on how my life's path had led me through the city and the wilderness. Both had something different to offer; both could be an adventure.

In California my first task was to develop a new, attractive package to catch the buyer's eye since the original packaging for Mooseltoe lacked the quality required for national distribution. While searching for a solution, I met Grabe Smith of Chan, Miller & Smith Co., an advertising agency in Oakland. After showing him the product, describing my plans, and explaining what I wanted, Grabe said, "I like your idea and admire the guts it takes to sell this crap nationally. We'll design the packaging and take care of your other marketing needs. As payment we want 5 percent of the net profit."

I was more excited than a moose in rut! Finally, someone in the business world would take on my crazy project for fun instead of purely for profit.

Grabe and his staff designed a unique package that looked like a Christmas tree ornament with an oval window so that the buyer could see the moose nuggets inside. They also completed a professional-looking display case that held twenty-four packages of Mooseltoe.

At one of our promotional meetings, Grabe explained that we needed a publicity release for the news media. The story of Mooseltoe with a photograph would be mailed out to magazines and newspapers throughout America. Why not promote sales through free publicity instead of paying for advertising? Everyone in the advertising agency agreed my product was bizarre enough to create newsworthy copy. Now we just needed an interesting photograph.

We decided to set up a picture of me, Mooseltoe, and a moose to help get our message across to the news media. But where could we find a moose in Oakland? After several telephone calls, Grabe sent one of his staff with a pickup truck to rent a trophy head mount from a taxidermist in San Jose. Several hours later, the man staggered back into the office, obviously upset. After pouring himself a stiff drink from the office bar, he told us his story.

"I had no idea a moose could be so huge," he exclaimed. "The head and antlers filled the whole back of the pickup, so everyone on the freeway could see the monster. I'd driven halfway back when another pickup, complete with gun rack and an NRA [National Rifle Association] sticker on the window, passed me, honked, and gave me the thumbs-up sign. They probably thought I shot the beast and considered me one of their hunting buddies. It made me feel a little proud, but what happened next sure didn't."

He mixed another drink before continuing. "A couple miles before the Oakland turnoff, a VW bug with a peace symbol painted on the side tried running me off the road while the hippies inside screamed, 'Murderer! Murderer!' and gave me the finger. It scared the crap out of me. Someone else can take the brute back."

We all had a good laugh, and he had another drink.

People had bought the Pet Rock because it was a clever, witty gift, but would buyers in the Lower 48 understand Mooseltoe's humor? I needed a funny instruction booklet and someone to write it.

The year before, I'd sold my novelty gift to the zany owner-editor of the *Wretched Mess News* in West Yellowstone, Montana. He'd sent me a complimentary copy of his newest book, *How to Fish Good*, plus his winter address in the Bay Area and an invitation to meet for lunch if I ever found myself in his neck of the woods. After calling Milford Patroon on the telephone, I knew I'd found the right person to write the booklet—his wild sense of humor was perfect for my product.

Milford enthusiastically accepted the job, and for the next few weeks we had many enjoyable meetings writing the brochure that I would include in each package. The humorous history of the invention of Mooseltoe included Umlaut, the Eskimo; He Who Stepped In It, a nearsighted Indian; and Exxon, the ex-ongoing explorer. But my favorite was the Mooseltoe guarantee.

"Your Mooseltoe is unconditionally guaranteed for one year against manufacturing defects, faulty parts, and other moostakes. Should you have cause for complaint, write to Chairman of the Moose Board, Alaskan Mooseltoe Co., Inc., Moosebox 2265, Homer, Alaska 99603. Describe the malfunction in detail and enclose 83¢ to cover mailing and handling costs of the personalized reply you will receive, plus a small beer for our Chairman as he reads your complaint."

On one of my visits to Milford's office he introduced me to two men from southern California. The reporter and photographer wanted to interview me for their newspaper. After writing down all the facts and taking my picture, they told me the story would appear within a week. On April 27, 1976, 1,200,000 people were greeted with the article titled "King of Mooseltoe Drops in on Lower 48" along with my picture on the second page of the *Los Angeles Times*.

I didn't mind that they made me the King of Crap; the story would help sell a lot of Mooseltoe. However, the amount of fan mail that came pouring in from the article surprised me. Even more surprising were the four written proposals of marriage I received—three from women and one from a man.

When I arrived in Los Angeles they didn't roll out the red carpet befitting my newly acquired royalty status, but I did get much accomplished. I purchased a truckload of damaged, plastic Christmas trees for the Mooseltoe sprigs. Next, I connected with Roger Gruen, Inc., which with its sales force and showroom would be my West Coast distributor. Before returning to Portland, I also hired two men to sell my product to retail stores as factory representatives.

Back in my Oregon office, I ordered 100,000 Mooseltoe packages from Fiberboard Corporation so that they would be ready when I got back to Portland from Alaska in three months. I had to return home for two good reasons. First, I needed to recharge my mental batteries by reconnecting with my life in Sadie Cove. Second, only during the summer months could I collect and dry a ton of moose turds.

Upon arriving in Homer, I hired Steve and his wife, Cheri, to run my Alaska operation. They would forward my correspondence, handle the mail orders, and organize the collection, drying, and mailing of the raw moose manure to my Oregon office. It would take 2 million moose muffins to make 1 million Mooseltoe packages, and if the idea caught on, I wanted to be ready for mass production. We placed an ad in the *Homer News* that read:

Wanted—Quality Moose Manure
Be your own boss and work out in the woods.
$8.00 per cubic foot.
Contact Steve or Cheri—Phone 555-1234

If a person picked up poop in an area with a healthy moose population, he or she could collect three cubic feet per hour. At $24 an hour, the woods were alive with willing homesteaders, summer visitors, and mothers with their kids, and the brown bombs started coming in by the sackful.

After the ad appeared, my project became one of the main topics of conversation in Homer. One Homerite wrote me a letter in which he expressed concern about how collecting too much moose manure might disturb the ecological balance of the area. To soothe his anxiety and stop a movement that could lead to submittal of an environmental impact statement, I made some calculations and wrote back to him:

Yearly Moose Manure Production
(averaged, of course)

	20	deposits per day per moose
x	100	nuggets per deposit
	2,000	total nuggets per day per moose

	730,000	nuggets per year per moose
x	180,000	moose in Alaska
	131,400,000,000	nuggets, yearly production

(Yes, there is plenty to go around!)

The bags of manure rolled in, but we needed three times the amount we had collected to achieve our goal. We decided to expand our collection area by advertising in the local newspaper for Kenai and Soldotna. These communities were on the fringes of the Kenai National Moose Range, so we expected good results from the ad. When Steve drove the eighty miles north to Soldotna to make the connection with the poop pickers, the response was amazing. He pulled into the parking lot to find twenty pickup trucks overflowing with moose scat. In one afternoon we collected our quota of the essence of Mooseltoe and could now move on to the next phase of the project.

In the three years I'd collected moose poop for the Alaska market, I dried the droppings in my oven at home. Now I needed to dry whole mountains of manure and hoped I could solve the problem in Homer. While living in Sadie Cove, I had brought my laundry to the Homer Cleaning Center whenever I came to town. I knew the owners, Red and Nelda, and over the years they had enjoyed my stories of life in the Bush and Mooseltoe. So I paid Red a visit and asked, "May I dry a ton of wet moose nuggets at your laundromat?"

He raised his eyebrows, crinkled his nose, and replied, "In the dryers?"

I laughed and answered, "No, that wouldn't work for several reasons, but Steve could build drying racks above your big boiler in the back room. The droppings have no odor, so it won't hurt your business operation, and he'll keep the area cleaned up."

Red liked the idea of getting involved in my wacky scheme and agreed to be the dung drier for the corporation.

I had one last matter to take care of before flying back to Oregon. Did I need a state or federal permit to ship and sell moose manure? I started telephoning government agencies to get an answer. On my first call I explained my situation and received the reply, "Let me get this straight. You want to know if there is a permit required to ship and sell moose shit? Is this a joke?"

When I assured the man of my sincerity, he replied, "Fertilizers are shipped throughout the world, and to my knowledge, no regulations apply."

My flight to Oregon took three hours compared to the six days required to drive the Al-Can Highway, and I arrived just in time to start receiving the shipments of dried moose nuggets. Every day I went to the Tigard post office and picked up ten to twenty cardboard cases. I was just another customer until the day one of the boxes broke open. The postal employees asked me about the brown berries scattered over the floor, so I related the story of Mooseltoe. My customer status skyrocketed, and whenever I appeared to pick up my mail, the clerks would smile, crack a few jokes, and ask about my business. A few even bought some Mooseltoe for Christmas stocking stuffers.

Somehow it seemed the right thing to do—I joined the Loyal Order of the Moose. After our meetings, a member usually asked what I did for a living, and my answer always created a lively topic of conversation. While traveling to different cities, I made a point of visiting my brothers in their Moose Halls, and I'm sure their support helped me keep my sense of humor.

The packages, instruction booklets, green sprigs, red and white yarn, dried moose manure, and shipping cartons were stored in the warehouse waiting for assembly. I knew the manufacturing costs would be my greatest expense, so I researched the alternatives to keep the overhead down and the profits up. After analyzing the expense of hiring the handicapped, setting up my own assembly line, or contracting production out to another company, the least expensive method would still cost twenty-five cents per package to produce. While considering my options, I received an order for 100 cases of Mooseltoe and started making them myself. Sitting there assembling my product, I learned I could only complete one case an hour. I needed help immediately if I hoped to manufacture enough Mooseltoe in time for the holiday season.

Thank God for mothers—mine took pity on me and volunteered to help. We started a production line in the den and were hard at work packaging poop when the neighbors dropped in for a visit. The Walkowitzes laughed as I explained the procedure and then asked, "Would you pay us to make Mooseltoe?"

"You bet," I answered. "I'll supply the materials, you can assemble them in your home, and I'll pay you ten cents per package."

They took home enough materials to make 500 packages. The next day they returned the finished products, received $50, and took home the makings for 2,000 more. The idea spread, and soon the whole neighborhood had Mooseltoe assembly lines in their homes. Mom had helped solve my production problems, so I promoted her to vice-president in charge of manufacturing. In one month our cottage industry produced 100,000 packages of Mooseltoe.

The warehouse overflowed with the finished product, but they weren't going to sell themselves. To create the demand, Grabe's advertising agency in Oakland arranged for a six-week publicity tour of California's major cities—Bakersfield, Fresno, Sacramento, San Diego, San Francisco, and Los Angeles. After receiving my schedule of appointments, I was more than a little nervous. Interviews for newspapers didn't bother me, but I'd never before talked on the radio or appeared on television. I knew the tour could help promote my product, so I packed a supply of courage, Mooseltoe, and pictures of my life in Alaska and headed for my first TV talk show in Bakersfield.

When I walked into the television station for my interview and met the crew, I almost forgot my own name. The show's host took me aside to discuss my story and calm my jangled nerves.

"Is this your first time on television, Keith?" he asked in a friendly manner.

"It sure is, and right now I'd rather be in Alaska facing a charging bear," I answered with a slight quiver in my voice.

He smiled and said, "Try to relax, and when we're on the air, just forget about the cameras. I'll ask questions and you'll answer just like a normal conversation. Believe me, you're going to enjoy it."

As we took our seats, he outlined what we would talk about, and the two cameras made their final adjustments. I took a deep breath, the red light came on, and we were on the air. I gradually relaxed as we discussed a topic I knew well—my life. We began by talking about my move from San Francisco to Alaska. Next, I described my life in Sadie Cove and showed a few pictures of the area and the home I built. The host then asked how I made the money to support myself, and I told him the story of Mooseltoe. Before I knew it, the show was over. On my way to the next appointment, I realized I had enjoyed the experience. The rest of the day was spent driving from one end of town to the other, talking on three different radio shows and doing an interview with the local newspaper.

The days grew more hectic as I progressed from city to city. The publicity Mooseltoe received went far beyond my highest expectations. On the national level the press releases worked well. Paul Harvey discussed my novelty gift, newspapers throughout the country ran articles on my bizarre product, and *Oui* magazine published the story with a photo of the moose and me. At the end of my six-week publicity tour of California, I'd appeared on fifteen television talk shows, sixty radio programs, and had my story published in every major newspaper in the state. I'd conquered my fear of the TV camera, made some good connections, and done my best to create a demand for the product.

Mooseltoe received more than a million dollars' worth of free publicity, but if I couldn't get retail stores to stock my novelty gift, people wouldn't know where to buy it. Distribution was the weak link in my marketing plan. My limited sales force consisted of two factory representatives, four small mail-order firms, Roger Gruen's company, and me, when I could find the time. The orders were coming in, but not as fast as I'd hoped.

In November I drove to Los Angeles to work with Roger's organization in a final big push before the holiday season. I sold Mooseltoe to the West Coast headquarters of J. C. Penney, but didn't have the sales force to get orders from the separate stores. I needed a big break to make the project a national success, and that opportunity arose my last week in Los Angeles.

Roger called me and in an excited voice said, "Let's meet for lunch. I've got some great news."

"You're going to tell me about the big orders you got?" I asked, hoping for the best.

"It's better than big orders," he said after a pause.

"What could be better than selling a warehouse full of Mooseltoe?" I asked.

"I'll tell you at lunch," he answered and hung up.

The news was so good I couldn't eat. Roger explained, "We have two good chances of getting Mooseltoe on Johnny Carson's show. First, my brother-in-law knows Johnny personally and said he would show it to him next time they played golf. Second, I received a call from the buyer you sold to at J. C. Penney's headquarters. He told me the Carson show sent over a person to make inquiries about any new, unique products they could use on the show. He gave him a package of Mooseltoe and told him how to reach you in Oregon."

My expectations were already making bank deposits. If my product appeared on the most-watched television talk show in America, Mooseltoe could be the next Pet Rock. I got so excited that I didn't pay any attention to the voice in my head that yelled, "Don't count your nuggets before they're dried!"

I returned to Portland to get ready for the flood of orders. Every night I watched "The Tonight Show," but Mooseltoe and I never got the call to appear. Chrismoose came and went, and even with a limited distribution network I sold 30,000 packages.

Before going back to Alaska, I visited the San Francisco area to thank those involved in my promotion. I also called my old buddy Neil to suggest we take a hike on the beach. As we slowly walked along the quiet winter shore, I said, "Isn't it interesting what different directions we've taken since our college days? You're a clinical psychologist in the city and I sell moose shit from my home in Alaska. What do you think, Doctor Steinberg, should I become one of your patients?"

"You're beyond therapy," he answered with a grin. "What's next for the Mad Viking from the North?"

"I'll return home to Sadie Cove for three months, and then I'm coming back." I answered. "My business made enough money to cover my expenses and repay part of the loan from my folks, but I'm not ready to quit. Besides, I still have a warehouse full of Mooseltoe and dried moose manure to sell."

During my year of promoting Mooseltoe, I bounced back and forth between the West Coast and Alaska like a yo-yo. The pressures of the city drained my energy while life in the Bush recharged my mental and physical batteries. Now I was going home for three months of therapy.

If Sadie Cove was my mental hospital, then *Green Death* was one of the psychiatrists. A ride across Kachemak Bay in the leaky, 14-foot skiff always cured me of city stress. If I didn't stay alert in *Green Death*, I died. When I returned to Homer in February, my boat awaited with my first treatment.

The weather seemed perfect for crossing the bay—except for the 20°F temperature, zero visibility, and snow. After an absence of four months, these obstacles didn't matter: I wanted to go home. I loaded *Green Death*, motored past the end of the Homer Spit, and took a compass bearing for Sadie.

Halfway across I sensed danger. Everything seemed normal, although I could see only 100 feet in any direction. The outboard motor chugged along as usual, I trusted my compass, and the skiff wasn't leaking too badly; so why was the hair standing up on the back of my neck? I'd just started thinking I had indigestion when a foghorn sounded. I knew the warning came from one of the oceangoing freighters that frequently came to Kachemak Bay, and it was very close.

Green Death wouldn't show up on the freighter's radar, and we were so small the crew wouldn't even feel a bump if they ran us over. I needed to warn them of my presence, so I grabbed a portable foghorn from the tool box and pushed the button. But nothing happened—no air! As a last resort I put on my cold-water survival suit. Now if we collided, my body could be recovered and receive a proper Viking funeral. Several tense minutes passed before the foghorn sounded again. I looked back and saw the ship's tall bow seventy feet behind me. I'd crossed the freighter's path and missed a trip to Valhalla by about five seconds. I finished the crossing shaken but wiser—next time I'd check the freighter schedules.

During the next three months at home, I totally recovered from the stress of the city. The hard physical labor got my body back in shape, and my mind relaxed in the peaceful setting. I even enjoyed the hours spent working out new marketing strategies. But all too soon it was time to return to the West Coast and try again.

The second year of my national promotion was easier than the first. With the company already established, I had time to concentrate on the weak points and work on the new moose-manure product I developed during my time at home.

I'd been on the West Coast for two months when I saw my friend Neil Steinberg in San Francisco. After shaking hands, he asked, "Still selling moose shit?"

"You bet, Neil. In fact, I've added a new item to my product line."

My friend raised an eyebrow and said, "I'm afraid to ask."

"Well, I had a ton of dried moose nuggets in the warehouse, so I invented Genuine Alaskan Moose Manure, or Poop for Plants." I answered. "It's a year-round product, and I'm trying to sell it nationally through plant stores. The packaging and instruction brochures are finished, manufacturing has started, and I've already sold more than 200 cases. With Mooseltoe and Poop for Plants, I know I'll make a pile of money. Can't sell from an empty wagon, you know."

Neil laughed, shook his head, and replied, "Keith, maybe you should become one of my patients."

I worked very hard at setting up the distribution for the two products, but for some reason I couldn't get a large national sales organization to peddle my poop. After six months, I could see my chances of becoming a millionaire were fading. At the Tigard warehouse, I filled the orders that came in, but my heart longed for home.

A voice in my head said, "Give it another try; you can do it. All you need is one big break."

Home could wait. I couldn't return feeling that maybe I'd given up just short of success. So I drove to a Safeway market, went to the produce section, where they sold a variety of fertilizers, and got the name of the buyer. Over the phone, I made an appointment with the man who did the purchasing for Safeway's ninety stores in Oregon and Washington.

Upon entering the large office complex with a case of Genuine Alaskan Moose Manure under my arm, I handed the buyer my business card, which showed a picture of my silent partner, the moose. He smiled and said, "You know, it's always been my dream to shoot a moose in Alaska."

I knew right then I would make the sale and said, "I could help you make your dream come true, but why wait—I have part of one with me now."

I opened the box of Poop for Plants and handed him a package. He grinned as he showed it to the people in the office. The whole room laughed as we entered his private office to write out the order. Safeway bought 300 cases of Genuine Alaskan Moose Manure, and the order grossed more than $14,000.

The next day I delivered the order, and the buyer said the stores would include Poop for Plants in their next newspaper ad. The following week they offered my product with other items in a two-page advertisement. It took all my patience to wait three days to find out the results. I nervously drove to a Safeway store and asked at the checkout stand where I would find the moose manure they'd advertised. The clerk answered, "It's in the plant department with the other fertilizers. If we're sold out, I can order more from our central warehouse."

I went to other stores, and they told the same story. In less than a week Safeway had sold more than half of what they'd ordered. My expectations went wild. I just knew the buyer would reorder 600 cases, and then I'd sell to all the Safeway stores in America. Next, K-Mart and other big chains would start selling my manure. Finally, I'd go international, become stinking rich, return to Sadie Cove, and live happily ever after.

To help the sales effort, I arranged to be on a television talk show in Portland the following week and called the Safeway buyer to see how he wanted me to plug his stores. He said he had to check with the company's main office and to call him back the next day. When I did call back, the excitement in his voice had vanished. He apologized and said a Safeway vice-president had ordered him to pull the remaining Poop for Plants from the shelves. The corporation's national headquarters had received complaints from a few stockholders who had seen the newspaper advertisement.

It was time to return to my life in Sadie Cove—the city adventure had ended. My two years of being an entremanure in the Lower 48 had been a success, even though I wasn't going home rich. I'd gained an education, met many fine people, and sold my share of shit. At least I'd tried!

The Good Life

Damn, it felt good to be home. After my two-year expedition to the West Coast I'd come back in a daze, and it took several days before I could smell the sea, hear the wind in the trees, and learn how to smile again.

I spent the first two weeks in Sadie splitting firewood, and the hard work slowly got my body and mind back in shape. One cold morning in February I grabbed my chainsaw to cut up a log that had washed up on the beach. With two feet of fresh snow on the ground, I used the wharfhouse porch to sharpen the saw. My concentration was focused on the work, so when I looked up and saw a full-grown wolverine less than eight feet away, my reactions were instinctive. I threw an empty gas can at the snarling beast and ran into the cabin to get my rifle.

When I came out of the wharfhouse, the wolverine stood thirty feet away and gave me a look that seemed to say, "What's your problem?"

As our eyes met, I calmed down and admired one of Alaska's fiercest animals. Wolverines have been observed chasing grizzly bear from their kill. They also have a bad reputation with humans. The largest member of the weasel family will break into remote cabins, eat any food they find, and then urinate on what they haven't destroyed.

The fellow facing me weighed about sixty pounds and had long, chocolate brown hair and a tan band running along both sides of its squat body. It displayed curiosity instead of aggression, but I knew it wasn't the kind of critter you made into a house pet. I could have shot it and sold the pelt for $500, but how could I kill a majestic symbol of the true wilderness, reducing it to an expensive fur coat for a rich city-dweller?

After several minutes, the wolverine sniffed the air, growled, and loped up the mountain. I grabbed my camera, shouldered the rifle, and followed its tracks through the deep snow until they disappeared into a small clump of dense brush. I saw no tracks leaving and hoped I could get a few pictures. After waiting an hour, I interrupted the silence and said to the beast in its temporary den, "I want to thank you for your visit, although you scared the crap out of me. This land is big enough for both of us, but I'll give you fair warning. If you try living up to your reputation as devil of the north by harming my home or pissing on my porch, I'll nail your hide to my wall!"

As I walked away, the wolverine answered with a deep-throated growl.

Green Death was still my main transportation to town, and although I tried picking calm weather to make the ten-mile crossing, dressing for a winter trip always proved to be a major ordeal. The long underwear came first, followed by heavy wool pants, two shirts, and three pairs of socks. Next, I slipped into insulated rubber boots with felt insoles and topped this with a down vest, coat, and full rubber rain gear. Waddling down the beach, I pulled on insulated gloves, a wool cap, and ski goggles. Before getting into the skiff, I'd take off half my clothes to relieve myself of the pot of coffee I'd drunk before dressing.

Whenever I crossed the bay in 10°F weather, both the skiff and I would be covered with a thin layer of ice. The forty-minute boat rides chilled my body, but now when I returned to Sadie I had the perfect way to get thawed out. During my trips home while selling moose manure in the Lower 48, I'd finished the sauna. The 10 x 14-foot log cabin that was my home for two years now served as a wood-heated bath house.

In the spring of 1978, I started another building project to provide more room for overnight guests. I also wanted a place to play at oil painting, putter with pottery, and do some carving, so I called my new cabin the Studio. After choosing a building site 100 feet up the mountain from the wharf, I cleared the land and put in pilings for the foundation. With this work completed, I designed the cabin, figured out my materials list, and went to see my neighbor about the lumber.

Slim Sidnal had come to Sadie the same year I did. He built his home and a sawmill to make rough-cut lumber out of beach logs. Slim had a unique policy; if I rounded up the logs, towed them to the mill, and helped him cut the boards, we'd divide the lumber equally. This allowed me to acquire most of the building materials for my new cabin. Instead of buying the boards, all I had to do was work for them.

By midsummer I had the 7,000 board-feet of lumber I needed to build the 16 x 24-foot cabin stacked on my wharf. Now all I had to do was haul it to the building site. I started carrying the boards and dragging the beams up the mountain. On occasion, people stopped by to visit and made the mistake of asking me if I needed a hand. Their help speeded up the process, but I knew there had to be a better way. Why not use my brain instead of my back and find some mechanical means to move the boards?

I looked through my junk pile, found the half-inch oil-drilling cable I'd bought the year before, and devised a high-lead system like those used in logging operations. I hung the metal cable between a tree next to the wharf and one up the mountain at the building site. From boards and two meat-hook rollers bought at a garage sale I built a carriage that rode on the cable twenty feet above the ground. With a block and tackle, I hoisted a small pile of lumber under the carriage and ran a long line to the upper tree and back down to the wharf. All I lacked was a motor to pull the load to the new cabin's foundation.

In the sauna that night, an idea popped into my head. The next morning I bolted a gas-powered cement mixer to the wharf near the lower end of my lumber-moving contraption. Then I tilted the cement bucket on its side and started the 5-horsepower motor. I wrapped the carriage rope around the revolving cement container, took up the slack, and watched as the load of lumber slowly slid up the steep slope. When it reached the top, I stopped the motor, tied off the line to the wharf, and walked up to unload. Not only did my idea save me work, my neighbors gave me the coveted Jury Rig Award for the year.

I figured I would haul every board, nail, window, door, and shingle needed for construction ten times before the cabin was finished. I also calculated the Studio would take two years to complete, but I wasn't in any hurry. I planned to enjoy the entire process.

Bruce, Slim, and I were the only year-round people living on the 12-mile coastline of Sadie Cove. We all came to Alaska for different reasons, but in Sadie we shared a common goal of making it our home. Through those early years of building, we shared a brotherhood that kept us moving forward. At times there were frustrations due to lack of money, knowledge, or female companionship, but when one of us felt down, the other two were there to pump him up. We helped each other physically and mentally, and I know it would have been much harder for me to begin my new life without the support of my two neighbors and friends.

Several times a week, the three of us got together after work for a few beers. Sometimes we met at Slim's for a fresh salmon dinner cooked in his fire pit on the beach. We held poker parties up the mountain at Bruce's, so when the game ended, Slim and I could slide down to our cabins. Whenever the sauna was fired up, I invited my neighbors to share the relaxing heat.

Every summer we had a big party on the Fourth of July. The two-day event included our summer neighbors Leon and Robbie Hickok, and we invited friends from around Kachemak Bay, Homer, and Anchorage. They arrived in everything from kayaks to large fishing boats, and everyone brought a variety of food and drink to contribute to the festivities.

The party began in the morning with the raising of the Stars and Stripes and a two-hour hike up the mountain to collect snow for making ice cream. On the beach, a variety of activities provided something for everyone. They included beer drinking, volleyball, rowboat races, water-skiing, beachcombing, kite flying, sailing, fishing, football, Frisbee, horseshoes, saunas, and more beer drinking. In the early evening, Slim fired his rifle and everyone gathered around his fire pit for dinner.

People brought, caught, and gathered a staggering variety of food. Whatever a person's tastes, he or she could find it among the crab, shrimp, clams, blue-shell mussels, salmon, halibut, octopus, moose and bear meat, venison, homemade breads, garden-fresh vegetables, salads, watermelon, pies, cakes, and homemade ice cream. The feasting continued until everyone sprawled out on the beach to watch the final event of the night.

How can anyone celebrate our nation's Independence Day without fireworks? Even in Sadie Cove, we honored our freedom by lighting up the night sky. Ever since our first annual summer party, Leon had taken charge of putting on the fireworks. Every year they got bigger and more flamboyant, and no one had more fun than our director of pyrotechnics. His first shows consisted of sparklers, firecrackers, and bottle rockets, but by the summer of 1978 they had grown to several hours of oohs and aahs. When the show ended, it was hard letting go of the day, but eventually everyone found a place to sleep and the cove became quiet again.

The first several years in Sadie, the population remained constant with we three bachelors. Then a new member arrived in our tiny community when Bruce married Jonnel. Slim and I were still waiting for the right ladies to be marooned on the beach, but we appreciated having a year-round woman in the cove.

Life wasn't easy for Jonnel. In the summer, we all had plenty of visitors, but the long, cold winters allowed few drop-ins, and her only company consisted of three men who were usually discussing past, present, and future projects. However, Jonnel and Bruce were happy, and she did well carrying supplies up the mountain, cooking on a woodstove, living with no electricity, and crossing the bay in an open skiff. Maybe someday I'd find a woman with her fine qualities.

We in Sadie Cove were also part of the Kachemak Bay community, which extends from the Fox River to Seldovia and from Halibut Cove to Homer. Our lives connected with these hardy neighbors, and more than once I gladly received their help.

The day before Thanksgiving I returned home to find one end of my wharf damaged by twenty huge logs that had washed up on the beach during the same storm that stranded me in Homer. With the +22-foot tides and another storm forecast, the danger wasn't over. All my neighbors had left for the holiday, so I went to work rolling the 40-foot logs down the beach with a Handyman jack. I only hoped I could complete the job before the storm blew in and destroyed my wharf and cabin.

As darkness descended, I slipped on the icy deck of the wharf and plunged ten feet to the log-strewn beach. I heard my ribs crack when I landed on my back, and for several minutes the pain made it very difficult to breathe. It seemed to take forever to crawl back to the cabin and call for help on the CB radio. Upon contacting Homer, I explained it wasn't an emergency injury, but I needed assistance to save my property. After signing off, I went to bed hoping someone would come to my aid.

Early the next morning, Kirk Rutzebeck arrived in his 70-foot fishing boat, *Wilson*, and on board were Wild Bill Slatter, Karen Eslin, Rene Rosie, and Big Johnny Lee. I couldn't roll logs but did help prepare the turkey they'd brought. With the work completed and my wharf safe, we all sat down to a Thanksgiving dinner. My first toast was to neighbors and friendship.

Working with neighbors, whether they lived in Sadie Cove or the larger community of Kachemak Bay, enabled us to take on bigger projects and made the work much more fun. One summer, Bruce, Slim, Leon, and I sat on the beach talking about how we could improve our lives if we had electricity in Sadie. None of us wanted to install a noisy generator, so we had three choices of alternative energy to generate power—sun, wind, and water. Each method had its advantages and disadvantages. Solar power would be great in the summer, but the winters had so little daylight that we probably wouldn't get enough energy to run an electric toothbrush.

Wind power had its problems too. Most of the time the cove was pretty calm, but when it blew, it could blow like hell. The Sadie Eighties might destroy a windmill, and none of us wanted to put in a spit-and-bailing-wire system that required constant maintenance.

The first time I saw my property in 1973, I knew the stream could generate hydroelectric power. Over the years, I'd read many good articles on the subject in *Mother Earth News* magazine. I didn't know much about electricity, but I did know the stream was the perfect location for a Pelton wheel. According to my calculations, there was enough water flow and vertical drop to provide all the energy we needed. I was sure getting tired of reading with a Coleman lantern.

The problem with putting in a Pelton wheel or any other alternative energy system was purely financial. The cost of installation would be like paying a utility bill ten years in advance, and none of us had that kind of money. So we decided to pool our resources and build a system that would produce enough electricity from the stream to supply all our needs. We each agreed to contribute $300 toward the joint venture, named our project the Northern Delight Power Authority, and toasted our new community project with ice-cold beers.

A month later, while on a trip to Anchorage, Bruce found just what we needed. The newspaper ad read "Pelton wheel for sale, built 1911, in good working order, 25,000-watt generator—$900." We bought the hydroelectric system and hauled the 4,000 pounds of equipment to Homer. Since none of us had a boat big enough to haul the Pelton wheel to Sadie, we stored it on the spit for the winter.

In early March, Dan Veerhusen, a commercial fisherman from Halibut Cove, approached us with a proposition that could help us all out. He had acquired a small barge, the *Shrimp of Juneau*, to haul building materials across the bay in exchange for painting its hull. Dan knew we wanted to move the Pelton wheel and suggested we all work together on both jobs. We agreed to the arrangement, and on a cold day in early spring, Bruce, Slim, and I met Dan in Homer to begin Operation Pelton Wheel and Barge Bottom.

With the help of a crane in the harbor, we loaded all the material aboard and towed the barge across the bay with Dan's fishing boat. We arrived in Sadie at high tide, so while the *Shrimp of Juneau* went dry on the beach next to the stream, we grabbed a quick meal. After the tide ebbed, we started unloading the 2,000-pound flywheel and 800-pound governor. Without a crane, we used the barge's mast and boom with block and tackle to move the heavy metal to the beach. Most of us had beards and wore heavy, wool, work clothes; so if someone had taken a black-and-white picture, it would have been hard to tell we weren't unloading the barge 100 years earlier.

The next high tide refloated the scow at 3:00 A.M., and we began the three-hour trip to Halibut Cove. Dan called ahead on his marine radio, so when we arrived, his wife Debbie had a big breakfast of eggs, bacon, homemade toast, and freshly ground coffee waiting for us. After a hot meal in the warm cabin, we all felt the lack of sleep but agreed to keep going and get the job done.

We towed the old barge to an equally ancient wharf, where we'd complete the unloading and bottom work. We needed to get up on the wharf to secure the lines, but it was fifteen feet higher than our deck, with no ladder for climbing. Bruce noticed a rope trailing over the high deck, gave it a tug to see if it was secure, and started up. We heard Bruce yell, "Oh, shit!" as the rope broke and he plunged into the freezing water.

When Bruce appeared sputtering and coughing at the surface, he was swimming the fastest dog paddle I'd ever seen. We quickly hauled him out and wasted no time getting him to the cabin before he became hypothermic. Once inside, his teeth were chattering, but we knew he was all right when he said, "Damn! I swallowed my Copenhagen."

Slim, Dan, and I returned to work and secured the *Shrimp of Juneau* to the wharf. The tide receded, exposing the hull, and Bruce joined us to finish the job. The bottom of the barge showed years of neglect, with rotted planks and worm holes from bow to stern. "The only thing holding this old scow together is the worms holding hands," Dan said as we started painting.

Dan took us home, and after a good night's sleep I had time to reflect on what had been accomplished. By working together we finished two large projects, and it only cost us our time and labor. I found great pleasure working with such versatile, competent men.

With the Pelton wheel in Sadie, we had come a long way from the day we formed the Northern Delight Power Authority. However, the next stages of the project would cost much more than we had already spent. We needed to build a small dam, install 2,000 feet of 12-inch high-pressure water pipe, construct a building for the generator, and connect our homes to the power source with heavy electrical wire. Lack of funds temporarily put our plans on hold, and we made do with what we had. Creating our own electricity with the Pelton wheel would be a long-term project.

During the cold months I usually worked alone building my home, but in the summer my "Help Wanted" signs in Homer brought me all the assistance I needed. Those who responded to my invitation did so for a variety of reasons. One California couple wanted to experience a life closer to nature before they tried it on their own. A group of four from Switzerland wanted to see a different part of Alaska and liked it so much that their planned three-day visit turned into two weeks. Many of those who worked with me in the cove became friends, and what they helped build made them a part of Sadie.

My life revolved around the cove, but I also had a strong connection with Homer. In winter I made the trip to town once a month, and in summer, sometimes every other week. The small community at the end of the road was my contact with the outside world, so I crossed the bay to pick up my mail, make telephone calls, buy supplies, visit, and raise a little hell.

A one-day trip to Homer could turn into a week if bad weather hit Kachemak Bay. And being stranded in town meant I needed a place to stay. The summer was no problem—I simply camped out—but in the winter, I relied on my friends for a warm bed and a roof over my head. Sometimes things didn't work out and forced me to make do with less-than-comfortable accommodations. One winter night I left the Salty Dawg late, having consumed a few too many beers. With nowhere to stay, I struggled into my bright orange survival suit and went to sleep stretched out in the bed of my pickup truck. The survival suit was designed to save my life if I ever had to abandon ship and jump into the sea, but that night on land I damn near froze my ass off.

Realizing the ideal situation would be to have my own place on the Homer side of the bay, I started hunting for land. I found I could afford a few acres if they were far enough out of town. While shopping for land, I met Seth and Norma from Connecticut, who were visiting my friends Wild Bill and Karen in Homer. During our conversation I explained my need for a place in town, and how land in the area was a good investment. The East Coast couple said they had some money to invest and asked if I'd be interested in becoming partners. Knowing we could buy more land at a better price per acre by combining our money, I agreed to the partnership.

A week later we bought a 20-acre parcel that was located eleven miles out East End Road. It had 1,200 feet of highway frontage and was heavily wooded with old-growth spruce.

While waiting for escrow to close, I designed a cabin and ordered the materials, and the day it became ours, Wild Bill, Seth, and I started building. Our first structure was an A-frame cottage we could use as a rental supplement for our land payments. The 16 x 20-foot cabin included an upstairs bedroom, kitchen, living room, and entry porch. The outhouse was around back. Wild Bill and Karen liked it so much that they became our first renters.

Seth, Norma, and I saw the need for low-cost rentals in the area and, since we had plenty of room for expansion on our twenty acres, agreed to build more cabins. They'd supply the cash, and I'd do the building. I still didn't have a place to stay in Homer, but I did have the land to construct my own cabin. I returned to Sadie for the winter knowing the investment could also help me gain my future financial independence.

It was January of 1980, and I had a bad case of cabin fever. I felt anxious because I'd made plans for a trip to California to be in a friend's wedding, but for the preceding two weeks the cove had been hammered by southeast storms that prevented me from crossing the bay to Homer.

Several times a day I listened to the marine weather forecast on KBBI, the local public radio station. It frustrated me to hear the announcer broadcast: "Forecast for Gore Point to Castle Cape— storm warnings, 90-knot winds, seas to forty feet." The huge waves pounded the northern beaches of the Gulf of Alaska on the other side of the mountains from my home; but the screaming winds weren't lessened by the snowcapped peaks, and they roared through the cove.

On the morning of the fourth day, the radio broadcast the same weather forecast, but the winds in Sadie had diminished to 20 knots.

Normally, I would have been more cautious, but with my desire to attend the wedding, I began preparing my kayak for the 5-mile voyage to Jakalof Bay, where I could catch a plane and fly to Homer. On the CB radio, I called friends who lived near my destination and told them to expect me by dark. Then I loaded the boat and started paddling out of the cove. If the lull in the storm lasted only a couple of hours, I could safely complete the hardest part of my trip south.

A mile from home the wind increased to 60 knots, and I cussed my impatient decision. The steep, cresting waves and howling wind drove me out of the cove with such force I constantly backpaddled to keep my speed under control. It only took ten minutes to surf to the entrance of Sadie, where I found some sheltered water in front of a protected beach. As my heartbeat return to normal, I realized I'd enjoyed the wild ride.

The last dangerous stretch of open water would call for a 1-mile sprint across the mouth of Tutka Bay to the Herring Islands. The wind and waves weren't any worse than in Sadie, and I didn't want to spend the long night camping out on the beach; so I took a deep breath and started paddling.

Whenever I extend my body to its physical limits and ride the razor's edge between life and death, my senses instinctively take control of my survival. Halfway across Tutka Bay, these instincts warned me of an unseen danger, and I looked back just in time to brace myself for the 6-foot rogue wave that buried me in an avalanche of freezing water and flipped over the kayak. It happened so fast I didn't have time to think. With all my strength I pushed with the paddle and somehow righted myself. The smaller waves washed over me as I sat in a boat full of salt water half a mile from the closest island. The kayak wouldn't sink because of the built-in air sacks, but I sure as hell could freeze to death before reaching shore. With no way to bail out the boat, the only thing I could do was try to reach the safety of land.

It took half an hour to reach a sheltered beach on the small, wooded island. As I dragged the boat out of the water, my teeth chattered uncontrollably. I knew hypothermia had dulled my senses, and if I didn't find shelter, I could lapse into a coma from which there was no journey back.

I spotted a summer cabin nestled in the trees and stumbled up the beach to get out of the howling wind. Upon entering, I yanked off my soggy clothes and struggled into the dry ones I'd brought in a waterproof bag from the boat. The cabin had a woodstove, but I saw no wood; so I looked around for another source of heat. In the kitchen stood a disconnected gas cookstove. It took me several minutes to find the propane tank in a back room. Leaving the shelter of the cabin to connect the gas, I felt like I was moving in slow motion. Hooking up a propane tank can be frustrating under the best of conditions, but miraculously I connected it on the first try. Back inside, I melted snow on the stove and drank the liquid heat. After swallowing what seemed like a gallon of hot water, my body quit shaking and I relaxed enough to realize I was out of danger. My situation improved even more when I found dry wood for a fire and a can of beans for dinner. As darkness fell, I went to sleep snuggled under every blanket in the cabin.

The next morning I felt recovered, but the wind still blew whitecapped waves past my tiny sanctuary. During the day, I spent my time keeping warm and listening to Homer radio on the battery-powered radio in the cabin. During the local news they announced I was missing and that a search would be launched when the winds died down. After hearing the world news broadcast its usual stories on crime, starvation, and war, I felt good about being marooned on an island in Alaska.

Two hours before dark I heard a strange sound. From the beach in front of the cabin I spotted a Coast Guard helicopter flying a search pattern a mile from the island. A few minutes later it hovered over where I stood. With nowhere to land, the crew dropped a message in a weighted plastic pouch with a long, yellow ribbon and flew off in a big circle to give me time to reply. "Are you in need of immediate medical attention?" the note asked. "If yes, wave your arms."

I stood with my hands in my pockets and watched as another message got caught by the wind and landed in the water sixty feet from the beach. I retrieved it with my kayak and read the note. "Are you Keith Iverson? If yes, wave your arms." As they passed overhead, I waved my arms and threw in a little jig for good measure.

The final message almost hit me on the head. "Do you want to be evacuated? If yes, wave your arms."

On their final pass I stood with my arms at my side, although I wanted to wave my thanks.

Back inside the cabin, I hunkered down next to the fire and silently thanked the Coast Guard for the great search and rescue work it performed. With the wind diminishing, I figured I could leave the island by morning. Just as darkness engulfed the cabin, I heard an outboard motor in the distance. I stepped outside in time to see Billy, a neighbor from Dunnings Lagoon, power up to my protected beach. "We're having a party at Sandi's in Little Tutka Bay. You want to join us or stay here?" he shouted.

It didn't take me long to tidy up the cabin, compose a thank you note with a promise to replace what I'd used, and load the kayak into Billy's skiff.

When we got to the party, I notified Homer with the CB radio that I was safe and then joined my distant neighbors to tell my side of the story. Sometime during the evening I realized that my friends in California were now on their honeymoon and I had no reason to continue my trip. The next morning I thanked everyone and returned to Sadie over calm seas. When I got to my beach I thought, nothing like a little adventure to cure cabin fever!

As winter slowly thawed into spring, only one nagging problem kept me from enjoying my life in Sadie—I needed money. Mooseltoe still brought in a small income from sales in Alaska, and the cabin rental helped pay for my Homer investment, but it wasn't enough to live on year-round. One night in the sauna, my mind sweated out an idea. Why not use a local resource and develop a small, gourmet-quality, smoked-salmon operation?

The first step was to gather information in Homer. After talking to companies and individuals who smoked salmon, I learned to listen most intently to those with the best samples. The library also supplied several books on the subject, and after a week's research, I knew enough to get started.

Next, I built a smokehouse in Sadie. The 6 x 6-foot wooden structure took two months to complete, and after making wire racks, installing a woodburning stove, and collecting dead alder for the fire, the smoker stood ready for its first batch of fish.

Finally, I went in search of salmon. The Tutka Bay Lagoon fish hatchery, four miles from my home, gave away their pink salmon after removing the ripe eggs and sperm. On arriving at the state-owned and -operated hatchery, the manager told me to take as many as I wanted. I felt tempted to fill *Green Death* with salmon, but although the new smoker could process 300 pounds at a time, my better judgment told me to take only twenty-five fish. I needed to learn the process and could always come back for more.

Back in Sadie, I filleted the salmon next to the stream and placed them in a salt brine for several hours. After sampling a bite of raw salmon to check its salt content, I placed the 1-pound slabs on the smoker racks to dry. All the next day I stoked the woodstove with alder branches to smoke and cook the fish. It took three days to finish my first batch, which I thought tasted pretty damn good, but I was a wee bit prejudiced. With an insulated box full of the fifty pounds of kippered smoked salmon, I skiffed into Homer for a final verdict.

I drove out to the rental cabin to let Wild Bill and Karen sample my wares. "What you're about to taste is my first try, so be honest and tell me what you think," I said while crossing my fingers behind my back.

"If this is as good as it looks, you've got a winner," Karen said as I handed them each a pink fillet.

Wild Bill took the first bite and gave me his answer: "Not too bad, not bad at all."

It wasn't exactly what I'd hoped to hear, so I waited for Karen's reaction. She put a thick piece in her mouth, wrinkled her nose, and spit it out. "God, I hate raw fish," she said in disgust. "Maybe you should smoke them longer and use fresher fish."

"Those spawned-out pinks from the hatchery are free, but they've lost most of their flavor," Wild Bill added.

With the verdict unanimous, I went back to Sadie disappointed in my first attempt, but resolved to try again. For the second batch, I bought red salmon from fishermen in Kasitsna Bay. The fish were so fresh that they flopped around the floor of my skiff as I transported them home. I followed the same procedure, and when they were completely smoked, I was amazed at the difference in quality. Back in town, Wild Bill and Karen appeared a little hesitant to try my second batch. However, after they each took a bite, Karen laughed in relief and said, "This is the best smoked salmon I've ever eaten! Can we buy some?"

"No, but I'll give you a couple of fillets for being so honest about the first batch," I answered.

The rest of the day I roamed around Homer passing out samples to people I knew. "This is great!" Bill Phillips said after consuming a pound of smoked salmon. "I know I can sell all you produce. I'm going back to Washington, D.C., this fall to enroll in law school and can establish the eastern markets. You smoke 'em, and I'll sell 'em. Working together we can both make some money. What do you think?"

I laughed, thinking it was a good thing Bill hadn't tried my first batch, and said, "Let's do it."

Now all I had to do was set up the operation and find out the requirements to produce and sell smoked salmon legally. For the rest of the summer, I worked sixteen-hour days on the project.

By the time Bill started packing for his move back East, I'd built a 30 x 40-foot wharf and put the roof on a 16 x 24-foot salmon-processing building. Bill helped me write for the information we needed on permits, and we also smoked 300 pounds of salmon for future buyer samples. We felt confident our operation could be filling orders by the next summer.

Bill left for Washington, D.C., and I returned to Sadie for the next phase of the project. Before finishing the fish-processing building, I took out the thick information folder on permit requirements and immersed myself in paperwork. My amazement grew as I studied the staggering number of regulations and the growing cost of equipment. After two solid weeks of filling out forms and making calculations, I called Bill back East. He excitedly told me of his progress. "The big fish buyers like our smoked salmon, and once we get the processing licenses, I'll be able to get some orders. How's it going with the permits?"

"Not so good," I answered. "In fact, that's the reason I'm calling. Since you left, all I've done is paperwork, and the twenty-two permits we need will cost $100,000 in equipment and building materials to pass the codes and get the licenses."

"Can't we use your smoker and cut down on the costs?" Bill asked.

"No way, Bill," I replied. "My wooden smokehouse would never pass inspection. Everything must be built of stainless steel. The metal smoker alone costs $40,000, and because it uses liquid smoke, I think it would diminish the quality of our product."

"Well, old buddy, what do we do now?" Bill asked.

I knew the answer to the question before calling. "Bill, I didn't come to Sadie Cove to deal with twenty-two permits, even if I had the $100,000, which I don't. It looks like we'll both have to look for another way to make money. But cheer up; we learned a lot and have plenty of smoked salmon for the winter."

Actually, I wasn't as cheerful as I sounded. After the phone call, I slipped into a blue mood and spent several hours feeling sorry for myself. It didn't take long to get tired of being down, so I had a serious talk with myself and started thinking positively again. I wasn't going to quit. All I had to do was discover another way to make a living. Besides, my Dad and Aunt Mabel were coming for a visit in two days—maybe they would have some ideas.

I enjoyed sharing my home with family and hearing about the rest of the clan in the Lower 48. Dad helped me with the chores, and Aunt Mabel contributed by cooking some of my favorite meals. They listened to my smoked-salmon story, gave me their support, and offered some suggestions; but I knew I was the only one who could solve my dilemma.

One morning while Aunt Mabel cooked breakfast and Dad fished on the beach, I sat in the unfinished building trying to come up with a solution to my problem. As I sipped my coffee, an idea exploded in my head. The more I thought about it, the more excited I became. So, feeling the need to share my brainchild, I ran down the wharf yelling, "I've got it! I've got it!"

Dad stopped fishing and Mabel put breakfast on hold while they listened to my idea. "I know the solution to my money problems," I began. "Since coming to live in Sadie, I've built a sauna, wharfhouse, and studio and started a new building; so I have enough to begin my venture. The cove is a perfect location for fantastic fishing, hiking, and wildlife photography, so I'm going to start a wilderness lodge!"

"Great idea," Dad said. "What are you charging us?"

I laughed and answered, "No problem, Dad, family is free."

"Do you need a seventy-six-year-old cook?" Aunt Mabel asked.

"You bet," I replied. "I'll put your name at the top of the list."

Dad wanted to know when I would start the new business, and I answered, "Next summer will be my first season. I've got the rest of fall, winter, and spring to prepare for my first guests."

"Why don't you give it a Viking name, like Valhalla?" Dad suggested.

"Good idea, but that name's already taken by another resort," I answered. "I'm going to call it Sadie Cove Wilderness Lodge."

We spent the rest of their visit discussing all the things I needed to accomplish before the next summer. When Dad and Aunt Mabel left, I was still making lists.

Sadie Cove Wilderness Lodge

I needed a list to keep track of my lists! Each page of notes represented a different project that must be completed before my first lodge guests arrived in the spring. I had marketing and promotion plans, building blueprints, calculations on costs (long list), a tally on cash in my bank accounts (short list), priority charts, and separate need, want, and wish lists. Just for fun, I made projections on the lodge's income and started a file on long-range improvements.

Once a week, I made the mistake of looking at the fat folder of projects, and the total amount of work involved in my new venture momentarily overwhelmed me. Whenever I got one of these anxiety attacks, I kayaked a mile up the cove and let the day breeze blow me back to my beach. While drifting, the beauty of Sadie soothed my troubled mind and I concentrated on what I'd already accomplished. By the time I hauled the kayak out of the water, my faith in myself and my project were renewed. I could do it if I completed one list at a time.

One of my biggest goals was to finish the building I'd started for the canceled smoked-salmon operation. This cabin would now be a living room, kitchen, and dining room for the lodge, and I named it the Oarhouse.

In early November, my friends Don and Nancy from Anchorage came to Sadie to help me with the project. Around noon of their second day, Nancy was in the Wharfhouse preparing lunch while Don and I nailed up rough-cut boards on the new cabin's outer walls. Pausing in my work, I saw four seals swim by only twenty feet from the wharf. I told Don they seemed to be in a big hurry just as Nancy ran out on the deck yelling, "Killer whales! Killer whales!"

One hundred feet off the beach two orcas surfaced, blowing a fine mist into the air. Their 5-foot black, dorsal fins cut through the water as we stood there with our mouths open. Two of the biggest, fastest creatures of the sea were swimming through my front yard. No wonder the seals were in such a hurry. Although killer whales weigh several tons, they can easily catch a seal in open water. Looking down the shore, I saw the four seals struggle up on the beach ahead of their enemy.

The killer whales seemed unaware of us or the seals as they headed out of the cove, and I wished there were some way to bring them back. Remembering that seals will sometimes slap their tails on the water, I hit on the idea of trying to get the whales' attention by creating the same sound. I grabbed a short length of scrap lumber and dropped it from the wharf. A loud "whap" sounded as it hit the water, and the two whales pivoted around toward us.

For the next half-hour, I dropped a board on the water each time they started to leave, and each time the sound made them return. I resisted the temptation to put my kayak in the water and paddle out to meet them. Although no known cases exist of orcas attacking people, my long, skinny, grey boat looked too much like a seal, and I didn't want to be the first recorded casualty. It was safer to watch the show from the shore.

The magnificent mammals finally tired of the game and didn't return when I dropped another board. As we watched them swim away, Nancy exclaimed, "They were so close I could smell their breath when they blew! Why didn't I have my camera with me?"

"It doesn't matter," Don said. "You could never get an experience like that on film, even with the best camera in the world. A picture can bring you back to the moment, but it can't capture the excitement of what we just saw."

Nancy turned to me and said, "The people coming to your lodge will love it here, Keith. Too bad the whales can't be trained to come back every time you have guests."

I thought for a moment and replied, "I'm glad I can't train the wild ones, because then Sadie Cove would be just another zoo or marine park. What makes this life so exciting is not having control over the animals or weather. I love surprises like we just experienced. That's what I can offer my lodge guests."

As we went in to eat lunch, the four seals slid back into the water and cautiously swam off in the opposite direction from where the killer whales had gone.

Don and Nancy returned to Anchorage, and I continued getting the lodge ready for business. The short days slowed my progress, but

I made up the time by working seven days a week. As Christmas approached, my neighbors all left to spend the holidays with their families, leaving me alone in the cove. To fight off the loneliness, I increased my work schedule and tried not to think about spending the holidays by myself.

I took a day off for Christmas and tried to make the most of the situation. After taking a midday sauna and cooking a duck for dinner, I sat next to the small tree I'd decorated and opened the presents my family had sent. I got a good laugh from the note on the greeting card my sister, Julie, attached to her gift. It read, "Dear Brother, I wanted to give you something that would make you think of me once a day." I tore open the box and pulled out a fancy, insulated toilet seat. The perfect gift—and I knew my future lodge guests would enjoy it as much as I would.

About 9:00 P.M. on New Year's Eve, I saw the lights of a big boat enter the cove. I turned on my CB radio just in time to hear, "This is the *Invader* calling the Viking of Sadie Cove. We've got a case of champagne, and it's party time. We'll be in as soon as we drop the anchor and put the skiff in the water. Happy New Year, Keith."

I forgot about going to bed early, lit every light in the Wharfhouse, and went out to welcome my unexpected guests. Dan and Debbie Veerhusen, along with their friends Bob and Diane, jumped out of the skiff, and we uncorked the first bottle of bubbly on the beach under a sky full of stars.

The party moved in to the warmth of the Wharfhouse, and as I poured champagne, Dan asked, "I heard you're starting a wilderness lodge. Are we your first guests?"

"The resort won't be ready until next May, but I just received the brochures I had printed at Fritz Creek Studios in Homer. Would you like to see one?"

As I handed out the literature on the lodge, Bob asked, "How will you let people know you are open for business?"

Before I could answer, Debbie asked the way to the outhouse. After giving her directions, I got back to Bob's question. "I don't have the money to promote the lodge at the sportsmen shows in the Lower 48, so my first year I'll concentrate all my marketing efforts in Alaska. I'm going to Anchorage in February to drum up some business. Besides leaving my brochure at all the travel agencies, I'll call on big oil companies and let them know what I have to offer."

As everyone read the brochure, Debbie returned and said, "Keith, your toilet seat's rusty!"

I figured she was kidding, since I'd just installed the gift from my sister, but before I could question her statement, Dan asked, "How will you be able to answer questions about the lodge with no telephones here in Sadie?"

"I already have the communications problem solved," I answered. "Beluga Lake Float Plane Service in Homer has agreed to be my message service. All I need is a VHF radio to make the connection."

Dan toasted my new business venture and said, "I have an old radio on the boat that still works. I'll donate it to your lodge."

After thanking Dan, I went out on the deck to answer nature's call. As I stood looking up at the stars, Debbie's comment popped into my head. How could the toilet seat be rusty? I laughed out loud when I thought of a possible solution to the mystery. To prove my suspicions, I followed her footprints in the snow. They went up the stairs toward the outhouse, but at the top she went left instead of right and into another small building. I lit a match, looked inside, and returned to the party. On entering the Wharfhouse I got everyone's attention and said, "Debbie, you were right. The toilet seat was rusty, but you didn't go to the outhouse. You took a wrong turn at the top of the stairs and peed in the metal stove I have stored in the smokehouse!"

Debbie blushed but, like the rest of us, got a big laugh out of her mistake. Later that night we toasted the birth of 1981, and the next morning I nailed up a sign pointing the way to the outhouse.

The rest of the winter I kept busy building and promoting the lodge, but with the coming of spring I started looking for help to run the resort. In Homer I hired Tim Gee to assist me in guiding, maintenance, and building. Marianne Orme became the cook, gardener, and housekeeper. I couldn't have asked for two more enthusiastic, hard-working, and supportive people. They wanted the lodge to be a success as much as I did.

Tim and I finished the Oarhouse and moved Marianne into her new kitchen, where she spoiled us with her cooking. Working, playing, and living together in an isolated area can be difficult and sometimes disastrous; but my crew proved to be very compatible, and we all became good friends.

By the end of May we were ready for business, except for one important part of the lodge's operation—reliable, safe transportation back and forth to Homer for the crew and guests. The time had come to retire *Green Death*. She had served me well for many years and deserved an honorable resting place. It took six people to drag her up next to the Studio, where we pointed her bow out to sea, filled her with dirt, and planted potatoes. On a wooden tombstone I wrote "R.I.P., *Green Death*, 1975-1980."

In Homer I bought a 16-foot skiff powered by a 50-horsepower outboard motor. The fast, seaworthy boat wasn't very big, but it would fill my needs for a couple of years. Fishermen say it's bad luck to rename a boat, but since this one had no name, I christened her *Valkyrie*. Naming her after the maidens who carried slain Viking warriors to Valhalla seemed fitting.

We had no guests over the Memorial Day weekend, and I was feeling a little concerned. However, when Jill from Beluga Lake Float Plane Service called on the VHF radio to inform me that I had two inquiries, my doubts dissolved. I wasted no time getting to Homer to contact what I hoped would be my first customers.

The first prospects turned out to be Bill and Delores, who owned and operated Kachemak Bay Title Agency in Homer. They wanted to know if my lodge could accommodate sixteen of their employees and families in the middle of June for their annual Christmas office party. Bill explained that his staff had voted to have the winter affair in the summer, and they wanted to come to Sadie for the day. I took his reservation and thanked him for the business.

My second inquiry was more difficult to answer. Jill's message said a man named Tom from Saudi Arabia wanted me to call him back, collect. The long-distance operator informed me that collect calls weren't accepted to the Middle East, so instead of losing the business, I took a chance and elected to pay for the call. Tom answered the phone and said, "Keith, I heard of your lodge from our office in Anchorage, and I'm interested in bringing my family of eight to Alaska for a week's vacation in July. Tell me what you have to offer."

This was my first opportunity for week-long guests, and I blurted out my pitch. "My resort is a full-service wilderness lodge, and the rates include transportation from Homer, three gourmet meals a day, and guiding for salmon, halibut, and wildlife photography. Your family will stay in two private cabins and eat your meals in the dining room located on a 100-foot wharf. You'll bathe in a large sauna on the beach, and our outside plumbing has one of the best views in Alaska. I've been building my year-round home and lodge in Sadie Cove for the past seven years and can guarantee you'll enjoy our facility's scenic location and old-fashioned hospitality."

His next question brought up a point I hadn't covered. "Since not everyone in my family is an avid fisherman, what else is there for them to do?"

"They can hike up into the mountains or stroll along the beach," I replied. "There's also bird watching, clamming, boating, berry picking, campfires, beachcombing, and just plain relaxing. I'll send you our brochure so you'll have a better idea of what we have to offer."

He thanked me for the call and said, "It sounds like you have just what I'm looking for. I'll contact you after I receive your booklet."

I didn't know if my $100 phone call would lead to Tom's family coming to the lodge, but sometimes you had to spend money to make money. After finishing my town business, I returned to Sadie to get ready for the Christmas party.

Sixteen men, women, and children arrived aboard the 50-foot boat I chartered to take them across the bay. Marianne, Tim, and I welcomed our first guests on the beach under a cloudless sky and escorted them to the wharf, where we had decorated a Christmas tree with shells and starfish. While my crew went into the kitchen to get ready for the big meal, I took my guests on a tour. I showed the way to the outhouse, explained the thousand-year-old pictographs in the cave by the stream, pointed out the horseshoe pit, conducted them through the different buildings, and told them to make themselves at home. "The seafood feast will begin in two hours," I promised.

The smell of homemade bread, pies, and cakes welcomed me into the Oarhouse, where Marianne was setting the table. Tim had gone to the garden to collect lettuce and radishes for the salads, and after checking our schedule, I left to prepare the main course. I started a fire on the beach, and several guests volunteered to help clean the thirty Dungeness crabs and huge pile of blue-shell mussels Tim and I had collected earlier.

I cooked the fresh seafood in big pots over a beach fire, took the steaming main course into the dining room, and rang the dinner bell. The hungry guests filed into the Oarhouse and sat down at the 16-foot-long table laden with crab, mussels, smoked salmon, baked potatoes, rice pilaf, salads, and homemade bread. After I poured the wine and gave instructions on the fine art of crab cracking, everyone got down to some serious feasting. When the group had finished eating, we passed out hot hand towels and served dessert and coffee out on the deck.

As the sun slid behind the mountains, the boat came to take the party back to town. Everyone thanked us for the great time, and Bill and Delores shook my hand and said, "We'll be back next year!"

We stood on the beach waving good-bye and then went back to work. After Tim and I straightened up the grounds, we joined Marianne in the kitchen to attack the huge pile of dishes. When everything was cleaned up and put away, we poured three glasses of wine and toasted the success of our first group of lodge guests.

The next day, Jill called on the VHF and said a reporter from the *Anchorage Daily News* was in Homer and wanted to do a story on the lodge. I jumped into *Valkyrie* and took off for town to pick up the writer. Amy spent the day asking questions, scribbling notes, and taking pictures. It was the first time the press had come to my lodge, and I sure felt better showing off Sadie than I had promoting moose manure in the big cities. During the ride back to town, Amy thanked me for the hospitality and said her story would appear within a couple of weeks.

Ten days later, there I was on the front page of the "Living and Leisure" section. Under a four-column picture of my lodge, the headline read "The Moose Nugget King of Sadie Cove." Amy's story began with a brief biography, which included Mooseltoe, and then turned to my newest venture, the resort. I laughed when I realized my main claim to fame remained moose shit. Without a doubt, the Moose Nugget King title would follow me to the grave. Even if I climb Mount Everest backward and blindfolded, my tombstone will probably read "Here Lies the King of Poop Peddlers." A dubious distinction, at best, but I didn't care what the story said as long as it brought business to the lodge.

In mid-August Bill Phillips, my smoked-salmon partner, brought a party of ten people from Washington, D.C., to spend three nights at the lodge. They flew to Sadie in floatplanes; then Tim, Marianne, and I escorted them to their rooms. Bill and I had discussed where everyone would sleep, so the guests knew there was a shortage of private accommodations. Actually, everyone had a place to sleep because the crew and I gave up our beds. Jack and Nini, the only couple in the group, took my room in the Wharfhouse, and I slept on the pantry floor sandwiched between Tim and Marianne. I didn't worry about not having enough private rooms—we would make up for it with our fantastic food and fishing.

While Marianne prepared dinner, Tim fired up the sauna and I recruited help to collect crab at the head of the cove. Bill and Jack helped me hand-pull the 60-pound crab pots into the boat. Each of my four pots contained eight to twelve Dungeness crabs, but after throwing the females back, we had just enough for dinner. We rebaited each pot with herring and started back to the lodge.

As we slowly motored down the calm fjord, Jack asked me if there was an easier way to catch crab. His question took me back to my first summer in Alaska, and I told him my story.

I dove for crab off the spit when I came to Homer as a cheechako in 1972. While camping out, I met another newcomer. Tom and I both had our diving equipment and decided to try to catch a few crab for dinner.

We asked a local merchant if anyone ever dove for crab off the spit, and he said, "Yup, they do it all the time." His answer spurred us to action. We put on our wetsuits, inflated an air mattress, spit into our masks, and waded into the sea. As the cold salt water leaked into our suits, we both let out a holler and quickly swam 100 feet offshore.

Neither of us had scuba tanks, which meant our dives would be limited to about twenty feet. Tom stayed on the surface with the air mattress as I made the first dive. Waves had churned up the sand, so on reaching the bottom I could see only two feet in front of me. The numbing cold and need for air brought me back to the surface, where Tom asked if I'd seen anything. I shook my head and made four more dives before letting my buddy try. His luck wasn't any better than mine—all we saw were underwater sand dunes.

We swam to a new location and, as we rested on the air mattress, discussed shooting our merchant friend, who was probably enjoying a good laugh at our expense.

I made another dive and this time noticed a shallow hole in the sand. The visibility immediately dropped to zero after I disturbed the bottom, but I continued to grope around in hopes of catching whatever had made the burrow. Something unseen clamped onto my finger, and the pain made me forget everything except getting to the surface. I exploded from the water like a breaching whale and probably took ten years off Tom's life. "We won't have to shoot that storekeeper after all," I yelled while prying the Dungeness crab from my finger. "I just discovered how to dive for crab."

I finished telling my story as we beached the skiff in front of the lodge. My assistant pot-pullers left to take a sauna, and I started cleaning our dinner.

The next morning, after a hearty breakfast that included crab omelettes, two floatplanes landed to take our guests silver salmon fishing. They would fly 100 miles across Cook Inlet to the remote bays and coves of the Alaska Peninsula, where 10- to 18-pound cohos had reportedly returned in record numbers. Fly-in fishing gives the pilot-guide the opportunity to see the schools of salmon from the air before landing. I felt confident my clients were on their way to doing battle with one of the finest fighting fish in the state.

Beluga Lake Float Plane Service called on the radio in the early evening to inform me that my guests would arrive at the lodge very shortly. As we walked down the beach to welcome them back, the two planes gracefully touched down on the calm waters of the cove and taxied into where we waited. The floats seemed to ride lower in the water than on the morning's takeoff, so I figured they carried more than just passengers. When Nini got out of the plane, I asked, "How was the fishing?"

With a long face, she replied, "Terrible! We got skunked! The commercial guys caught all the salmon."

Everyone else got out of the plane grinning from ear to ear, so I played along with her joke and added one of my own. "Damn, that's the second bad news of the day. A bear broke into the pantry and ate all the food. All we have for dinner is oatmeal."

Nini started laughing and said, "I'm kidding, Keith. We all caught our limit of six silvers, and I'm so thrilled I don't care what you feed us."

I couldn't help replying, "Great! Now we can have salmon with the oatmeal."

Marianne cooked a delicious dinner of fresh salmon with all the trimmings. While we ate, Jack told Tim, Marianne, and me about their successful fishing expedition.

"It took a little over an hour to fly across Cook Inlet," Jack related, "where we followed the coastline south until a large school of silver salmon attracted our attention. Several hundred fish were milling around the entrance to a small stream, and we landed right on top of them. Once we got on shore, everyone started fishing, and I caught a big, feisty, 15-pound male on the first cast. What a fighter! That salmon must have jumped ten times before I landed him. It took only two hours to limit out, and boy was it hard stopping with all those silver beauties jumping in front of us. After devouring the lunch you packed, we took off to do some flight-seeing. We flew over the McNeil River Brown Bear Sanctuary but unfortunately didn't see any bears. On the way back to the lodge, our pilot said you've guided over there, Keith. When would be the best time to get a good look at the brown bears?"

"If you're interested in photographing the coastal grizzlies at the McNeil River, you need to apply for the permits in winter and fly over in June. It's one of the greatest experiences in Alaska."

Nini looked confused and asked, "What's the difference between grizzlies and brown bears?"

"There is no difference," I explained. "Until recently, most people referred to them as separate types of bear. However, the big-game biologists have now proven they are the same species."

"How do they explain the difference in size?" Jack asked. "I've read that a brown bear can weigh up to 1,500 pounds and a trophy grizzly won't weigh over 800."

"The brown bear lives on the coast, where the winters are milder and the food more abundant. The grizzly roams the interior and must work harder to find enough fish and game to survive," I answered.

Before I could continue, everyone at the dinner table started bombarding me with questions about the bear sanctuary at the McNeil River. Instead of answering each one separately, I told them all about my adventure in the land of *Ursus arctos..*

In the spring of 1976, Kachemak Bay Wilderness Lodge paid me $50 a day to guide two photographers at the McNeil River Brown Bear Sanctuary. At the McBrides' lodge in China Poot Bay, I met Virgil and Ken, who had photographed wildlife throughout the world, including several safaris in Africa. Jon of Beluga Lake Float Plane Service picked us up in his Cessna 185 floatplane for the 100-mile trip across Cook Inlet. During the smooth flight we flew over the island volcano of Mount Augustine. Jon circled the steaming mountain so we could photograph the smoking, boulder-strewn crater, and as I looked down I thought, this land hasn't really changed in thousands of years—nature is still in control.

We landed gracefully in a protected cove and taxied to shore. Larry and Mo, the wardens of the bear sanctuary, greeted us and introduced the four other photographers sharing the camp. After unloading the plane, Jon flew back to Homer.

The camp consisted of a small, wooden cook shack and a tall food cache to keep everyone's groceries away from the bears. The McBrides had provided all our equipment, including a new dome tent and an old canvas tarp, and I knew instinctively which was my shelter. It took only a few minutes to set up my pup tent, but the dome wasn't as easy. After a lengthy struggle I managed to get the right poles in the right holes and moved Virgil and Ken into their new home. Next, I mixed them their evening cocktails and headed for the cook shack to prepare dinner. During the meal everyone told Alaskan bear stories, so when I finally slid into my sleeping bag I had only one thing on my mind—the largest land carnivore in the world.

In the middle of the night, something big woke me out of a deep sleep as it rubbed against my tent. When the bear's nose pushed in the side of the canvas and touched the top of my head, my heart almost exploded. As I lay there in the blackness listening to the bear sniff my flimsy shelter, I tried to kill the fear that surged through my body. What the hell could I do?

I considered blasting the beast with the 12-gauge shotgun or .44 magnum pistol that lay at my side. What would happen if I screamed for help? Maybe I should ask Virgil and Ken if I could sleep in their tent. I started chuckling to myself when I considered the limited choices. I didn't know if any of these plans could save my life, but I did know all of them would shoot the shit out of my reputation as a wilderness guide. I finally decided to do nothing. If it was time for me to enter Valhalla, so be it. As the bear moved away, I took a deep breath, rolled over, and went back to sleep.

After breakfast the next morning, Larry and Mo, who would guide us to the river, called everyone together to tell us about the bears and explain the rules. Mo began, "The brown bear by nature is a loner and only socializes with its kind during the mating season or while feeding on spawning salmon. Over the years, the bears of the McNeil River have become more tolerant of humans because of the abundance of food and their protected status in the sanctuary."

"To protect yourself and the bears, please remember the rules," Larry continued. "Don't surprise a bear—let it know you are near by making noises. Stay on the trail and don't wander off by yourself. Don't disturb a sleeping or feeding bear, and keep a safe distance from a sow and her cubs. Following these rules greatly reduces the chances of a bear attack and could save a bear from getting shot."

Larry picked up his shotgun, and the rest of us shouldered our packs full of cameras. As we hiked the one and a half miles to the river, our guides answered questions about the area and the subjects we came to photograph. The bear trail we followed through the flat, treeless land made for easy hiking. Even my client Virgil, who was seventy-nine years old, had no problem completing the trek.

We arrived at the McNeil River, and there to greet us was the Alaska brown bear. Within 200 feet of where we stood on a small knoll overlooking the river, fifteen big bruins fished and fed on the thousands of spawning salmon fighting their way up the rapids. Everyone watched the scene wide-eyed and silent until one of us remembered we were there for photographs; then out came the cameras.

I looked across the 120 feet of water to the far shore, where a 500-pound sow fished for salmon to feed her two fuzzy cubs. She had just caught lunch and flipped it up on the bank toward her off-spring. The cubs batted at the flopping fish with their small paws, obviously enjoying the game. The mother bear took a bite out of the salmon's belly, exposing the pink eggs, and dropped it in front of her young as if to say, "Don't play with your food."

As I watched the sow and cubs, I noticed she suddenly became very alert. She stood up, sniffed the air, and kept looking up the bank into the heavy brush. Suddenly, she charged into the alder and attacked a larger bear. One of the wardens explained that the sow, named Katie, was protecting her cubs by chasing the male, Zeke, out of her territory. Larry and Mo were so familiar with the bears they had given them all names. I was glad Katie and her cubs were across the river from our observation area.

The other bears remained preoccupied with catching and eating salmon and seemed totally unconcerned by our presence. Some locations along the bank and out in the rapids provided better fishing, and the bears had long since figured this out. The biggest bears usually controlled the prime spots while others sat behind them waiting their turn.

The bears knew several ways to catch the salmon, but the old step-on-it technique caught the most fish. A furry fisherman would trap the salmon against the bottom with its front paw, secure it in its jaw, and carry the frantic fish to the beach. Most of the bears ate only the skin, belly, and eggs, which contain the most nourishment, but nothing went to waste—hundreds of squawking sea gulls fought over the scraps.

For several hours I watched three bears, each about 300 pounds, team up and bully their way into the best fishing spots. I asked Mo about them, and she said they called them the Marx Brothers. They had lived and traveled together since their birth three years earlier.

The young of all species must learn to survive, and the Marx Brothers were about to go back to school. The professor ambled out of the brush upriver from our location, and as he advanced, I noticed a change in the three adolescents. The newcomer was a 900-pound male, monarch of the land, and he knew it. His huge body rippled with raw power as he walked toward the best fishing site. The Marx Brothers had become accustomed to having their own way, and I smelled challenge in the air as the trio lined up in front of the advancing bear. As the big male approached, I expected a bloody fight to follow. The bear kept coming and somehow communicated a message to the youngsters blocking his path, because suddenly all three broke ranks and ran into the brush. I don't know what was said, but the bullies got the message, and the king lumbered to the river to get a bite to eat.

Most of the photographers had expensive cameras and a variety of lenses. I used a Pentax with one 55mm lens. With the bears so numerous and close, it didn't make any difference—anyone could have taken good pictures with any kind of camera.

One 500-pound bruin caught fish only fifteen feet away from us, and I was so engrossed taking pictures I didn't see danger approaching. The Marx Brothers must have regrouped downriver after their encounter with the big male and were headed back to the fishing grounds. I looked up to see them walking straight for us. I started yelling, Larry grabbed his shotgun, and the three bears stopped ten feet from where we stood. They looked at us with small, piggish eyes and sniffed the wind. Bears have excellent senses of hearing and smell but poor eyesight. Even so, at such close range I couldn't believe they didn't see us. We all shouted and waved our arms until they got nervous and ran off the way they'd come. Unfortunately, few pictures resulted from our encounter; the action was too close for the big lenses.

When everyone exhausted their film supply, we headed back to camp. Later that night, I took a walk along the beach to be alone and think about the incredible experience I'd just lived. I was very glad the government had designated the area a sanctuary so that one of Alaska's greatest adventures would be protected for future generations.

I guided Ken and Virgil for three more days, and all too soon the floatplane arrived for our return to Kachemak Bay.

After finishing the story for my guests in Sadie, I said good night and left everyone to talk about bears while sipping cognac by candlelight.

On the morning of the group's departure, my crew and I served breakfast, packed up the cleaned fish, and carried the luggage down to the waiting boat for the ride back to Homer. Although they left 100 pounds of silver fillets with me to smoke and mail out later, they returned to Washington, D.C., with more than 600 pounds of fresh salmon. When we said good-bye to my last bookings for the season, Jack and Nini shook my hand and said, "We'll be back next summer."

As the end of my first year in the lodge business approached, I analyzed what had been accomplished. The $4,000 I took in from the two groups barely paid my expenses, but at least I'd broken even. I knew building a business took time and felt confident the lodge would do better the second year. The money generated from Mooseltoe sales during the Christmas season would take me through the winter.

Tim and Marianne had only two weeks before they would return to Homer, but we still had plenty of work to do. We discussed the past season and agreed on our strong and weak points as a lodge. The meals of fresh seafood, saunas, fishing, wildlife, and the beauty of Sadie Cove would be hard to improve upon; but we definitely needed more private overnight accommodations. So Tim and I started building a new cabin.

I named it the Bunkhouse. This new structure's design included two separate rooms, each with a private entrance. Both rooms would have a double bed, a single bed in the loft, and an indoor bathroom. (After hearing bear stories during dinner, a few of the guests weren't too happy about trekking to the outhouse in the middle of the night.)

As with the other cabins, I planned to build this one out of rough-cut lumber from my neighbor's sawmill. It would provide the additional space we needed so that when we had a dozen guests, the crew and I wouldn't have to give up our beds and sleep on the pantry floor.

By mid-September we had a good start on the Bunkhouse, which I could finish during the winter months. The time came to take Marianne and Tim back to Homer, and as we hugged good-bye, I said, "I never could have done it without you. You're both welcome in my home anytime."

I was sorry to be leaving my summer family in town and returning to Sadie alone; but we would meet again, and I had plenty to do getting ready for the next lodge season.

Building a Business

For the next four years, 1982 to 1986, my life revolved around Sadie Cove Wilderness Lodge. Each spring I interviewed and hired two employees to help me during the summer season. The transition from living alone to sharing my home with others wasn't always easy, but I had no desire to be a hermit and enjoyed the change.

My employees didn't get rich on what I paid them, but money wasn't the main reason most wanted to work in the Bush. They came to experience a part of Alaska few individuals ever get a chance to see. Living and working in Sadie was an adventure.

The summer Sue Parker ran the kitchen, we shared an experience that made us both realize the thrill of living in the wilds of Alaska. About 4:00 o'clock one morning, I was awakened by a noise out on the wharf. At first I thought it was Sue on her way to the outhouse, but then something started scratching on my window. I rolled over, looked out, and immediately snapped fully awake. A big black bear was trying to break into my cabin.

I yelled, grabbed the .357 magnum pistol next to my bed, and bolted downstairs. The bear stood facing me twenty feet down the deck as I ran out of the Wharfhouse. Its menacing growl and curled lip made me yell even louder, but when I fired five shots into the air, the beast took off running up the hill. I hoped he would keep going, but on reaching the garden he halted, turned, and looked at me like I was a pork chop on a plate.

This bear hadn't scared easily, and if he wanted to eat me for breakfast I needed more firepower. I sprinted into the Oarhouse and grabbed my 12-gauge shotgun from the rack. As I loaded the shells into the magazine, Sue asked from her loft bedroom, "Are you all right?"

"Yeah, I'm okay," I answered in an excited voice. "But there's a bear outside!"

It occurred to me that she might think I'd gone crazy after waking her up with gunshots and then busting into her cabin stark naked. "Is it a grizzly?" she asked with a hint of sarcasm in her voice. "Hell no!" I answered while pumping a shell into the chamber. "It's a big blackie, and I didn't scare it away."

Sue finally believed me, and I ran out to find my pants and deal with the bear.

The cause of the commotion had disappeared, but I hurried up to the garden to make sure. Luckily, the only sign I found was a fresh pile of bear scat next to the rhubarb patch. At least now I could prove my sanity to Sue.

The bear never came back, but Sue became hesitant about venturing out alone. I convinced her it was safe if she made a lot of noise, and from then on the entire cove knew when Sue was headed for the outhouse—a shrill blast from her bear whistle always announced her intentions.

In 1984 I began constructing the big house. This 1,500-square-foot building constituted my biggest project to date, and its design included a bar, office, shop, large storage area, full bathroom, greenhouse, and a new bedroom for the Viking. I knew it would take two or three years to finish and require the efforts of many different people, so after framing the walls and completing the roof, we worked on the interior one room at a time.

Not all of my building projects involved new construction. No matter how well I designed and built a wharf or cabin, the forces of nature had the power to destroy them. Earthquakes, volcanic eruptions, hurricane-force winds, and pounding surf weren't everyday events in Sadie Cove, but the potential for damage or destruction was always present.

When I built my log sauna next to the stream, I didn't give much thought to what had formed the stream's deep gorge. If I had, I would have built it in a different location. The conditions were perfect for a catastrophe. It had been cold and snowy for weeks, but then the weather pattern changed and we were hit with warm winds and pelting rain off the Gulf of Alaska. Eight hundred feet up the mountain behind the lodge, the saturated snow broke free, avalanched, and dammed the already swollen stream. When the dam broke, it created a flash flood that sent boulders and uprooted trees roaring down the canyon, barely missing the sauna. The main force of the water slammed into the cliff next to the bath house and then knocked it over. Luckily, no one was taking a sauna when the flood occurred!

Repairing the badly damaged sauna took longer than building it, and during those three months I went back to bathing in a small, galvanized tub. The short winter days and freezing weather slowed down my work, but I finally finished the repairs and fired up the stove. Sitting in the 150°F heat, I once again relaxed in the sauna's tropical warmth.

During those four years of building my lodge business, I also spent much time and money on boats. In the winter of 1983 a combination of events took place that taught me another expensive lesson. I crossed the bay to Homer in *Valkyrie* in the middle of January to buy groceries. On arriving in town, I learned a big storm was forecast to blow in that tonight, so I hurried back to Sadie.

I made it home just in time. By the time I anchored the skiff off my beach the wind began increasing. When I sat down to eat dinner it was blowing 80 knots. As I crawled into bed for the night, big gusts were shaking my cabin.

The next morning I awoke in the dark and went through my morning ritual of making coffee and visiting the outhouse. The winds had diminished to 60 knots, but I felt uneasy and kept looking out into the darkness toward my anchored skiff. When it became light enough to see, my concern turned to anguish—*Valkyrie* had disappeared.

I felt sick as I searched Sadie with my binoculars. All I saw were whitecapped waves marching out of the cove. As I puzzled over what to do next, my neighbor Slim knocked on the door. After I got him a cup of coffee, he said, "I noticed your skiff's missing and came over to help. If you want, I'll launch my boat and we'll see if we can find it."

"Thanks," I answered, "but with these big waves crashing on your beach, it would be too dangerous to get your boat into the water. I'm going to look for the skiff, but I'll use my kayak."

My beach was better protected from the southeast storms than Slim's, so I wouldn't have too much trouble launching the kayak. I had been out in worse weather than this, and if I stayed close to shore I would be able to get to the beach if I capsized.

As the 4-foot waves pushed me out of the cove, I hoped the low tide had beached my missing boat. If I could find the skiff before high water, I had a chance of saving her.

I searched all day but never found even a trace of *Valkyrie*. However, I did find what destroyed her. Washed up on a beach, I discovered an island of ice two feet thick and 200 feet long. During the night, the wind must have broken this small iceberg loose from the pack at the head of Sadie. When the ice hit my skiff, it tore *Valkyrie* from the moorage and swept her out to sea. The experience taught me a costly lesson, and from then on I stored my boat on land in winter.

Fortunately, I didn't have to look very long for another boat. Nancy Hickson, a new year-round resident of Sadie, had one for lease. After inspecting the old wooden craft in Homer, we made a deal. I could use the boat in exchange for doing its much needed repair work.

The *Povo* was Alaska history. The Libby Salmon Company had built her, plus hundreds of others just like her, to fish for red salmon in Bristol Bay during the 1930s. The 31-foot, double-ended boats were originally powered by sail and gained a reputation for being very seaworthy.

My new used boat now ran on diesel power, and although she was slow, she could haul 6,000 pounds of cargo. It took two hours to cross the ten miles from Homer to the lodge (I once kayaked the distance a minute faster), but I didn't care; I had safe transportation for the next lodge season.

Between 1982 and 1986 the lodge business doubled every year. Each season, Kachemak Bay Title Company returned for their summer Christmas party, and the group from Washington, D.C., came back to fish for silver salmon. With this repeat business and new customers from within Alaska, my prospects seemed bright.

Early one spring I received a contract for some unexpected business from a local source. An old quarry at the mouth of Sadie Cove had supplied rock to rebuild the Homer Spit after the 1964 earthquake. Homer reopened the site to provide rock for a harbor expansion, and my lodge would house and feed the construction crew for the three-week job.

Fortunately, I had plenty of help. Sue Parker and my mother, who was visiting from Oregon, cooked and cleaned while four young men I'd hired in Homer helped me with outside jobs. When the ten-man construction crew arrived, it took a few days to work out the kinks in our operation, but finally the lodge and quarry crews settled into their daily routines.

Every night after taking the men back to the lodge, I would usually join them for a few beers. During one of these bull sessions, I mentioned my plans to build a good moorage. Before I could finish discussing my ideas, the dinner bell rang and the topic was forgotten. The next day when I picked up the crew at the quarry, Don, whom I'd known for years in Homer, surprised me with some good news. "I found the perfect anchor for your moorage," he said. "Today, while pushing dirt, I unearthed a 3,000-pound boulder with a drill hole through its center."

I could see its potential as well as one small problem and asked, "How am I going to move a one-and-a-half-ton rock from the quarry to the front of my lodge?"

Don thought for a moment before answering. "You get the chain, line, and floats for your moorage, and we'll figure something out."

The last day on the job the quarry crew had time to help me with the project. Don collected beach logs with his huge front-end loader and dumped them in the water, where I tied them together to make a raft. Then we attached a heavy chain to the rock, and loaded it onto the makeshift barge. Most of the rock and logs were submerged, but they floated enough for me to tow my new anchor back to the lodge.

I said good-bye to the crew, thanked them for their help, and started for home. The sea was calm when I started, but by the time I arrived in front of my beach, the wind had kicked up 2-foot waves to complicate the final phase of my plan.

The makeshift barge rolled uneasily in the choppy sea, but at least it was over the spot where I would attach the 200 feet of line and floats to the rock, cut the rope holding the raft together, and send the anchor to the bottom. Everything worked perfectly except for one small detail. The raft came apart and dropped the boulder to its final resting place before I could connect the anchor line. There was nothing I could do but cuss my luck and try to remember where it went down.

As I collected the scattered logs, I thought of an idea to salvage my anchor. I called my Homer fisherman friend, Billy Choate, over the marine radio and asked him if he would come to Sadie with his diving gear. Later that day Billy came on his boat, the *Whale Song*. We dropped his anchor where I guessed the rock went down, and he made his first dive. As Billy followed the boat's 100-foot anchor chain to the bottom, I stood on deck watching the air bubbles rise to the surface and crossed my fingers for luck.

Billy popped back up fifteen minutes later and gave me the thumbs-up sign. As I helped him on board he said, "Good guess, Keith. Your rock's only ten feet from my anchor."

With a smile stretching from ear to ear, I said, "I owe you for this, Billy. What a great ending to the quarry crew job. I enjoyed them as guests, made some money, and as a bonus acquired a good moorage and twenty logs to cut into lumber at Slim's sawmill."

Besides guests from Alaska and the Lower 48, I started attracting groups from foreign countries. The Japanese love nature and fresh seafood, and since Sadie Cove supplied both, every summer I entertained one or two parties from the Land of the Rising Sun.

One such group came with enough equipment to supply a small army. As we unloaded their mountain of gear, the party's leader, Takeshi Kaiko, explained, "We travel all over the world to remote areas in search of good stories and photographs for the books we write. Sometimes we arrive to find few of the things we need, so we have learned to bring our own."

"What kind of books do you write?" I asked while carrying a huge cooking pot up the beach.

"We write articles for Japanese *Playboy*, picture books on fishing, and cookbooks," he answered. "I am so sorry to say this trip we brought no geisha girls, but we did bring a famous Japanese cook."

At this point he introduced me to the chef, who bowed a lot but spoke no English. Kaiko then made two rather unusual requests. First, he asked, "To write our cookbook, you will please let honorable chef do all the cooking?"

I saw no problem and informed my own cook that she could help with the kitchen cleanup and lend a hand when asked. My crew would eat with our guests, and we eagerly awaited sampling the Japanese cooking.

Then Kaiko made his second request. "Our company has already made books on salmon and halibut, so please help us catch other kinds of seafood."

"Kachemak Bay is one of the richest marine habitats in the world, so we'll have no problem getting what you want," I said. "Today let's gather crab and mussels for dinner and plan the rest of the meals around shrimp, clams, octopus, sea cucumbers, and a variety of tasty bottom fish."

After Kaiko interpreted what I said, the cook bowed his thanks and went to work in the kitchen.

The next morning, my crew and I received a big, steaming bowl of homemade Japanese soup for breakfast. Although it smelled delicious, we lost our appetites when the fish heads floated to the surface. It was definitely unsettling having our meal watch us eat. After that, we got up earlier than our guests and ate a good old-fashioned American breakfast.

Most of the guests we entertained in Sadie Cove came to catch salmon and halibut, but none were more fanatical about fishing than the Germans. One group of six from the German Alaska Club, led by Fritz, came in mid-August, eager to test their skills on what we had to offer. Halibut fishing was excellent, but the silvers were running later than usual in Kachemak Bay that year, so I decided to fly my guests to the Rocky River, where I knew the fishing would be better.

Beluga Lake Float Plane Service picked up the first four men and flew them twenty miles over the mountains to the Gulf of Alaska. When the pilot, Jon, returned for the second group, I'd finished packing the emergency gear we needed if the weather turned bad. As we approached the remote river, Jon said, "I'll pick up both groups at high tide down where the water flows out of the canyon."

He circled and pointed out the location. I nodded and asked, "Why can't you pick us all up on the lake we'll be landing on upstream?"

"If you catch many fish, the plane will be too heavy to take off from that small a body of water. Better to be safe than sorry," he answered.

Jon would pick us up in six hours, so when we landed, I led Wolfgang and Hans to a good fishing spot on the river and started off with my first load of gear.

A short distance downstream I caught up with the first group of guests. "Make sure everyone gets to the pickup point by high tide," I said to Fritz. "I'll drop this gear to mark the spot and return for the second load. If you fish your way downstream, you can't miss it."

Fritz was so excited that most of what he said came out in German. "Das is fantastic fishing. We catch already six fish unt one ist twenty pounds!"

I left the happy fishermen and continued downriver. Since there were no trails, I fought the brush most of the way and arrived at the pickup spot wringing wet with sweat. My trip back was easier without the 60-pound pack, but it still wasn't a stroll in the park with all the blown-down trees I had to crawl over and under.

I found Fritz and his group even more excited than when I had left them. The four men had already caught their limit of silvers, and although each man hauled about seventy pounds of fish, they were beaming.

To save time, I left the river and hiked over a hill to the lake on which we had landed. With the last load of gear collected, I returned to the river to find Hans and Wolfgang. They weren't too much farther downstream from where I'd left them, and they, too, had caught their limit of six salmon.

Wolfgang was sixty-five years old and was having a hell of a time carrying his fish. Neither man spoke English, but Wolfgang understood me when I volunteered to carry half his catch. I tried not to think of how much weight I carried and concentrated on getting downriver.

We were still a quarter-mile upstream from the pickup spot when I heard the plane. As we rested, I took out my hand-held radio and called Jon. "This is the ground to Beluga Lake Float Plane Service. I have the last two guests with me, and we only have to cross the river one more time before arriving at the canyon. See you when you return from the lodge."

"Roger. I'll be back in thirty minutes," came his reply.

I started to ford the knee-deep river where I'd crossed before, but something was wrong. The high tide had backed up the water. I had only one choice—lift the pack over my head and get wet. When the cold water filled my hip boots I began muttering, but by the time it reached my chest I chuckled at the absurdity of the situation. Hans and Wolfgang stood on the bank obviously amused at my predicament. I hoped they would still be laughing when it came their turn to cross.

I dropped my pack on the far bank and went back to help them. They took the dip in good stride, and after emptying our hip boots, we continued.

We reached the entrance of the canyon, but could go no farther. The water was too high to get to the pickup point at the other end. I knew Wolfgang couldn't climb the cliffs to our final destination, and it would be dark before the tide went down enough to get through the gorge. It looked like we were going to spend the night. This wasn't a life-threatening situation, but a hot meal, sauna, and warm bed back in Sadie sure beat spending a long night on the cold ground.

Wolfgang and Hans sat shivering as they looked at the steep-walled canyon. I wished I could explain the situation, but since we didn't speak the same language, any attempt would only confuse them. So I reached into my pack, pulled out a bottle of peppermint schnapps, and asked, "Would you like a drink?"

They both grinned and answered, "Ya, ya!"

That broke the language barrier, and as we passed the bottle around, I heard the plane. I turned on my radio and informed Jon of our situation. We couldn't make it through the canyon, but maybe he could come to us. The wind and water were calm, so he tried. The floatplane slowly taxied through the narrow gorge with only two feet clearance off each wing tip. As we loaded our gear, I said, "Thanks, Jon. You went above and beyond the call of duty on this one."

We made it safely back to the lodge, and during dinner I proposed a toast. "To a great day of fishing, and congratulations to Wolfgang and Hans, who in fording the Rocky River, experienced their Alaskan baptism."

One of the best groups I ever had the pleasure to entertain at my lodge came from the Lower 48 and Europe. I had watched two members of this party, Billy Kidd and Jimmie Heuga, win silver and bronze metals in slalom skiing for the United States at the 1964 Winter Olympics in Innsbruck, Austria. What made their visit so special was the reason they and the rest of their party came to Alaska.

After Jimmie Heuga won his bronze metal, he became ill with multiple sclerosis (MS), a condition that can cause partial to complete paralysis. As his condition worsened, Jimmie fought back, and not only did he continue skiing, he devoted his life to raising money to fight the crippling disease.

Jimmie, with a group of famous, talented, and caring people, came up with an idea to help his cause. They acquired corporate sponsors who pledged to donate $1 million to MS research if they could ski 1 million vertical feet in a day. They called this fundraiser the Jimmie Heuga Express.

They chose Alyeska Ski Resort, near Anchorage, as the location for the event, and the group contacted my friend Dave Hamre of Girdwood to set up the in-state logistics. Through Dave they made arrangements to come to Sadie Cove before skiing the mountain.

The sixteen guests flew to Homer during one of the worst spring storms in many years. When they arrived, I had the pleasure of meeting not only Jimmie Heuga and Billy Kidd, but Steve Lathrop, Phil Mahre, Jan Helen, Stein Eriksen, Bernard Russi, Leif Grevle, and Jean-Claude Killy. These were some of the greatest skiers in the world, and news of their arrival would soon be all over town. But before they could sign any autographs, I shuttled them to the harbor and aboard the boat that would transport them across the bay.

Bruce, the captain of the 50-foot *Sunday*, met me on the dock. "The weather is pretty bad, Keith," he warned. "Do you think we can get them to the lodge?"

"The wind is decreasing, so let's give it a try," I answered. "Dave and I will go ahead in the smaller skiffs we'll need to unload your boat. I just hope it's not blowing a Sadie Eighty in the cove."

When we arrived at my beach, the wind had diminished to 30 knots and we made it safely ashore. As we carried the gear to the lodge, Jan Helen came out of the newly completed bar wearing my horned Viking helmet and yelled to Stein Eriksen, "Look what I found! It makes me feel like I'm back home in the fjords of Norway."

I smiled and said, "Everyone here is a Viking, whether they're Scandinavian or not, for joining in such a great cause. Welcome to my home and lodge."

With twenty guests and crew, the resort was packed, but it didn't matter. We ate well, caught fish, and enjoyed each other's company.

The day they left it rained, and while saying good-bye to Jimmie and his gang, I apologized for the stormy weather. Jean-Claude replied, "It makes no difference, Keith. The rain is a part of the experience. Thanks for sharing part of your Alaska with us."

These men truly had connected with the essence of my life in Sadie Cove. The storms weren't bad; they were just another part of nature. I would be bored waking up every morning to warm, sunny weather.

On my next trip to Homer I heard that the Jimmie Heuga Express had skied a million vertical feet in one day at Alyeska.

In building the lodge business, I gave my guests what they wanted, and many of them came back year after year. I also spent money on promotions to let more people know what the resort had to offer. One spring I took the entire $4,000 of my advertising budget and bought a Sony video camera, television set, and two VCRs.

Now I could capture the grandeur of Kachemak Bay and Sadie Cove, as well as its wildlife inhabitants. I didn't want network television in my home, but the TV allowed me to monitor what I filmed. The two VCRs made it possible to make my own "movie" to promote the lodge at sportsmen shows in Alaska and the Lower 48.

Using my video camera to record the antics of local wildlife gave me many hours of pleasure. I kept the camera ready at all times so that I could photograph bald eagles as they flew by, killer whales in my front yard, and mountain goats descending the cliffs to the beach.

Early one morning as I walked along the wharf to the kitchen to make coffee, a movement on the beach caught my eye. Three river otters were feeding at the water's edge. Postponing coffee, I sneaked inside to get my camera and started filming about 150 feet away from the sleek, brown creatures. Then, step by step, I crept down the beach with the camera whirring. The otters were so engrossed in feeding on small crabs, worms, and shellfish that I was able to get within twenty feet of them before they noticed me and nervously swam away. I didn't need coffee that morning to wake me up.

Not all my movie-making was so spontaneous. The first fall after buying the camera, I set aside two full weeks to do nothing but photograph the spectacular life in and around Sadie Cove.

With the coming of colder days and longer nights, I planned a trip with Beluga Lake Float Plane Service to do some filming from the air. Jon took me up on a perfect, clear, windless day in his vintage DeHavalin floatplane, and we flew over the starkly beautiful ice fields and glaciers that encased the mountains behind my home. On our way back, we dropped into the high valley behind the lodge and spotted a bull moose and its harem of females. I shot the moose with my movie camera and smiled, knowing in two days I'd be back with my friends, the Sidelingers, for our annual moose hunt. Like other Alaskans living in the Bush, we harvested wild game for food—not for trophies.

Kevin, Cindy, and son Bowman came the next day in their 20-foot skiff loaded with camping gear and four llamas. "The forecast looks good for the next three days," Kevin said as they unloaded. "I hope there's a big, fat moose in the back valley so we won't starve this winter."

I never was good at keeping secrets. "Yesterday I flew over our hunting grounds and filmed our winter meat supply," I answered.

"After dinner and a sauna, I'll start the generator, and we can watch a preview of the star of our coming action."

The next morning we loaded the long-haired llamas, named Boone, Poncho, Jim Bridger, and Ashu. They stood patiently watching us with large, brown eyes as we filled their specially built packs.

Kevin led the way up the steep trail with Poncho and Ashu. Five-year-old Bowman came next, leading Boone, and Cindy brought up the rear with Jim Bridger. As the camera man, I ran ahead to find the best locations to film our pack train.

The first part of the mile-and-a-half trail to camp was the most difficult, and the only ones not sweating when we stopped to rest were the llamas. "I'm sure glad we have the llamas along on this hunt," I said as I relaxed next to a cold, clear stream. "If we shoot that bull moose in the back valley, it would take us a week to haul out the meat ourselves. How much can each animal pack?"

Kevin watched the llamas feeding quietly on the high, green grass next to the trail and answered, "They'll carry about 100 pounds apiece. If we bone the meat and carry some ourselves, we can pack out a medium-size moose in one trip."

Cindy added, "They also make our hunting trips more enjoyable by hauling in more camping gear than we could pack by ourselves."

As I filmed Poncho nibbling on the bright pink flowers of a fireweed, Kevin said, "Not only are they great beasts of burden, they're healthy, live to be twenty years old, and are so gentle we consider them pets."

"Yeah, but we don't let them in the house 'cause they'd mess on the floor," young Bowman remarked.

We all laughed as he continued, "And you know what, Keith? Mom lets me help brush the llamas, and we save the hair to make into socks to keep our feet warm in winter."

Cindy passed around a bag of granola to munch on, and I asked, "Have you ever met a bear with the llamas?"

"Yes, we have," Cindy answered, "last season when we were packing out a load of moose meat from a valley near our home in Halibut Cove. We came around a bend in the trail, and there was a big blackie feeding on salmonberries only thirty feet away."

"Tell him what happened, Mom," Bowman shouted.

"Well, it was pretty exciting," said Cindy. "The llamas all bunched up, faced the bear, and started making this strange chirping sound. We yelled as loud as we could, and that ol' bear got so scared I bet it's still running. The llamas did fine, but it took a while for my heart to stop pounding."

"A good thing that bear didn't get any closer, 'cause the llamas would have spit on him," added Bowman. "Boy is that stinky stuff!"

As we got ready to go, I asked him, "I take it you like the llamas?"

"They're my friends," he answered. "When I grow up, I'm going to live in the woods with my llamas and be just like my Mom and Dad."

Kevin, Cindy, and I smiled as we headed up the trail, and I said, "Bowman, at five years old you're already a mountain man. If I had a son, I'd want him to be just like you."

We arrived tired and hungry at our campsite around 3:00 o'clock in the afternoon. After unloading the llamas and putting them out to graze, we set up the tents among a small grove of short, wind-blown spruce trees. Cindy prepared lunch with Bowman's help, Kevin took out his spotting scope, and I hauled water from the nearby pond. This crystal clear pool was the headwater of the stream that cascaded 1,400 feet down the mountain to my lodge on the beach.

Our campsite overlooked a larger valley than the one we had just hiked through and was the ideal location from which to spot game. We sat eating smoked salmon, cheese, and Cindy's home-made bread and silently appreciated the beauty before us.

A sparkling stream wound its way through the narrow valley, with steep mountains rising up more than 2,000 feet on both sides. With the llamas grazing in front of us and snowcapped peaks in the distance, I did more filming than eating. As I photographed the long valley for the second time, I spotted something through the camera and said, "I see a big ol' black bear, and it looks like it's coming this way."

Kevin looked through his spotting scope. "You're right," he replied. "I don't see any cubs, and from its size, I'll bet it's a male."

"You promised me bear meat for the winter, Kevin," said Cindy.

"We only have a couple hours before dark," he pointed out.

My mouth watered as I thought of sinking my teeth into a medium-rare bear steak. "Let's do it," I said. "We might not get another chance with such perfect conditions. Kevin, you shoot the bear, and I'll record it with my camera."

Cindy and Bowman stayed in camp while Kevin and I quickly loaded up two llamas with what we needed and ran down through the brush to the valley floor. When we got into position, Kevin loaded his .30-'06 rifle and I put fresh batteries in my camera. Now all we had to do was wait for the bear and hope it was still headed in our direction.

Thirty minutes later the bear ambled over a small knoll 500 feet from where we sat waiting. I started recording, and two seconds later Kevin fired. The deafening shot made me jump, but I kept the camera going and watched as the wounded animal rolled over, scrambled to its feet, and charged straight at us.

Three more shots ran out as the bear crashed through the brush. It was hard keeping the charging beast in the viewfinder of my camera, knowing we were in big trouble if Kevin didn't stop him.

The bear was less than 100 feet away when it suddenly veered off, ran up the mountain, and disappeared into a large patch of alder. I stopped recording, looked at Kevin, and said, "Damn, that's one tough bear. You hit him all four times, and he still kept coming."

"It's not over yet," my friend said as he reloaded his rifle. "We'll wait fifteen minutes before going into the brush after him."

The valley was very quiet as Kevin and I waited. We watched the brush for any movement and cautiously walked to where the bear had fallen. "Not much blood," Kevin said as we searched the ground. "This time of year the bear's winter fat can plug up a wound."

He paused, then added, "It's time to get the job done."

We entered the alder where the bear had disappeared. Kevin carried his rifle with a shell in the chamber, and I followed with my camera. Tracking a wounded bear in heavy brush was not my idea of an enjoyable wilderness experience, but we had no choice. If the bear was still alive, we wanted to end its suffering. If it was dead, we didn't want to waste the meat. We were both committed to finishing what we had started.

Slowly, we started up the mountain. After climbing several hundred feet, we agreed that with darkness approaching we would split up so that we could cover more ground. Kevin paralleled the slope, and I descended at an angle. As I crept through the dense brush, I thought about the possibility of videotaping my own mauling.

Kevin was out of sight when I saw the wounded bear. Its jet black body lay among green ferns thirty feet below me. I thought it was dead until I heard a deep, sinister growl. I didn't need my sixth sense to tell me I was in great danger. Adrenalin surged through my body as I shouted to Kevin and scrambled uphill as fast as I could go.

I've never been happier to see anyone in my life. Kevin came crashing through the brush just as the bear started to get up. He fired the final shot and the beast rolled down the hill—the hunt was over.

Kevin gutted the 300-pound bear while I filmed the process. I didn't plan to use this part of the hunt in my lodge movie, but what I photographed would be a good record on field-dressing wild game.

In the fading light we loaded the butchered bear onto the two llamas, which were surprisingly calm. Cindy's campfire guided us back to camp, and after a long, exciting day, we feasted on fresh bear steaks under the twinkling stars.

Two days later, Kevin shot the bull moose I'd filmed from the air. Due to heavy rain I wasn't able to tape the hunt, but the trip had been a great success. We had enough bear and moose meat to feed us through the long, cold winter, and I now had some great action footage for a movie on the lodge.

Trouble in Paradise

Would I spend the rest of my life as a bachelor? At age forty-three, maybe I was getting too cantankerous to share my good life in Sadie Cove with a woman. I would soon find out. Falling in love wasn't on any of my project lists, but it happened anyway.

The relationship began in September 1985 while I sat talking to Tony, a halibut charter captain and my good buddy. As we relaxed in the Land's End Bar on the Homer Spit, I noticed a fine-looking woman sitting alone across the room. I wanted to meet her, but I didn't want to make a fool of myself by starting a conversation with a line like "Haven't we met before?" or "Are you new in town?" With no way to be properly introduced, I continued talking to Tony.

When the bartender took our order, I told him to serve the woman with the long, brown hair a drink and put it on my tab. He did and two minutes later returned with a cocktail for me. "She wants to return the favor," he said with a grin.

I looked over to where she sat, raised my drink in thanks, told Tony we'd talk later, and walked across the room to introduce myself. "Hi, I'm Keith Iverson. Thanks for the drink."

She looked up with sparkling brown eyes and said, "Well, thank you for the same. My name's Lila Mae McEwen."

Sometimes I'd rather face a charging bear than start a conversation with a woman, but with Lila Mae I felt relaxed and wanted to talk.

I liked her firm handshake and asked, "Are you in Homer on business or pleasure?"

"Both, actually," she answered after asking me to join her. "I'm a family nurse-practitioner from Eagle River, near Anchorage, and came down to give physicals to the school bus drivers. After catching some king salmon in the Kenai River this summer, I vowed to fish for halibut in Homer before the season ended. Tomorrow I'm going out on a charter. I really love this area."

She looked out across the bay to the distant mountains and asked, "Do you live around here?"

"Not in Homer," I answered. "I'm from over there where you're looking. My home and wilderness lodge are in Sadie Cove."

Lila smiled at me and said, "I thought that was you. Several years ago I saw your picture in the *Anchorage Daily News* with an article about your lodge and Mooseltoe."

I laughed and replied, "Yup, that's me. I wear several different hats to match the different parts of my personality."

She seemed interested, so I continued. "To make it easier to understand myself, I've named the two main parts of me. My middle name is Austin, and that's who you're talking to right now. Austin is fun-loving, a little bit crazy, and a Viking. But don't worry; I don't go around ravaging and pillaging. Austin is just adventurous."

Lila Mae touched my arm and said, "That's interesting! I have the same philosophy about my inner self. In fact, you're talking to Mae. It sounds like your Austin and my Mae have much in common. What's Keith like?"

"Keith is just the opposite of Austin," I answered. "He's all business, reserved, serious, a little shy, and, as far as Austin is concerned, boring."

Mae laughed and said, "I don't believe it—you just described Lila. Which part of you created Mooseltoe?"

"Austin invented the product and collected the moose manure," I answered. "Keith planned the marketing campaign and did most of the worrying. We both had our moments peddling the poop."

She laughed again, and I ordered us another round. Lila Mae asked, "Which one of you lives in Sadie Cove?"

"We both do," I answered. "Keith does the building, runs the lodge business, and counts the money. Austin prefers to climb mountains, go fishing, and raise a little hell in Homer."

Austin was feeling more and more attracted to this lovely lady and wanted to know her better. "Are you a doctor?" I asked.

"No, I'm a family nurse-practitioner, but several years ago the state of Alaska passed a law making it possible for me to start my own medical practice. Lila, my serious side, established an office and started taking care of a few patients. Actually, I was the first to take advantage of the new law. Now, Lila is very busy and Mae doesn't have much time for fishing or dancing."

Both sides of Lila Mae's personality impressed me. "How about joining me for dinner?" I asked. "Why don't we make it a double date? Austin can take Mae, and Keith can escort Lila."

Lila Mae accepted, and we had a fantastic evening. After dinner we went dancing, and while Keith and Lila discussed literature during the waltzes, Austin and Mae gyrated to the rock and roll.

The next day, Lila Mae canceled her halibut fishing trip and we crossed the bay to Sadie Cove for the weekend. The cold, windy weather didn't matter—we were too engrossed in each other's company. Lila rolled up her sleeves to help Keith with the chores and spent several hours discussing the lodge business. The next day Austin took Mae on a hike up the mountain. All too soon I skiffed Lila Mae back to Homer so that she could return to her medical practice in Eagle River. After we said good-bye, Keith Austin agreed that Lila Mae combined those special qualities he was looking for in a woman.

In early December my new friend returned to Sadie Cove to help with my last duck-hunting group of the season. Lila Mae did a great job cooking for our six guests from Anchorage while I guided the lively party, who called themselves the Duck Brothers. The frigid, blustery weather made our work difficult, but we performed well as a team. At the end of the four-day hunt, Lila Mae returned with the hunters to Homer on a chartered boat. As I watched them leave the cove, I knew my life had changed—Keith and Austin had fallen in love.

We'd agreed to spend the holidays together, but on the drive to Eagle River I became more and more nervous. Although Keith and Austin were scared spitless, they both wanted to make a commitment.

Two days after Christmas, at a fancy restaurant in Anchorage, I summoned all my courage and asked Lila Mae to marry me. When she said yes, I was speechless. My heart felt like it would burst from too much love. After a long embrace, I regained control of my voice and ordering champagne. While sipping bubbles, we chose June 1, 1986, as our wedding date. My life in Sadie Cove had begun on that day twelve years earlier, and we agreed it would be the perfect time to start our new life together.

I couldn't wait to share the good news, and although it was 3:00 A.M., I telephoned my parents in the Lower 48. When my folks woke up enough to understand why we were calling, they seemed to breathe a sigh of relief. "It's about time," Dad said. "We thought you'd be a bachelor for the rest of your life."

Then Mom asked, "Are you getting married in a church?"

"We're getting hitched in Sadie Cove," I answered. "It's our chapel."

"Where are you going on your honeymoon?" Dad inquired.

As I grabbed Lila Mae and gave her a hug, I said, "We're going to spend a few weeks on the beach."

"Hawaii's a great place," Mom replied. "You'll love it."

I laughed and set them straight. "I'm talking about the beach at Gore Point. After the ceremony, we'll fly over the mountains to the Gulf of Alaska and spend our honeymoon camping out. Instead of suntan lotion, we'll take insect repellent."

Before they hung up, my folks added, "We're very happy you're not alone anymore, Keith. The whole family will be up for the wedding."

On returning to Sadie, I learned I wasn't the only one with a good reason to be so happy. My neighbor Nancy had married John Hillstrand, a fisherman from Homer. During a break in the winter weather, they'd flown to Mount Augustine in a helicopter and were wed on the beach of the volcanic island. It looked like Sadie Cove was about to experience a population explosion.

I'd spent most of my winters in Sadie alone, but now the isolation had become too difficult. I wanted to be with Lila Mae. We talked several times a week over the VHF radio, but our conversations weren't enough. Rather than prolong my misery, I went back to Eagle River in February so that we could be together and plan our future.

During my stay, I met Tom and Mona, a couple interested in working at the lodge the next summer. I had a lodge guest from Anchorage who wanted to experience spring in the Bush, and since her reservation was in March, we agreed that would be a good time to meet in Sadie for a trial run. Going home knowing that Lila and the others would be down soon, made it much easier to concentrate and get ready for their arrival.

Two days before their scheduled trip to Sadie, Mount Augustine volcano erupted. This show of nature's force sent a cloud of ash and smoke 35,000 feet up into the winter sky, but the strong southerly winds blew it north to Anchorage. Kachemak Bay received no ashfall, so I made the crossing and picked up the group without mishap. It felt damn good having Lila Mae back in Sadie Cove, even if we weren't alone.

Our first night at the lodge, the wind shifted enough to bring a light dusting of ash and the coldest temperatures of the winter. The next morning the outdoor thermometer read 0°F as I lit the stove and put on coffee. Tom, Mona, and Jane, my guest, joined Lila Mae and me in the kitchen. As we sat down to breakfast, I turned on the radio to hear the latest news about the eruption. The announcer told us to expect light ashfall for the next two days and warned of the possibility of a tidal wave if the volcano erupted again.

Everyone stopped eating and looked at me as I casually poured myself another shot of coffee. "We get tsunami warnings every time there's an earthquake," I said. "It's all part of the adventure of living in Alaska."

Jane still looked nervous, so I continued. "The radio will alert us if we're in danger, and we'll have plenty of time to reach safety. The upper cabin is 100 feet above the beach, and I've stocked it with food just in case of such an emergency. So let's relax, finish our breakfast, and enjoy our time in Sadie."

I didn't tell them the biggest tsunami ever recorded happened in Lituya Bay in southeast Alaska. An earthquake caused a large chunk of coastal mountain to avalanche into the water, creating a wave 1,700 feet high.

I was about to suggest clam digging after breakfast when something caught my eye. While adjusting the focus of my binoculars I said, "What's a mountain goat doing on the beach?"

"Where?" everyone shouted.

Pointing at a white speck about a mile down the beach, I handed them the binoculars and answered, "It's kneeling at the base of a cliff; maybe it's hurt. The tide's coming in, but there's time to hike to where it's lying."

"I'll come with you," Tom said.

"Good, we'll take the video camera, some rope, and my .357 magnum pistol. If the goat's too badly hurt, we can stop its suffering," I said as we started packing.

Walking down the beach, I told Tom that the mountain goats always wintered on the cliffs next to the lodge, but that they rarely came down to the beach.

We arrived unobserved at a point 100 feet from the goat. As I took the camera out of my pack, I whispered to Tom, "From its horns

I can see it's a male. Give me time to sneak up on him and get some pictures before you join me. When we get close, be careful—that billy knows how to use those horns!"

It took twenty minutes to crawl to a large boulder thirty feet from the most magnificent mountain goat I'd ever seen. As I focused I realized I was living out a once-in-a-lifetime opportunity.

The beauty of the beast held me in awe, and a chill of excitement rushed through me. He knelt on the beach, serenely watching the small waves gently rattling the gravel. The light wind ruffled his long, white body hair and the six-inch beard that dangled from his chin. His perfectly formed, jet black horns curved upward to the sky like a crown on his regal head.

"The waves are at his feet, and he still hasn't moved," I whispered as Tom joined me. "He must have fallen off the cliff. I'm going to show myself and walk toward him."

Tom nodded as I stepped out from our hiding place. With the camera running, I slowly approached the kneeling billy. At ten feet he saw me but only for a brief moment showed any sign of alarm. He merely noted my presence and turned his head to watch the waves.

I circled to his front and started talking in a soft voice, to let him know I meant no harm. At I approached, he slowly turned his head and gazed at me. At that instant, the sun broke from behind the clouds and the slanting rays sparkled in his gold-flecked eyes. Our eyes locked, and for a moment I looked into his soul. I saw no fear— only the serene strength of a wild, noble beast.

To my amazement, he stood up. I sprang backward and yelled, "Look out! Give him room to escape!"

I thought he might charge, but then realized he was too weak. We were in no danger. He staggered up the beach gasping for air. The highborn creature was dying.

We watched him painfully make his way off the beach and lie down under the gnarled branches of an old spruce tree. He gazed over at us, and I said, "If we hadn't interfered, he would have let the sea take him."

Tom nodded his head in agreement. "He won't last through the night," he said. "Let's leave him to die in peace."

"When my time comes, I hope I'm here in Sadie," I said as we slowly walked back to the lodge. "Who knows, maybe that old billy and I will meet again!"

The next morning we found the lifeless body of the goat lying where we had last seen him. Even in death he was magnificent. His remains would be recycled by the elements and become a part of the land. I believed his spirit now roamed the cliffs above the cove.

Mount Augustine continued erupting; but the wind carried the ash north, so we could make a safe crossing back to town. Tom and Mona took the job at the lodge, Jane said she would be back in the summer, and Lila gave me a long good-bye hug. An hour after they left, I felt the wind change direction and watched, fascinated, as a huge, ominous cloud from the volcano headed for Homer.

We were in for it now. The sun's rays highlighted the billowing, grey outer edges while the turbulent interior looked like it was boiling. The maelstrom in the sky rained down ash and, when it arrived over Homer, turned daylight to dark. The automatic streetlights came on and gave off an eerie light, silhouetting scurrying people caught outdoors. I imagined the end of the world could be no worse.

Ashfall continued for two hours. Finally, the gloomy cloud swung to the south, leaving Homer coughing. By the time I returned home, the volcano had stopped erupting and the sun had reclaimed the sky.

Lila Mae and Tom returned to Sadie the first day of May. Mona would join us as the lodge cook after her city job ended later that month. While Tom and I worked long hours finishing the new bedroom, Lila kept busy preparing our meals and cleaning cabins. In our spare time, Lila and I sent out 400 invitations to our wedding, which was less than a month away.

Maybe it was the pressure of getting the lodge ready for the summer, or tension from planning a big wedding, but things weren't going well between us. Two people really get to know one another living in the Bush, and we discovered some new sides to each other's personalities.

Austin and Mae were fighters, but their clashes lasted only a few minutes because they both solved problems by dealing with them immediately. Keith and Lila were fleers who avoided dealing with disagreements. When Keith and Mae or Austin and Lila clashed, life could be hell. We tried working out our problems, but life at the lodge kept getting hotter and hotter.

Was it our inability to change major parts of ourselves that caused our love to fade? Perhaps one or both of us were afraid to make the final commitment and get married. I didn't know, but by mid-May we had agreed to call off the wedding.

Lila Mae returned to her medical practice in Eagle River, Tom decided to join Mona in Anchorage after they learned she was pregnant, and I hiked into the mountains to think. From past experience, I knew that the only way to cure a broken heart was by going to work. So I returned home, finished building the bedroom, and began looking for new employees.

On the first of June, I was alone at home trying not to think about what that day could have meant, when I heard a skiff pull up to my beach. My fisherman neighbor, John Hillstrand, jumped out of his boat, threw me a bottle of champagne, and asked, "Where are all the people?"

I tried to be cheerful, but failed. "Sorry, John, I couldn't contact you out on the high seas. We called off the wedding," I replied. "You're welcome to come up, but I'm not very good company today."

He said he understood, handed me another bottle of champagne, and left. As I slowly walked up the beach, an old adage came to mind: It's better to have loved and lost than never to have loved at all. I believed in the words, but they offered little comfort now. I put the unopened bottles of sparkling wine in the bar and went back to work.

On Friday, June 13, 1986, I hurried through Homer getting supplies for a group of lodge guests scheduled to come in three days. I hadn't found a new cook, so I planned to take care of the party of four myself. McDonald's had just opened a restaurant in town, and I popped in for a quick sandwich.

After gulping down a hamburger, I darted into the men's room before continuing my in-town chores. The next thing I knew my feet shot out from under me, I fell over backward, and blacked out when my head slammed into the tile floor. When I regained consciousness my brain felt like it was on fire. Voices drifted through the darkness, and when I struggled to sit up, somebody held me down and said, "Just lie still."

As the person put an oxygen mask over my mouth, he continued, "You've had a bad fall, and we're taking you to the hospital. We're paramedics from the Homer Volunteer Fire Department, so try to relax. Before we load you into the ambulance, I'm going to put an IV needle in your arm, so you'll feel a little pain."

I felt something gooey on my hand and strained to see what it was, but in the darkness I couldn't see a thing.

"Are the lights out?" I asked the paramedic.

"No," he answered. "Can't you see?"

"I'm blind!" I gasped.

The loss of my sight scared me more than the searing pain in my head. A moment later I asked, "There's something wet on my hand; is it blood?"

"No, that's soap, and it's all over the floor," the medic answered. "You must have slipped on it when you came into the bathroom."

I vaguely remember the ambulance ride to the hospital. People were talking to me, but they seemed a long way off. Then, as I regained my senses, a voice asked, "Do you know your name?"

After answering, the voice replied, "Sorry, Keith, I didn't recognize you behind the oxygen mask. This is Dr. Bell, and we're transporting you to Providence Hospital in Anchorage. With your blindness and seizures, they have better facilities to take care of you."

A familiar voice said, "Doctor, I'm John Rogers, and this is Tim Gee. We're friends of Keith. Is there anything we can do?"

Before the doctor could answer, I said, "I've got lodge guests coming."

"Don't worry, Keith," John said. "We'll take care of everything."

"I'll call your folks," Tim added. "You just take it easy and get back on your feet. You're too ornery to be down for long, you ol' sea dog, you."

The next thing I remember was waking up to a nightmare. My arms wouldn't move, the room bounced up and down, and a roaring noise hurt my ears. "Where am I?" I yelled out in alarm.

"You're on a chartered jet flying to a hospital in Anchorage," answered a woman's calm voice. "You're strapped down to keep you from rolling around in the turbulence. I'm a nurse, so try to relax. We'll be landing in twenty minutes."

Being blind and in pain scared me, but I laughed at the irony of it all. I'd lived in the Alaska Bush for fourteen years, and now I might die from slipping on a soapy floor in the bathroom of McDonald's. Maybe this was what they meant by a "Big Mac attack."

We finally landed, and they rushed me to the emergency room of the hospital. A doctor examined me, and I felt very relieved to be able to see the light he shined in my eyes. After a CAT scan, they wheeled me through a maze of hallways to a bed in the intensive care unit.

I'd been alone in the room for only a couple of minutes when someone walked in and said, "How ya doing?"

After recognizing John Rogers' voice, I answered, "Much better, buddy. I can see your form but not your face. They say my vision will come back, but my head feels like it's going to explode. How did you get up here so fast?"

"I flew up on a commuter flight," he answered. "I'll stay in Anchorage until you're better. Tim said to remind you—pain is good!"

When I laughed, my head erupted. At that moment a nurse walked in, and John implored, "Can't you give him a shot for the pain?"

"I'm sorry," she said with a starched voice, "but with a head injury all we can give him is aspirin."

After I took two extra-strength aspirin, John left with a promise to check in later, and I finally relaxed enough to sleep.

For two days they kept me in intensive care, where I regained my sight and the pain in my head slowly subsided. Except for an occasional seizure, I felt much better. At first, I enjoyed the food and being able to watch television (even the advertisements were entertaining), but by the second day I became restless. What I needed was something to take my mind off the accident—and, boy, did I get my wish.

While I was resting in bed, switching TV channels, and feeling sorry for myself, a naked man burst into my room. The barrel-chested intruder looked at me through glazed eyes and yelled, "It's time to take a shower!"

I wasn't sure if he was telling me or asking me. "Help yourself. I took one earlier," I answered, a little annoyed.

He looked at me really hard and said, "If you're looking for trouble, you've come to the right place."

That did it. I'd had enough. After a month of slogging down the muddy road of life in leaky hip boots, I was in no mood to deal with some nut. "Get the hell out of here!" I yelled as I started climbing out of bed.

Before my feet hit the floor I had another seizure. When I regained consciousness, Lila Mae was sitting there holding my hand. She told me that the nurses had recaptured the mental patient and that he wouldn't bother me again. We talked for a while longer, and when she left, I knew we were still friends.

The next day I was moved to the progressive care unit, hooked up to a heart monitor, and put through a long series of tests. The doctors didn't know what was causing the seizures and wanted to keep me in the hospital for observation. If I did have another seizure, the heart monitor would record it.

Time passed, and I settled into the monotony of hospital life. The only distractions were John's daily visits and telephone calls from family and friends. After five days John had to go back to Homer, and I missed his company. Looking for distraction from my inactivity, I paced the hall by my room, joked with the friendly nurses, and did push-ups to see if the exercise affected my heart rate on the monitor.

On my seventh day in the hospital, Carol, a long-time, special friend, came to visit. She sat down on my bed and said, "I told you eating at McDonald's was bad for your health."

I'd had plenty of time to think about the accident, and any mention of the golden arches set me off. "That clown has no integrity," I fumed. "I don't care that they didn't send flowers or a get-well card, but they could have at least acknowledged that I damn near died from a soapy floor in their restaurant."

"You haven't heard from McDonald's?" Carol asked.

"Not a word," I answered.

"They're probably afraid of getting sued," she replied.

"Many people in Homer fought to keep them from coming to town. Now I can see why," I said. "Their big city way of doing business doesn't fit in a small community."

"You could choose not to eat there," Carol said.

I answered, "I rarely do—just my luck it was Friday the thirteenth!"

"They do support worthwhile charities," she responded.

"I know; I've seen their advertisements on the hospital television set," I said. "In my case, they sure didn't practice what they preach."

When Carol left, I walked her to the exit. I'd forgotten about my heart monitor, but the nurses hadn't. As I headed back, the public-address system broadcast, "Keith Iverson, please return to your room!"

When I got back, three distraught nurses explained that I'd gone beyond the range of the receiver, and my monitor showed me with no heartbeat.

Later that day, the doctor came in, and I pleaded, "Please, Doc, let me go home. I haven't had a seizure in five days, and watching more TV soaps will drive me crazy!"

He disconnected my heart monitor and said, "Okay, you can leave today, but check in with your doctor."

After flying to Homer, I stopped in to see Dr. Bell, who gave me a prescription for my seizures. On my way to the boat harbor I passed McDonald's and cringed. While crossing the bay, Austin took out the bottle of pills, threw it overboard, and yelled, "I'm not taking these stinking pills!"

Being back home was the best medicine, and I celebrated by going to work. The next day I kayaked out to my anchored skiff to go fishing for dinner. While warming up the motor, I moved forward to untie the moorage. When I leaned over to grab the line, everything went black.

I felt very cold and couldn't breathe. I'd fallen in the water, and instinctively my legs started kicking. I fought my way to the surface and came up next to my boat. After a long coughing fit, I crawled into the skiff, and Keith exploded at Austin, "You stubborn fool! If we don't take those pills, we're both going to die!"

Austin didn't say a word on the trip back to Homer.

Dr. Bell examined me and rewrote my prescription. "How long do I have to take the pills?" I asked.

"For a year," he answered. "Then we'll slowly lessen the dosage. If you have another seizure after that, you might have to keep taking them for the rest of your life."

That wasn't the worst of it.

"I must warn you not to stop taking the pills without my supervision," he added. "If you do, you could have a massive seizure and die."

I left the doctor's office mad as hell. My frustration needed a scapegoat, and I knew exactly whom to blame. I drove to a small, wooden office across town, walked through the door under a sign that read "Lawyer," and said to Martty Friedman, "I want to sue McDonald's."

Martty reminded me of Abraham Lincoln in physical appearance and in his honest outlook on life. He listened to my story, took some notes, and outlined the legal procedures. Before leaving his office, I asked, "How long will this case take to settle?"

"It's hard to tell right now," he answered. "It could take as many as five years."

The thought of a long legal battle didn't improve my mood, but I knew I would win. McDonald's was responsible for my accident and continuing medical problems. Their sloppy housekeeping had disrupted my life physically, mentally, and financially: they would pay.

For the rest of the summer the lawsuit constantly intruded on my life. I wanted to forget about the accident, but I couldn't. Whenever people asked about my injury, I relived the suffering and anger, and as a result, my mental attitude deteriorated.

In August, I visited my friends Gale and Al in Homer. As we sat in their kitchen drinking tea, Gale said, "I understand you're suing McDonald's."

"Yes," I answered.

"Why?" she asked.

After telling them the story, Gale said, "McDonald's didn't put soap on the floor so that you'd slip and fall. It's possible the bathroom was messed up by someone else."

Gale's questions and concern made me think. Why *was* I suing McDonald's? Before the accident I hadn't believed in lawsuits of this kind, so what made me change my mind? Did I want revenge for the impersonal way they handled my accident? Maybe it was easier to blame them than myself. After struggling with the problem, I saw the solution: I had to take responsibility for my own actions. What would happen if I fell in the woods? Would I sue Mother Nature?

I thanked Gale and Al, drove to my lawyer's office, and told Martty to drop the lawsuit. After explaining my reasons, I said I wanted to pay him for his time and expenses. He smiled and said, "You don't owe me a thing, Keith."

Martty could teach McDonald's a lot about integrity.

My decision to drop the lawsuit made me feel better, but the rest of my life was a mess. Back at home in Sadie, I poured myself a big glass of whiskey and tried to forget my troubles.

The Battle

Chapter 12

My depression consumed me!

Fourteen years earlier I'd come to Alaska seeking a more meaningful and independent lifestyle, and I'd found it while building my home in Sadie Cove. I'd learned to survive in the Bush, but now a new struggle raged inside me. This battle wasn't with the elements or with other people—it was with myself.

Only five months before, everything had seemed practically perfect. Lila Mae and I were getting married, the lodge business looked promising, I had a positive mental attitude, and my body was in its prime. How could life have changed so quickly? Now I was alone, unable to operate my business, taking pills to avoid seizures, and had no money in the bank. My problems were destroying my existence and sucking me into a whirlpool of despair. I knew I had to do something to get out of my depression, but what?

Social drinking had always been a part of my life, but now I started drinking heavily. Budweiser and Crown Royal were my preference, but I drank anything handy. Whether alone in Sadie or in the bars of Homer, I developed a pattern of hitting the bottle every other day. I had little money but somehow could always buy a bottle or a drink. Booze didn't solve my problems, but it did help me forget them.

As my life deteriorated, alcohol became my main problem, and it added to those I wouldn't face. Drinking caused more seizures, both in the bars and at home, although I continued to take my pills. The booze that poisoned my body and mind started me on the fast track to self-destruction. My hangovers were monumental, and though I tried to convince myself I could function normally with a pounding headache, upset stomach, and bloodshot eyes, I knew it was a lie.

My mental health joined my body on a toboggan ride to hell. When I was sober, my negative attitude turned to anger. During my drinking bouts I became argumentative and explosive. I'd lost my pride and forgot how to smile.

If I didn't like myself, how could my friends and family? I lost friends, but the best stayed with me even though they must have tired of my perpetual negativity. My family lived in the Lower 48, but they were there with long-distance support. As my condition worsened, I ventured out of Sadie less and less. By not dealing with my problems and isolating myself from those who could help, I became even more depressed.

What little money I had was spent on whiskey, so my financial situation became desperate. With no lodge business, my only income source was Mooseltoe, and I couldn't count on that until the December holiday season. With taxes, unpaid debts, and my food supply getting low, I had to do something soon to bring in some bucks. What could I do? What did I have of value to sell? Suddenly, I saw money as my only salvation and, in my madness, decided to sell the wilderness lodge. All my problems seemed solved, until I realized that by sacrificing the lodge I'd also be surrendering my home, my dream, perhaps even my soul. Was there no way out of this prison I'd created?

I staggered down the beach in front of my home with a half-empty bottle of whiskey in one hand and a .357 magnum in the other. It was a bright, warm, fall day in late September, but my black mood made it feel like the darkest, coldest night of winter. The beauty of Sadie Cove sparkled all around me, but I was blinded by despair. Decision time had arrived, and there were only two choices—life or death. One more step would send me to a land of no return, and the gates of Valhalla would be bared to me forever.

As I teetered on the brink of doom, an image of the mountain goat on the beach that spring flashed into my mind. It gave me something to grab, and I took one step back from extinction. I remembered his long, white hair blowing in the breeze, and the pride and courage that shone from his golden eyes. We both had come to the beach to die, but he had no choice and I did.

Wallowing in drink and despair had blinded me to the pain of suicide—not for me, but for others. How would the news that I had killed myself affect my family and friends? After thinking about the answer, I knew ending my own life was no longer a choice.

I poured out the whiskey, unloaded the gun, and dove into the sea. The bone-chilling cold made me live only for the moment, and I thanked God for helping me return to reality. It was time to get back in control of my life. I knew I'd won only a battle, not the war. My problems still existed, but I made a promise to myself to stop drinking, face my responsibilities, think positively, and go back to work. Suddenly, it felt so good to be alive!

For the next two weeks, I cut firewood to get physically and mentally back in shape. Splitting gnarly rounds of spruce put calluses on my hands, sweated out the alcohol, and gave me something real on which to release my pent-up emotions. My aching muscles actually felt good, and each day the pile of firewood grew until I'd built up enough for the entire winter. The hard work had also helped restore my pride, and I had no desire to go bar-hopping during my next visit to town.

My Homer post-office box overflowed with mail. Letters spilled out from my family and future lodge guests, but the most touching simply said, "Dear Keith, Come see us. We love ya! Kevin and Cindy."

Crossing Kachemak Bay to Halibut Cove was rough and cold, but it didn't matter. I was going to see friends who had supported me through my dark days.

The Sidelingers met me at the dock on Ismailof Island, and as we walked through the woods to their cabin, Kevin said, "Cindy and I know the hard times you've been having, and we want to help. You need a break this winter, so we're giving you enough money for a vacation. Go see your family and then visit somewhere hot and dusty. When you return home, everything will look much better. We're behind you 100 percent."

No words could express how I felt at that moment, so I just gave them each a hug and walked away to be alone for a while. As I sat on a cliff overlooking the water, I thought back over all the years I'd known these strong, caring, hard-working, Christian folks. They didn't preach their faith; they lived it. We'd shared a friendship through good times and bad, and I loved them and their son, Bowman. They were a major part of my Alaska family.

The last night of my visit, the four of us sat out on their porch talking and eating popcorn. Bowman was at the stage of his childhood where he thought he knew everything about everything—and was willing to bet on it. After several minutes of taking advantage of the situation, he owed me ten cords of split firewood. He was a good sport and said," Uncle Keith, how about waiting a while for me to chop the wood? I'm too small to pick up the ax."

"You bet, Bowman," I said with a smile. "Let's wait about twenty years; then I won't be able to pick up the ax."

With no children of my own, I looked forward to watching Bowman grow into a man.

As Cindy put Bowman to bed, Kevin and I started talking about how I could increase my income. We agreed I should continue with the lodge and Mooseltoe and look for another method to generate a more consistent cash flow. As we finished our conversation, Cindy rejoined us. "You've been living an exciting life, Keith," she said. "Why don't you write a book?"

"Are you kidding?" I answered. "I sweat blood writing a letter that's more than one page long. Bowman is a better speller, and I have a hard time sitting down long enough to eat a meal."

"Well, it was a thought," she replied.

I accepted my friends' financial help, paid off a few pressing bills, and took a much needed vacation. After visiting my sister and brother in California, I spent some time with my folks, who were retired in Arizona. I put on weight with Mom's home cooking and took it off by hiking in the desert. In Isla Mujeres, Mexico, I lay on white-sand beaches; swam in the warm, clear ocean; and tanned my pale northern skin. My last stop was Houston, Texas, where I visited my Swiss friend, Peter, and helped him remodel the home he'd just bought.

Peter introduced me to his friends, including a cute, fun-loving lady named Diane Desmond. Diane and I began spending time together, and she taught me the Texas two-step while I told her stories about Alaska. One night several weeks after we'd met, Diane and I were finishing the fine meal she'd prepared when I said,"You can cook at my lodge any day."

She looked at me with a sparkle in her ocean green eyes. "When do we leave?" she asked.

Diane wasn't kidding, and neither was I. One week later we headed north. After arriving back in Homer, we stayed in town just long enough to pick up mail, buy groceries, celebrate Diane's twenty-ninth birthday, and adopt a black lab puppy we named Teal.

We skiffed into Sadie Cove the first week in February, and although the days were short and the weather cold, it was great to be home. Diane put on so many clothes she looked like a colorful snowball, but she adjusted well to the transition from Texas to Alaska. We both slipped easily into a winter routine, with our activities controlled by weather and daylight. During the day, we did outside chores, taught Teal to retrieve, took slow walks along the beach, went fishing, and washed each other's faces in the snow. After dark, we enjoyed Diane's culinary talents, took long, hot saunas, read, discussed the summer lodge business, and hugged a lot. We were a couple with a dog, and that winter I had a family in Sadie.

As winter melted into spring, Diane and I prepared the lodge for guests. During May and June we entertained only three small groups and had no more bookings for the rest of the summer. Seventy percent of my business normally came from big oil companies, but with the low price of oil, they could no longer afford my $300-a-day rate. Diane needed more money than what I could pay her; so she took a job cooking on a fishing boat, and we parted friends.

The summer of 1987 was a lean lodge season. I needed to promote the business but didn't have the $25,000 needed to sell my services through winter sportsmen shows in the Lower 48. What could I do to publicize Sadie Cove Wilderness Lodge that didn't require much money? As I sat sweating in my sauna, the answer hit me like a bucket of cold water—why not write a book?

Ever since Cindy Sidelinger suggested the idea a year earlier, I had met and talked to several writers. A few were published; others were still working on their first book; and some just wrote for the fun of it. What they told me about the writing process sounded challenging but rewarding.

Why not try! How hard could it be to write a book?

Operation Viking

My screams of frustration echoed off the cliffs of Sadie Cove. No, I wasn't experiencing flashbacks to blacker times: the stress came from sitting on my butt for three days trying to begin my book. My office looked a mess, with crumbled yellow paper, broken pencils, and dirty coffee cups scattered everywhere. My bloodshot eyes, nervous pacing, and chewed fingernails revealed my anxiety. To make matters worse, the weather was perfect. Why couldn't it be raining? I wanted to be outside working or playing—anything besides sitting indoors writing. I'd already put off starting my book by changing the generator oil, cutting down a wicked patch of devil's club, and digging out the outhouse. My commitment to write my autobiography was still there, but I couldn't remember any project ever being so hard to begin. The truth was, I didn't know how to start.

The solution to my problem came to me while walking on the beach. I was overwhelmed by the enormity of writing a book, so I needed to divide the project into small, manageable segments. My formula for starting new ventures could work for this one too. I would read books on writing, talk to writers, and study published autobiographies.

I named my project Operation Viking and divided the work into its major components—writing the manuscript, finding a publisher, and financing the undertaking. To accomplish these objectives, I would devote eight hours a day to the enterprise and set a goal of one year for completion.

The title I chose, *Alaska Viking*, had a double meaning. I claimed the name Viking from my Norwegian ancestors and the similarities between our wilderness environments and lifestyles. But I also used the word for its original meaning—to pursue adventure.

My adventures in the city and the wilds gave me the stories for my book. Now, all I had to do was learn how to tell my tale. After dusting off my dictionary and thesaurus, I started reading. I bought

The Elements of Style, by Strunk and White, and Zinsser's *On Writing Well.* A hardback copy of *How to Write the Story of Your Life,* by Frank Thomas, caught my eye in the Homer Bookstore, and it joined the stack of publications already on my desk. Before leaving my city life in San Francisco I'd read and studied Helen and Scott Nearing's *Living the Good Life* and, after some searching, found it on one of my shelves in Sadie Cove. The last addition to my how-to library was a subscription to *Writer's Digest* monthly magazine. These tools could help me prepare, but I still wasn't ready to put words on paper.

I needed to talk with writers, to learn from their experiences. Surprisingly, Homer is home to quite a number of published authors. Tom Walker, for example, had published several books of his writings and photography. He had also written articles for *Alaska Magazine* about life on the Last Frontier. From the first time we met he was very supportive, gave me good ideas, and asked questions I needed to answer.

"Have you started writing?" Tom asked during one of our conversations.

"No, and I'm feeling a little guilty about putting it off," I answered.

"Just remember, the only way to produce a book is to write," he remarked.

I took Tom's advice and began outlining the chapters. After 200 hours of organizing, I was ready to begin writing.

The big day finally arrived. I got up a 4 A.M., drank a huge pot of coffee, and put two hissing Coleman lanterns next to the yellow writing pad on my desk. After an hour I had three pages of doodles. Maybe it would help if I made a list of the important dos and don'ts I'd learned from books on writing. The list included the following:

- Show, don't tell.
- Write like you talk.
- Use close, middle, and long views.
- Remember what, where, when, why, who, and how.
- Don't forget dialogue.
- Utilize flashbacks.
- Engage the senses of taste, touch, smell, hearing, and sight.
- Add suspense.

- Build characters.
- Don't use clichés or the passive voice, switch tenses, or write too formally.
- Watch transitions in sentences, paragraphs, and chapters.
- Keep it simple!

After composing that list, I wrote another one, which read:

- Take a deep breath.
- Relax.
- Let it flow.
- One sentence at a time.
- Write, you fool!

I tacked the two lists to the wall in front of my desk and began writing the chapter on Mooseltoe. Once started, I couldn't stop. Four hours later, I put down my pencil and smiled—I'd just broken the book barrier!

My first chapter took two weeks to complete. I took it to Anne Marie, who owned and operated Paisley Publishing in Homer. She typed it into her Macintosh computer and made a copy with a laser printer. Her services cost me money, but at this stage of my project I had neither the cash to buy a computer nor the hours to learn how to operate one. As time passed, my stack of finished chapters piled up like the snow outside my window.

The most important part of Operation Viking was writing the book; however, I also needed to find a publisher and raise the cash to continue. On a trip to Anchorage, I tried to get a loan from the University of Alaska's Small Business Development Center. They couldn't help me with the money, but they did connect me with a local writer who might be able to assist me in finding a publisher. If I could get a royalty advance on my book, I might not need a loan. Steve Levi was already a published, full-time author when we met, and he gave me some good insights into the craft and business of writing. During our first conversation, I asked him about finding a publisher.

"For a first-time author writing an autobiography, it's very, very difficult," he answered. "How do you feel about rejection?"

"I know it won't be easy," I said, "but when my manuscript is finished, I'll send a copy to every publishing house in America."

He chuckled and replied, "I'm not talking about publishers. Today, most publishing companies won't even read your book unless it's submitted by an agent, and they're as hard to interest as a publisher."

"How did you find your agent and publisher?" I asked.

To my surprise, he said, "I have neither."

"But I've seen your book, *Sourdough Journalist*," I said. "How did that get printed?"

"I got tired of rejections and self-published," he answered.

Steve proceeded to explain self-publishing; but it sounded costly, and I didn't have the money or knowledge to do it myself. I thanked him for his help and headed back to Homer. Maybe a local author could come up with a better way to get published.

I had met Tom Bodett shortly after he and his wife, Debi, moved to town. While building houses for a living, he had had some success writing humorous stories about everyday life in Homer and reading them on our local public radio station. His commentaries became so popular that KBBI sent his tapes to National Public Radio, where they were broadcast nationwide. Tom's popularity grew, and he hung up his carpenter's belt to concentrate on his new career. He had published his first book, *As Far as You Can Go Without a Passport*, and was working on his second. Perhaps Tom could give me some pointers on finding a publisher.

I called him and made a date to meet for lunch. After describing my writing project, I asked Tom for his advice. He thought for a while and said, "Keith, I'd like to help, but my route to getting my book published probably won't help you much. My radio commentaries gave me so much public exposure that a publishing company contacted me to write my first book."

Tom's road to publication simply wasn't open to me, so I took a harder look at self-publishing. After reading *The Self-Publishing Manual: How to write, print & sell your own book*, by Dan Poynter, I knew I could do it. In the end, I realized that it might be the only way my manuscript would ever become a book.

My first act as a publisher was to spend $25 for an Alaska business license as R&P Publishing, an abbreviation for "Ravage and Pillage." I didn't want to hurt anybody—my definition of R&P was to attack and overcome all obstacles keeping me from producing my book. With Operation Viking, the biggest battles would be with myself.

The Self-Publishing Manual helped solve the mystery of what a publisher does by dividing the process into five categories: editing, design, printing, marketing, and financing. Most of the first three I planned to contract out, but I looked forward to promoting the book myself.

The financial aspect was another matter. I calculated that it would cost about $35,000 to print and market the first 5,000 copies of *Alaska Viking*. How could I raise the money? I knew celebrities were paid for endorsing companies' products and services, so why not get sponsors for my book? I'd never heard of anyone doing this for an autobiography, but that didn't mean it wouldn't work.

To become a sponsor, a business would have to provide me with cash, products, or services. In return, I would promote what the business was selling. I designed a sales kit to assist me in presenting my idea to potential backers. The Operation Viking portfolio contained an explanation of the project and outlined the chapters of my book. It described my successes with Mooseltoe and Sadie Cove Wilderness Lodge and included photographs and articles from local, national, and international publications. I also included a brief outline of self-publishing and my marketing strategy. The next section listed what the sponsor would receive, including a tax write-off as a cost of advertising, an advertisement in the back of the book, and time at my lodge. I offered $1,000, $5,000, and $15,000 sponsorships and invited companies to become backers of Operation Viking and ride my longship to economic success.

I needed some current publicity to kick off my sponsorship campaign, so I called the *Anchorage Daily News*. They sent a reporter and photographer to Sadie Cove, where I explained my project. The story appeared in the newspaper three weeks later. It filled the first two pages of the "Lifestyles" section under the headline "Like A Viking." One of the pictures showed me on the beach wearing a horned helmet and shaggy coat while holding a rusty logging ax.

This was exactly what I needed to complete the Operation Viking portfolio. I made up twenty-five sales kits, mailed twenty presentations to companies in Alaska and the Lower 48, and made appointments to see others in Homer and Anchorage. The first six local businesses I approached said they found the concept interesting, but they couldn't afford to take part. The winter of 1987 was tough for most Alaskans. Banks failed, and bankruptcies quadrupled while I asked some of the surviving companies to invest in my untried idea. I couldn't wait for another financial boom, so I just kept trying.

Carl Wynn lived in a log mansion on the bluffs overlooking Homer, and his was my next presentation appointment. I drove down the tree-lined, gravel road to his home, hoping my seventh attempt would break the sponsor barrier. After introductions, the tall, friendly founder of Wynn Oil Company invited me into his living room with its million-dollar view of Kachemak Bay. "Are you the same Iverson my late wife bought a case of Mooseltoe from about ten years ago?" he asked.

After I admitted that I was the one, he continued, "You know, she had a lot of fun with your clever gift that holiday. Now, what can I do for you today?"

I handed him the red portfolio with the Viking helmet on the cover and presented my program. He reviewed the pictures after I'd finished and said, "I'll have my secretary mail you a check for $5,000."

We shook hands, and I floated out the door in a state of shock. I believed in my Operation Viking project, and now Mr. Wynn did, too. My first sponsor gave me more than I would have received as a royalty advance from a publisher, and I still hadn't finished the book.

I wanted to share the good news, so I visited my friends Gregg and Helen Parsley. They owned South Central Sports in Homer and offered a boat taxi and rental service on Kachemak Bay. Gregg congratulated me on my success with Mr. Wynn and said, "We believe in your project, too, but don't have the cash to become a sponsor."

"How about a trade?" I suggested. "You transport guests to my lodge in your boat taxi in exchange for a $5,000 sponsorship. That way we both win."

"Where do we sign?" Helen asked.

Over the next two weeks, I acquired five additional sponsors: three more for $5,000 and two for $1,000. Going back home to continue writing my book, I didn't need a boat. I could have walked on the water. Operation Viking had $27,000 in sponsorships!

It took all winter and spring for me to complete the rough draft. After 200 hours of organizing and 300 hours of writing, my twelve-chapter manuscript finally lay on the desk. I felt very proud until I re-read it. The stories were good, my grammar fair, but the writing style was terrible. For two days, I questioned my ability to become an author and finish the book. Depression tried to suck me into the void of despair, but I fought back with reason. This was the rough draft and my first attempt at writing. Did I expect to be Hemingway? The road leading to the completion of my autobiography would be much longer than I had imagined, but now I could build on what I'd learned.

I wanted to start rewriting the rough draft, but it was time to put Operation Viking aside until fall. During the winter I had stopped taking my pills and hadn't experienced any more seizures, so with summer just behind the next storm, I needed to hire some help and get the lodge ready for business.

Hobo Jim, an Alaskan entertainer/songwriter and an old friend, introduced me to my cook for the summer. Anne was a twenty-eight-year-old, fine-looking, feisty blonde who knew how to work. After a trial visit to Sadie Cove, she quit her bank job in Anchorage and moved to the lodge.

June and July of 1988 were the hottest, driest months I could remember in Alaska. On August first, Anne and I had just finished getting ready for five dinner guests who would be arriving soon from halibut fishing all day with Tony aboard his charter boat, the *Sea Otter*. While Anne set the dining room table, I put on my hip boots to move a boat down the beach. That morning had been stormy, with 50-knot winds gusting through the cove, but the weather had turned bright and calm. After tying the skiff in front of the sauna, I looked up and waved to Phil and Mauri, my summer neighbors. They were standing on the top of a 60-foot cliff, pointing up the mountain and yelling to get my attention. I couldn't hear what they said because of the rushing stream at my feet. Turning to look where they pointed, I thought maybe they'd spotted a bear. What I saw sent a full charge of adrenalin surging through my body. My big Studio up the mountain was on fire.

I ran toward the burning building bellowing, "Fire! Fire!" Even wearing hip boots, I flew up the steps three at a time. Smoke and flames shot out from under the empty, wooden cabin that normally housed overnight guests. I knew the Studio would be a total loss even though a 1,200-gallon water tank stood only twenty feet away; the fire had too big a start and the water too little pressure. Now I had to contain the blazing inferno to save the rest of my home and prevent a major forest fire.

Anne rushed up carrying five-gallon buckets and helped me tear off the top to the water tank. She threw water on the fire while I ran down to call the Homer harbor office on the VHF radio. "Alert the state fire fighters," I gasped. "We have a cabin fire in Sadie Cove and will need help if we can't put it out. I'll call back with more information."

"We can see the smoke from here," answered the concerned voice. "Good luck!"

I returned to the fire just as my neighbors began to show up. They hauled hoses, shovels, and buckets up the 100 steps from the beach and started a portable, gas-driven pump to get water from the stream to the burning brush and trees. As I cut firebreaks with a chainsaw, two commercial fishing boats sent their crews to help. Tony came with my dinner guests just in time to join the bucket brigade from the beach to the blaze. We were gaining on the fire around the burned-out cabin when we discovered the woods burning a hundred yards up the mountain. Luckily, the area was close enough to the stream that we could quickly put out the flames.

After four hours of back-breaking work, we had the fire under control, and the sooty-faced fire fighters left with my heartfelt thanks. As Anne made coffee and sandwiches, I used my marine radio to call KBBI radio station in Homer to give them a message to read over their Bay Bushlines, announcements read daily for people without telephones. My thank you note read: "To the neighbors, friends, and strangers who came to my aid with the fire at my home in Sadie Cove—words can't express enough gratitude. The bucket brigade up the mountain damn near killed us, but we put the fire out. It's people like you who give special meaning to the word Alaskan. Thanks, from Keith."

The fire was still smoldering, so Anne and I went back to work. We continued pumping water on hot spots on the ground for another thirty hours and didn't quit until we knew it was dead out. As we finished mopping up, I wiped a sooty smudge off Anne's tired face and gave her a hug. "You are one hell of a fine woman," I said, fighting back tears. "I couldn't have done this without you."

The Alaska State Troopers flew in the next day to inspect the charred remains. "How did it start?" they asked.

"I don't know," I answered. "No one had been in the building for three days, and it didn't have any electricity. Maybe the fire started by spontaneous combustion in the wood I had stored underneath it."

Somehow I knew their final question. "Who's your insurance company?"

"None of my buildings are insured," I answered. "It's too expensive living in the Bush."

The Studio was a total loss, but at least the fire hadn't destroyed everything I'd built in Sadie. My misfortune could only be treated as a learning experience, and I held a meeting with my neighbors to learn more about fire prevention and suppression. If the fire had started in the morning during the 50-knot winds, all our homes could have burned down.

As the cottonwood leaves turned from green to gold, Anne returned to Anchorage, and I went back to Operation Viking. After blowing the dust off my manuscript, I sat down and read it aloud. Unlike good whiskey, it hadn't improved with age. It was time to learn how to rewrite.

Tom, my writer friend in Homer, suggested adding for clarity, subtracting the surplus, and correcting my technical errors. Using his technique, I totally rewrote the manuscript. Anne Marie at Paisley Publishing keyboarded each chapter and gave a printed copy to my local editors, Kathy and Polly. Like protective mothers, they kept me from humiliating myself in print.

Two months into my rewrite, I made a trip to Homer for supplies and ran into Art Davidson, the author of *Minus 148°*. He was a participant on the first successful winter climb of Mount McKinley, and I'd read his book before leaving my city life in San Francisco. "Are you still living in Sadie Cove and running the lodge?" he asked as we shook hands.

"Sure am," I answered. "But now I've taken on a new project—I'm writing my autobiography."

His rugged face broke into a grin. "That's great!" he said. "I'd like to read some of your work. Why don't you send me a couple of chapters."

I cringed inwardly, knowing I had a long way to go as a writer. But I wanted his help, if he was willing, regardless of my ego. "I'd like that, Art," I replied. "A few people have read my writing and given me positive feedback, but I need constructive criticism." He promised to be brutal.

The two chapters I mailed to Art came back in three weeks. Each page was covered with red-inked comments, Xs, and question marks. He also sent a three-page letter pointing out the good, bad, and unneeded. Art's helpful comments definitely improved my writing.

I had completed the rough draft and was halfway through my rewrite before experiencing writer's block. One day I wrote eight pages in six hours, and the next day it took the same amount of time to write one paragraph. How could my mind shut down after writing for so long? Was this the end of my book? It felt like it. For a week I waded through mental turmoil, trying everything I could think of to coax my mind into giving me words to fill the blank pages. I drank pots of coffee, did sit-ups, stood on my head, doodled, read about miracle cures, cussed, cracked my knuckles, thought about acupuncture, and rejected alcohol. Nothing worked. I felt like I was doomed to float around in writer's hell forever.

Finally, I took a break from my madness and went spring skiing in the mountains above Sadie Cove. The four days I spent alone, camping in the snow and yodeling through the back valley, relaxed my anxious mind. When I returned to my desk, the words flooded onto the paper so quickly that my hand couldn't scribble fast enough.

As I wrote, I also worked on other aspects of Operation Viking. During trips to town, I continued presenting my program to companies until I had eighteen sponsors, totaling $50,000. Most of the work of self-publishing wouldn't take place until after my manuscript was finished, but I didn't want to forget a step that could hold me up later. So I wrote letters inquiring about copyright forms and ISBN numbers, asked printers for prices, and planned my marketing campaign.

I completed my rewrite the first week of March 1989. My twelve-chapter manuscript took twice as long to finish as I had planned, and I still had much work to do to self-publish; but with no major setbacks or catastrophes, I would have *Alaska Viking* in the bookstores within six months.

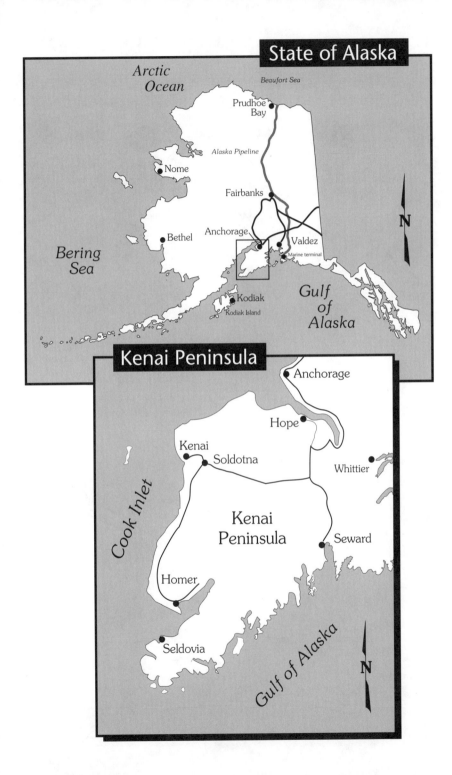

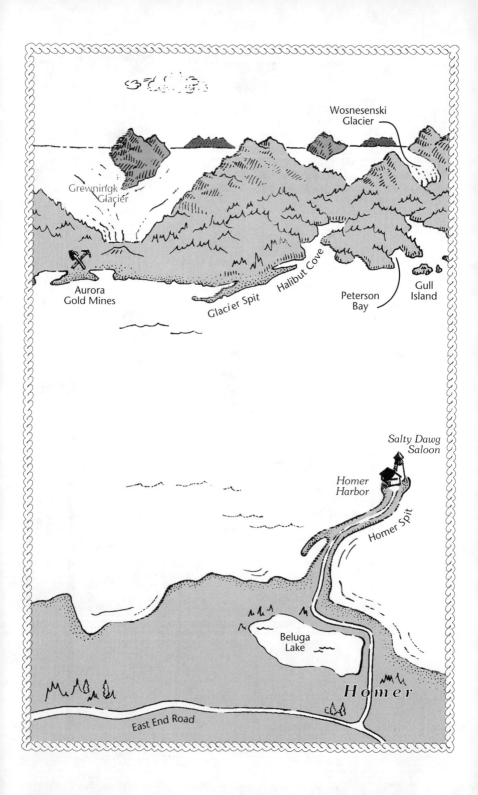

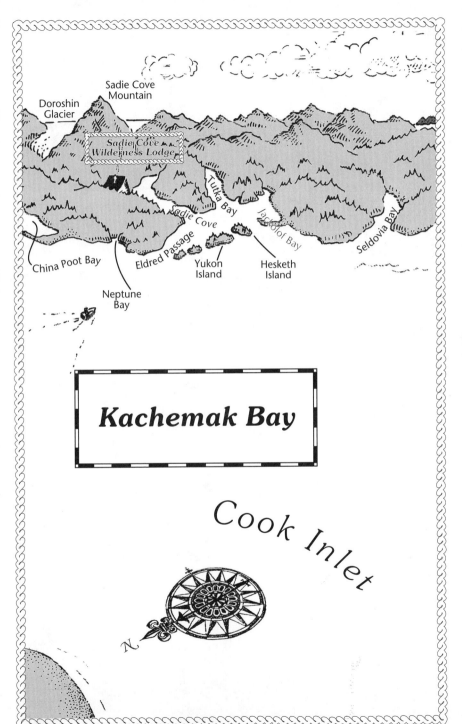

Kachemak Bay

Cook Inlet

N

Illustration by Matt Johnson

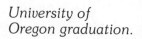

Mom, Dad, and me.

*With grandpa on
Coeur d'Alene
Lake.*

*University of
Oregon graduation.*

Driving to Alaska.

Alaska pipeline—
1972.

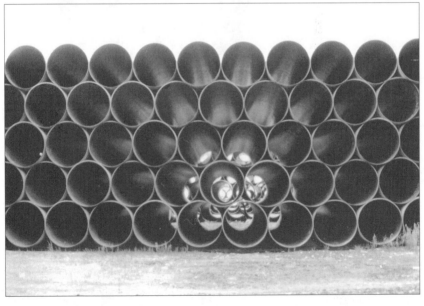

High country wanderer.

Kayaking, Yukon River.

Have boat, will travel.

*Bald eagle—
freedom on the wing.*

©1992 Tom Walker

Skilak *ready to splash.*

©1992 Hal Gage

Throne with a view.

First building project.

©1992 Hal Gage

Morning meditation.

©1992 Hal Gage

Liza—Sadie Lady.

Mom and Dad in Sadie Cove.

©1992 Hal Cage

Sauna on the stream.

Hand-dug pilings for the wharf.

Building the wharf house.

King crab for dinner.

Subsistence fishing for silver salmon.

Green Death, 1975-1980.

National Mooseltoe
Campaign.

My business
partner.

Promoting Poop
for Plants.

©1992 Tom Walker

The wonder of it all.

Kippered smoked salmon.

Sadie Cove Wilderness Lodge at high tide.

Povo in Homer Harbor.

Sadie Cove Wilderness Lodge at low tide.

Building the oarhouse.

Marianne serving dinner.

Lodge guests arriving.

Tim with lunch.

*You catch 'em,
we clean 'em.*

*Brown bear—
monarch of the
land.*

*Highborn
mountain goat.*

*Sadie Cove—
steep and deep.*

©1992 Tom Walker

©1992 Tom Walker

Firefighting Anne.

Viking in the doghouse.

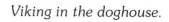

Lila Mae fishing.

Kevin and Cindy on moose hunt.

Bowman and a day's harvest.

Home Sweet Home, 1990.

©1992 Hal Gage

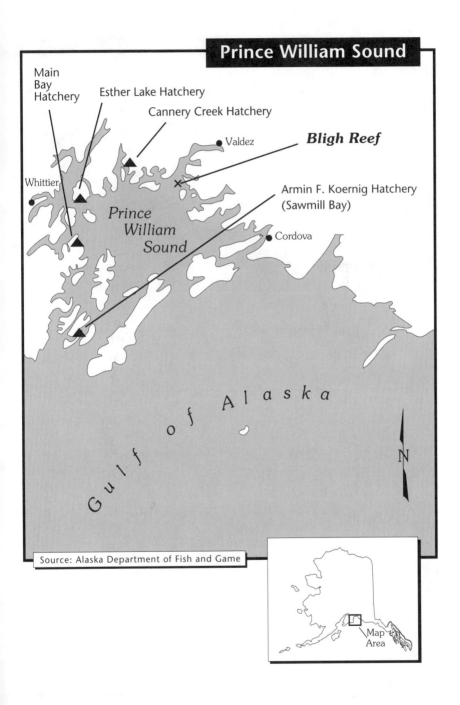

Prince William Sound

Main Bay Hatchery

Esther Lake Hatchery

Cannery Creek Hatchery

Valdez

Bligh Reef

Whittier

Armin F. Koernig Hatchery
(Sawmill Bay)

Prince William Sound

Cordova

Gulf of Alaska

N

Source: Alaska Department of Fish and Game

Map Area

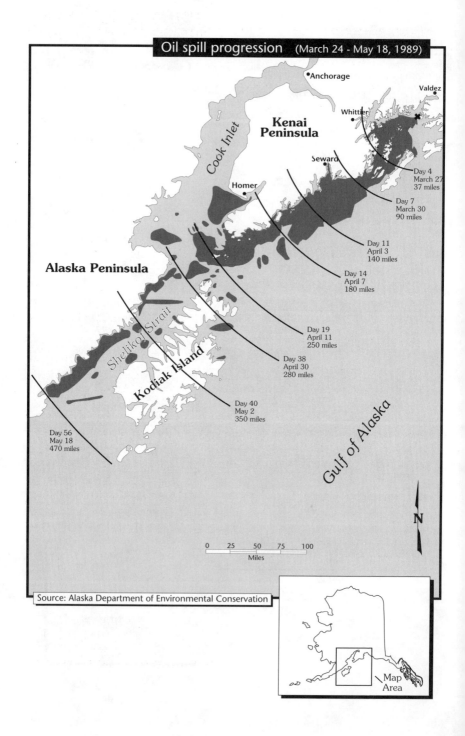

Oil spill progression (March 24 - May 18, 1989)

•Anchorage

Valdez

Whittier

Kenai
Peninsula

Cook Inlet

Seward

Homer

Day 4
March 27
37 miles

Day 7
March 30
90 miles

Day 11
April 3
140 miles

Alaska Peninsula

Day 14
April 7
180 miles

Shelikof Strait

Day 19
April 11
250 miles

Day 38
April 30
280 miles

Kodiak Island

Day 40
May 2
350 miles

Gulf of Alaska

Day 56
May 18
470 miles

```
0    25    50    75    100
           Miles
```

N

Source: Alaska Department of Environmental Conservation

Map
Area

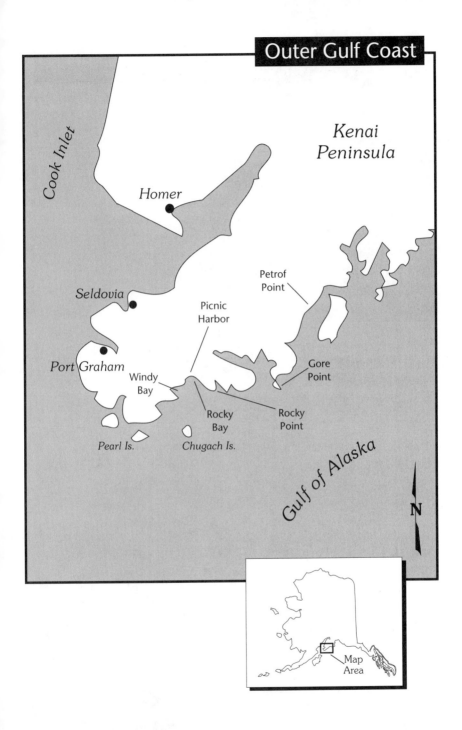

Cook Inlet

Kenai
Peninsula

Homer

Petrof
Point

Seldovia

Picnic
Harbor

Port Graham

Windy
Bay

Gore
Point

Rocky
Bay

Rocky
Point

Pearl Is.

Chugach Is.

Gulf of Alaska

N

Map
Area

©1992 Randy Brandon

Exxon Valdez *at
Naked Island.*

©1992 Randy Brandon

First oiled bird captured on spill.

Oil spill beach crew.

Oiled otter in critter hospital.

©1992 Randy Brandon

©1992 Randy Brandon

The Exxon Valdez Oil Spill

Early on the morning of March 24, 1989, the *Exxon Valdez* ran aground on Bligh Reef in Prince William Sound and created the biggest oil spill in U.S. history by dumping 11 million gallons of crude oil into the sparkling waters of south-central Alaska. On the same day in 1964, the Good Friday earthquake (8.5 on the Richter scale) rumbled through the Last Frontier. These catastrophes took place exactly twenty-five years apart, and the epicenter for the largest earthquake in North America was less than fifty miles from Bligh Reef. These events only proved that lightning can strike the same place twice. However, the disasters differed in one major respect: natural forces cause quakes while humans are responsible for oil spills. I can accept nature's destruction because the earth's geological processes are beyond my control, but oil spills are the result of human carelessness and can usually be prevented. The Good Friday earthquake caused mass destruction and death—what would be the end result of the Exxon oil spill?

Homer was buzzing with anger when I arrived in town to buy supplies on the first day of the spill and learned of the tragedy. After the initial shock wore off, I tried finding answers to a long list of questions. How could a modern supertanker equipped with radar and sonar hit a reef known to everyone who fished in Prince William Sound? Who was on the bridge at the time of the accident? Was the captain, Joe Hazelwood, drunk? Why didn't the Coast Guard radar station warn the ship that it was in danger? Was anyone cleaning up the 11 million gallons of crude oil? No one knew the answers!

On the second day of the spill, the newspapers reported that the oil covered an area four miles wide and eight miles long. Worse yet, the crippled thousand-foot tanker, still stuck on the reef, continued leaking crude oil into the once clean, clear waters of Prince William Sound. Forty-two million gallons remained on board, and no one seemed quite sure how to safely unload the oil from the *Exxon Valdez* while keeping her stabilized.

The more I read, the more questions I had. The oil that fouled the sound belonged to Alyeska Pipeline Service Company. Alyeska was established to build, operate, and maintain the 800-mile Trans-Alaska Pipeline from Prudhoe Bay to the port of Valdez. What was the company doing to clean up the spill? Would it destroy Prince William Sound's $100-million-a-year commercial fishing industry? How would it affect Alaska's tourism business? Who was responsible? Nobody could answer my questions, but I knew someone who might be able to help explain the tragedy and the cleanup effort.

John Wolfe, a friend from Homer, had worked on the 1987 Cook Inlet oil spill, where the tanker *Glacier Bay* leaked 126,000 gallons of oil after hitting a rock during the peak of the commercial salmon harvest. I drove to his home and banged on the door. John's girlfriend, Karen, greeted me with a hug. We'd been friends for a long time, and I could see that she was tired. John waved from his office. "He's been on that damn phone *ever* since yesterday morning, when we first learned of the spill," Karen said in frustration.

"Have they called him in?" I asked. "After working on the Cook Inlet spill, you'd think he'd be one of the first called."

"Hell no!" she thundered back. "John called Alyeska, Exxon, the Coast Guard, the governor's office, and everyone else involved. Nobody knows what's happening."

John hung up the phone and joined us. His bloodshot eyes and stern look told me how he felt. "I've left messages all over the state," he began. "The response is totally disorganized, but the early stages always are. They'll eventually get it together. While we're waiting for my return calls, let's watch some videos of the Cook Inlet spill."

As I watched fishing boats trying to contain the floating oil with small, plastic booms and then the difficulty of removing the gooey mess from the water, I began to realize what we were up against. If our most advanced technique was using a backhoe parked on a barge to dip oil out of the water and into garbage bins on deck, a massive spill simply could not be picked up in time to save the shoreline. We've put men on the moon, but our method of cleaning up oil spills is still primitive.

"We used what we had and kept trying until we made it work," John remarked as the video ended.

I understood their method of getting the job done—I'd used the same approach in Sadie Cove.

John went back to making phone calls while Karen and I watched a television news special on the spill that answered a few more of my questions. When the ship hit Bligh Reef, it ruptured eight tanks and immediately spilled more than 6 million gallons of oil. It continued leaking at a rate of about 600,000 gallons an hour until the spill totaled almost 11 million gallons in seven hours. Alyeska took twelve hours to get any equipment to the crippled tanker, even though it was only twenty-five miles from Valdez. The Coast Guard wasn't monitoring the ship on its radar because there weren't any other ships in the area, and after the accident, they stopped all traffic from entering or leaving the port of Valdez. Alyeska reduced the flow of crude oil in the pipeline from 2 million to 1.2 million barrels a day at 42 gallons per barrel.

After the broadcast, I stuck my head into John's office and said, "I'm going to Valdez and volunteer to help clean up the mess."

"Good luck!" he answered. "I'll see you there."

Before leaving town, I stopped to see my fisherman friend Billy Choate. He was listening to KBBI when I walked in. "What's the latest news?" I asked.

"Alyeska and Exxon are flying in oil spill experts and equipment from all over the world," he answered. "But that's like closing the net after all the salmon have escaped. Their contingency plan said they were ready for any size oil spill, but you can see how totally unprepared they really were."

And so were we, I thought. "Have they decided what to do about the *Exxon Valdez* or cleaning up the oil?" I asked.

"Yes and no," he answered. "They're just beginning to pump the remaining oil into the *Exxon Baton Rouge*, but nothing's being done to clean up the 11 million gallons already spilled. I hear they're considering dispersants."

"What's a dispersant?" I asked.

"It's a chemical sprayed on the floating oil from specially equipped aircraft," Billy answered. "The dispersant breaks up and sinks the oil but doesn't get rid of it. So instead of killing everything on the surface of the water and the beaches, it kills everything underwater, including the bottom. I think the chemical dispersant is as bad as the oil, and it doesn't solve the problem of oil spills, it adds to it!"

"What else have the oil-industry experts got to clean up the spill?" I asked.

"They're talking about burning it, too," he replied. "Neither method has ever been tested on this size spill or in this environment. Right now they're concerned that burning would endanger the cargo still aboard the tanker.

"Without dispersants or burning" Billy continued, "oil on the surface probably will kill most of the birds and mammals it fouls, and what about the millions of migratory birds passing through the sound on their way north this spring? But, if they do use the chemicals to sink the oil, what will happen to the fishing industry? In April the herring return to spawn, and hundreds of millions of salmon fry leave the streams and hatcheries and swim out to sea. What about adult salmon returning to Prince William Sound later this summer?"

It was time for me to get going. I needed to find out some things for myself, and that meant getting closer to the action. "I'm going to Valdez to help with the cleanup," I told Billy.

"What about your book?" he asked.

"This is more important," I answered. "Who knows, maybe I'll add a few chapters about the spill."

Billy looked out the window at my rusted-out, road-weary car, and asked, "How will you get there? Your rig will never make it."

"I'll drive till it drops and then hitch-hike," I replied.

"How you fixed for money?" he inquired, knowing that most Alaskans were short of funds this time of year.

Before I could answer, he said, "I'll loan you a few bucks, and you can borrow one of my pickups. The camper shell is uninsulated, but it'll keep you dry if you need a place to sleep. I wish I could go with you, Keith, but I need to get ready for my fishing season."

What a godsend—reliable transportation and enough money for the trip. I thanked Billy for his help, packed my gear, and on the third day of the spill began driving the 525 miles from Homer to Valdez.

While heading north to Anchorage I concentrated on the icy road, but my mind was on oil. I thought about what I knew of the oil industry and its relationship with Alaska.

The courtship began in the mid-1950s, when Alaska, still a U.S. territory, was economically lean and hungry. Richfield Oil Company began searching for oil at Swanson River in the 2-million-acre Kenai National Moose Range, south of Anchorage, the largest city in the state with a population of 40,000 at that time. The federal government under the Eisenhower administration allowed no leasing of federal land, but Richfield began a campaign to change this law. The Wilderness Society and other environmental groups fought to restrict development of public lands, but the oil company won. In July 1956, Richfield acquired leases in the moose range. The marriage between Alaska and oil was consummated in 1957, when Richfield discovered black gold at a drill sight on the Swanson River.

Richfield evolved into ARCO, and after finding giant oil reserves on the North Slope of Alaska, ARCO joined seven other oil companies, including British Petroleum and Exxon, to form Alyeska Pipeline Service Company. Alyeska built the Trans-Alaska Pipeline connecting the Prudhoe Bay wells to the coastal town of Valdez on Prince William Sound. With the completion of the 800-mile pipeline in 1977, supertankers began transporting North Slope crude oil to refineries in the Lower 48. When the first loaded tanker left Valdez, the Last Frontier officially became an oil state. In 1989, Alaska supplied 25 percent of our nation's oil production.

Until 1989 most Alaskans probably would have agreed that oil had contributed greatly to Alaska's growth and prosperity. Oil helped Alaska become a state by proving to the federal government that Alaska could pay its own way. To date, the oil companies have paid nearly $30 billion in taxes and royalties to the state. Oil lease income created the Alaska Permanent Fund, which in 1989 paid every resident more than $800 as a dividend. The Last Frontier also has no state sales or income taxes because of oil revenues. Even in Sadie Cove, most of my lodge business came from oil companies.

Everyone in Alaska has benefited from oil dollars, and now we all would pay the price. By means of their expert opinions, lengthy contingency plans, and big public-relations campaigns, the oil companies seduced us into believing that they could prevent or contain any oil spill. And we were naive enough to believe them when they said, "Trust us." When would we understand that corporations have only one goal—to make a profit for their owners? Now the biggest oil spill in U.S. history had changed black gold into black death—for Prince William Sound and possibly much more of Alaska's coastline. I knew even Sadie's shores could be fouled.

As I slid through an icy turn, the voice on the radio announced, "On day four of the Exxon oil spill, Governor Cowper declared the area a state disaster. While the major effort focused on stabilizing the crippled *Exxon Valdez*, several skimming boats recovered 12,600 gallons of floating oil."

"What's that compared to 11 million gallons?" I yelled aloud.

Day five of the spill found me pacing the floor of a repair shop twenty miles north of Anchorage: Billy's truck needed emergency service. After spending the night in the pickup, I wasted no time getting back on the road. I switched on the radio and caught the last part of a spill update: "Northeast winds, gusting to 70 miles per hour, have stopped all cleanup efforts. Aircraft have been grounded, and boats sought shelter in protected coves. The high winds spread the floating oil over a large area and caused it to mix with salt water to form what the spill experts call 'chocolate mousse'. Two thousand feet of oil containment boom arrived at Esther Island fish hatchery northwest of the grounded *Exxon Valdez*. Cordova fishermen and workers from various state agencies are battling to save the salmon hatchery at Sawmill Bay on Evans Island."

A state official called the response from Alyeska and Exxon "pitiful." The broadcast ended with the news: "Gasoline prices have risen twelve to twenty cents throughout the Lower 48."

Now I knew who would ultimately foot the bill for the spill— every American would pay for the tragedy.

The last stretch of my journey took me through Thompson Pass, site of Alaska's record seasonal snow accumulation of 550 inches. I started singing to keep awake and noticed a flash of light shoot across the dark sky. The heavens came alive with more dancing lights, and I pulled off on the shoulder to watch the show. The aurora borealis snapped and crackled as it shimmered a hundred miles above me.

I felt more relaxed as I resumed driving and thought about the first time I drove into Valdez during my visit to Alaska in 1972. The original community had been destroyed by a tidal wave in the 1964 earthquake, and the town was soon rebuilt at a safer location. My first glimpse of Valdez included a few small stores, plywood houses, trailers, and hundreds of acres of pipe stacked and waiting for the pipeline construction to begin. Work hadn't started due to the efforts of environmental groups, Cordova fishermen, scientists, and a few politicians who wanted the pipeline routed through Canada to avoid transporting the oil over water. Their efforts failed, but they succeeded in having the project postponed long enough to complete environmental impact studies and to obtain assurances from Alyeska that it could prevent or contain any foreseeable oil spill. (The experts said an 11-million-gallon spill was possible once every 220 years.) It took 70,000 workers four years and $8 billion to complete the pipeline—the biggest private construction project ever completed.

I had considered working on the pipeline but instead chose to build my life in Sadie Cove. Now, returning to Valdez after seventeen years to help clean up the spill, I was stunned to find a modern town on the shore of Prince William Sound. The glare from its lights blotted out nature's light show in the sky.

First Days in Valdez

Chapter 15

The clock in the lobby of the Westmark Hotel read 1:00 A.M. when I asked for a room. The tired-looking receptionist said there wasn't a vacancy in town, so I headed for the lounge.

I ordered black coffee at the busy bar, took a sip, and relaxed after the long drive. The man sitting next to me sighed, "It's been a long day."

"Yeah, and it's bound to get longer," I said. "After driving from Homer, I looked forward to a hot shower and soft bed, but there's no room at the inn."

He smiled and said, "Not with a town full of folks looking for work, oil company executives, Coast Guard officers, state and federal officials, and hundreds of media people from all over the world. I arrived two days ago and was lucky to find a room not much bigger than my bathroom back home. I'm Pat Daugherty, a writer from San Francisco, here to cover the spill. Wish I could suggest a place to stay."

"Thanks, but I can sleep in the back of my truck." I said. "Maybe you can fill me in on what's been happening."

Pat ordered another drink and said, "Well, it just turned day six, and both Alyeska and Exxon are trying to unload the oil still on the *Exxon Valdez*. Cordova fishermen with the help of Alaska's Division of Emergency Services are attempting to protect the fish hatcheries. Besides a few oil skimmers working near the crippled tanker, there isn't much cleanup. A couple hundred workers have been hired, but so far they just sit aboard that big tour boat you see out in the harbor. Mostly, the power people are all still trying to come to an agreement on what to do next."

I asked, "Are they taking volunteers?"

"They won't take volunteers because of the potential liability," he explained. "There's a press conference tomorrow morning to bring everyone up-to-date."

I thanked Pat for the information and drove to a quiet street to get some sleep. It was a cold, noisy, restless night. I got up early, ate a frozen banana, and drove to the state employment office. Even at 6:30 A.M., I was tenth in a line of guys who looked like me in heavy work clothes and beards. We stomped our feet to keep warm and kept our thoughts to ourselves. At 7:00 A.M. the doors opened. When my turn came to fill out the lengthy employment application, I learned from the friendly but frazzled staff that VECO, the general contractor for the spill cleanup, wouldn't need anyone for five to ten days. As I left to get my morning coffee, the line of foot-stomping hopefuls extended far down the block.

A few hours later I walked into the well-designed, plush civic center for my first press conference. The stage and seats were separated by a large open area, filled to capacity with news people and their extensive equipment. They stood shoulder to shoulder in a semicircle in front of the stage.

Security was relaxed, but not the people waiting for the first speaker. I could sense the stress and hear the emotion in the voices of those who sat around me. I decided to keep quiet and just take notes when the conference began. There were plenty of other frustrated Alaskans in the room to ask questions.

As the speakers walked onto the stage, Michael Neece from Homer took the seat next to me. A Harvard-looking executive type introduced the first speaker, Exxon president Bill Stevens. Stevens cleared his throat and began speaking: "We want you to know we are doing everything possible to deal with this tragic situation."

A rumble of protest erupted from the audience, but he continued. "In the past twelve years, Alyeska has shipped 6.6 billion barrels [2.772 trillion gallons] of North Slope crude oil out of Valdez!"

Someone in the audience yelled, "What's Alyeska doing now to clean up the spill?"

"Since it is an Exxon ship that went aground," he answered, "we have taken over control of the operation. Alyeska is giving us all the support they can."

Stevens then introduced the president of Exxon Shipping Company, Frank Iarossi. He looked out over the gathering, took a deep breath, and said, "I will give you an update on the situation and then answer any questions you have. The oil slick is moving thirty miles a day in a southwest direction. The *Exxon Baton Rouge* is pumping oil off the *Exxon Valdez*, and our company along with the Coast Guard are investigating the cause of the accident."

"Can you confirm the report that Captain Hazelwood was drinking?" asked one of the news people.

"The matter is under investigation," Iarossi answered. "Our priority is stabilizing the *Exxon Valdez*, but we are moving ahead on the cleanup effort. As you know, we tested dispersants on the oil, but with the calm seas we didn't get good results. When we did get the wave action we needed, the high winds grounded the aircraft we used to drop the dispersants. Now the spill is spread over such a large area that this method would be ineffective. However, we are still considering its use in places where the oil is concentrated."

A woman to my left asked, "Aren't the dispersants just as toxic as the oil?"

He answered, "Our experts say they are safe, and we have approval to use them on the spill."

I leaned over and whispered to Michael, "If that's true, why is it illegal for me to use dishwashing detergent to disperse small amounts of spilled gasoline on the water?"

He shrugged his shoulders and said, "You're not a giant oil company with a staff of experts."

From the stage Iarossi continued. "The cleanup of the oil is very difficult in such an isolated area, but we are bringing in containment boom, skimmers, and spill experts from throughout the world."

A reporter pointed his portable tape recorder at the speaker and asked, "Alyeska had a contingency plan for spills in Prince William Sound, so why are you using the remoteness of the area as an excuse?"

"Alyeska did follow the contingency plan," he answered.

That did it! Most of the audience jumped to their feet and started jeering. "It took Alyeska twelve hours to get to the grounded tanker when the contingency plan said it would take five!" shouted one irate man. "Where were the trained oil-spill crews, skimmers, booms, and barges?"

As more questions were thrown at the stage, Michael said to me, "When the spill began, Alaska's fishing fleet was all geared to start harvesting herring. I designed a method to protect the bays and coves with herring seine nets and the suction pumps the fishermen use to get the fish on board. I submitted my plan to the governor's office, the Department of Environmental Conservation (DEC), and

Alyeska. They all said no and gave no reason. Damn, Keith, we could have sucked up a lot of oil in those first calm days if they'd given us the go-ahead."

The crowd settled down, and Iarossi took more questions from the floor. "Who exactly is in charge of the cleanup operation?" asked Pat, the writer I'd met the night before.

"A commission has been established with representatives of the Coast Guard, state of Alaska, Alyeska, and Exxon," answered the Exxon executive.

"This commission may make the decisions, but nature is in control of the spill," I said to Michael.

"How far will the oil spread?" asked a man from across the room.

"The Coast Guard is monitoring its movement, and we will keep you informed; but nobody knows how far it will spread," came the answer from the stage.

"What's happening to the wildlife in the sound?" asked a woman with more than a little emotion in her voice.

"To date, only a few fouled birds have been found," Iarossi answered. "Exxon will provide the money for the collection and care of all affected birds and animals."

An angry fisherman, dressed in worn rubber boots, overalls, and a stained wool cap, jumped up and shouted, "What's going to happen to the fish, shrimp, and crab?"

"Prince William Sound will be as clean as before the spill," Iarossi answered in a stern voice.

"Then let's get going and do it," came back the fisherman. "Put a bounty on the oil, and let the fishermen do the job. We've got the equipment, boats, and knowledge of the area. This sitting around waiting for you to make decisions is destroying our fisheries and driving me nuts!"

The crowd cheered.

Iarossi didn't address the question, but turned the remainder of the press conference over to local groups and environmental organizations, including Greenpeace, Sierra Club, Earth First, and the Prince William Sound Coalition. The last speaker, Dr. Riki Ott of the Cordova District Fishermen United, summed up local feelings: "From the beginning of the oil pipeline, the question wasn't if there would be a spill, but when and how big. Now we know. Our worst nightmares have come true!"

On day seven, the frustration of standing in lines while the oil spread spurred me to try other job possibilities. I went to the headquarters of Alyeska and Exxon but couldn't get past the security guards, who told me to sign up with VECO. Next, I tried the local laborers' union hall and, after standing in line for two hours, paid my $12 dues and joined the AFL-CIO. I succeeded in getting my name on another list, but the prospects didn't look good with 300 names ahead of mine.

Upon entering the press conference that morning, we couldn't help but notice armed security guards who stood watching as we took our seats behind a forest of television cameras facing the stage. After Exxon board chairman Lawrence Rawl restated his company's commitment to clean up the spill, Exxon Shipping's Iarossi presented his update. The oil-spill task force had grown to almost 600 people, but no one had started to clean up the beaches. Besides pumping out the *Exxon Valdez* and a few skimmers nibbling on the flanks of the spreading crude, it seemed the task force was suffering from analysis paralysis.

Some decisions had been made, however. There would be no land-based camps, so all operations had to be conducted from the growing fleet of boats. The captain of the *Exxon Valdez* was fired for failing his alcohol test and for leaving the bridge before the accident. Although he wasn't tested until ten hours after the tanker hit Bligh Reef, his blood alcohol measured 0.14, the equivalent of four quick shots of 86-proof whiskey.

During questions and answers, the main topic was when VECO would start hiring more workers to clean up the oil. VECO, an oil-field service company prominent on the North Slope, was no different from Exxon or Alyeska in most people's eyes. Alaska had lived with the oil companies' superiority complex for a long time, but now their arrogance fueled the emotional fires of frustration and anger. They gave us no answer on future beach cleanup, but what could we do? The self-appointed generals remained mired in the trenches of indecision.

After the press conference I went to the city library. This warm, quiet building full of books had become my office and a place to escape the franticness of the crisis. While researching events leading to the spill, my mind drifted back to a personal disaster—the fire at my home and lodge in Sadie Cove. Several days after the flames were out, my neighbors and I met to evaluate and learn from the accident.

We wanted to be better prepared in the future, so we discussed the four stages of any disaster: prevention, response, containment, and cleanup. These criteria helped us develop our fire safety program in Sadie Cove and would also prove useful in evaluating the Exxon oil spill.

The key is to keep accidents from happening. Prevention and response to any potential oil spill along the 800-mile pipeline route, in Valdez, or out in Prince William Sound was spelled out in Alyeska's oil-spill contingency plan, a lengthy set of reports published in the 1970s that few ever knew about or read. To better understand the present tragedy, I looked back at the history of Alyeska, the pipeline, and contingency planning:

1970 Alyeska formed.

1971 Department of Environmental Conservation (DEC) created to oversee pipeline construction.

1977 DEC approved Alyeska's first contingency plan.

1977 Pipeline completed, first oil shipped out of Valdez, legislature gave DEC authority over oil-spill response.

1981 Alyeska disbanded its full-time oil-spill response team.

1982 Alyeska replaced Coast Guard–approved, oil-recovery barge with smaller, secondhand, unapproved barge.

1989 March 24, oil spill.

Prevention and early response had failed because DEC never forced compliance with the contingency plan. When the *Exxon Valdez* hit Bligh Reef, what the plan directed and what Alyeska did differed dramatically. For example, the full-time response team described in the original plan had been replaced by dock and office workers with no spill expertise. Instead of thirteen skimmers, only five were in Valdez, and the only oil-recovery barge was in dry dock for repair.

After the initial response, the second most important emergency action is the call for help. Alyeska didn't know who to call, even in its own chain of command. Those in charge ignored the most valuable cleanup force close at hand—the fishermen of Prince William Sound. Though oil and fishing interests have at times been at odds, in this emergency Alyeska and Exxon should have immediately engaged those who had the equipment and knowledge to save the sound instead of blundering through on their own.

The oil companies also failed in the third category of emergency action—containment. They were preventing the 42 million gallons of crude oil still on board the *Exxon Valdez* from escaping the tanker, but they couldn't keep the 11 million gallons spilled from spreading throughout Prince William Sound.

It was too early to evaluate the fourth category—cleanup. By day seven, a few skimmers were nibbling on the giant spill, but no cleanup had started on the beaches. From the beginning of pipeline construction, oil company experts told us what we wanted to hear—everything was under control. In 1971 a British Petroleum specialist for Alyeska stated that BP could clean up any oil spill, even ones involving tens of millions of gallons, with minimum effect on the environment. Alyeska's contingency plan said 50 percent of a spill could be cleaned up, but other experts stressed that only 25 percent could be collected under perfect conditions. A 10 percent to 15 percent recovery was deemed realistic. During spill drills, Alyeska crews picked up hundreds of oranges dumped in the water to simulate oil cleanup. Put into the current spill perspective, these crews would have had to retrieve the entire citrus crops of Florida and California as a comparative exercise.

I sat in the library with my scribbled notes spread out on the table and evaluated the oil companies' performance. To date, Alyeska had made a profit of $45 billion but at the same time had cut back on oil-spill equipment and experienced response crews. In their contingency plan, the oil companies said spill prevention and containment would be effective using modern equipment and the knowledge they had gained from fighting oil spills all over the world. The only thing they learned from experience was the fact that they could neither prevent nor contain oil spills of even moderate size. They lied! But we let them get away with it.

By this time I had signed up for cleanup work with two other organizations—the Cordova District Fishermen United (CDFU) and the Alaska Department of Environmental Conservation. With four lists to sign every morning, my daily rounds were taking longer. Luckily, I met two Homer men, Doug and Steve, who were also in Valdez to find cleanup work. After discussing the employment runaround, we decided to join forces. Early each morning, we would sprint to separate lines and sign up all three of our names.

While eating lunch, we ran into another guy from Homer. "Here to work on the spill?" I asked Kurt.

"I came to help out at the wildlife hospital," he answered. "We're getting set up now."

"Have any critters come in yet?" Steve asked.

"Just a few sea ducks and a loon," Kurt replied. "The volunteer vets are putting together separate cleaning and care units for the birds and sea otters. I'll be working with the otters. If you get a chance, come over and we'll put you to work building cages. We figure it's going to get very busy, real soon."

It felt like old home week when later that day I met another Homerite, a commercial diver working on temporary repairs to the hull of the grounded *Exxon Valdez*. When I asked how the bottom looked, he just said she had a few holes. "Just a few holes," I found out later from a reporter, turned out to be eight major gashes in her hull. The two largest holes measured 8 by 15 feet and 6 by 20 feet— big enough to drive a car through. Maybe my diver friend was told not to talk about the damaged supertanker.

On day eight, Steve, Doug, and I got up early, finished our sign-up in record time, and joined Kurt for breakfast. He mentioned that the day before, he had met several members of Greenpeace, including a videographer sent up from the group's San Francisco office to prepare a spill documentary. They invited him to join them at the Valdez harbor while they interviewed boat owners returning from the spill area. Several people waved them away, but finally a grizzled old seaman standing on the bridge of his oil-stained boat began conversing with them. As they talked and the video camera rolled, a man wearing a VECO cap ran up and told the old fisherman he was fired. He said later that he had been warned not to talk to the press. So much for freedom of speech and the press on an oil spill.

The first thing I noticed on entering the 11:00 A.M. press conference that day was the increased security. Valdez police and private guards were everywhere. I took a seat next to Kurt, and as we talked, Michael Neece came over and asked for our help. He said, "Greenpeace has found a dead, oiled otter, and they plan to bring it into the conference. We want you to go out and casually talk to the guard at the front door of the building. While you're distracting him, someone will walk in with the otter in a pack. Exxon has said they haven't found any dead or sick otters, so now we can do something to focus attention on the wildlife affected by the spill."

Starting a conversation with the Valdez policeman at the front door turned out to be easy—he was friendly. After exchanging a few

Alaska stories, we got around to discussing the spill, and I told him I thought the police had done a good job keeping the peace with all the confusion and angry people in town.

As we continued talking, I wondered what happened to the person with the pack. We'd been out front for twenty minutes. Maybe plans had changed. The conference was just starting as Kurt and I went back inside.

Exxon's Iarossi reappeared with his usual updates: overnight, the oil traveled thirty-seven miles in a southwest direction; work continued on unloading the the damaged tanker; and Exxon put $10 million in a contingency fund to clean up the spill. After more facts and figures from the stage, a reporter asked, "Does your company have a gag order to keep spill workers from talking to the press?"

The Exxon official looked uneasy as he barked an emphatic "No!" Kurt and I looked at each other and shook our heads. We knew better.

A fisherman stood up and started begging Exxon to send protective boom to the oil-threatened salmon hatcheries. As we waited for a reply, several angry people jumped to their feet and demanded action. About that time, we heard loud voices and an excited woman yelling for help from the hallway. This caused half the news people to charge out of the conference room to catch the commotion. Kurt, plus others from the audience, dashed off to see what was happening. I stayed to watch the Exxon people panic and run out a door behind the stage. The remaining press frantically grabbed their gear and rushed after them, only to be stopped by the security guards.

The excitement ended as fast as it had begun. "The lady with the pack finally showed up," Kurt said when he returned. "The police looked surprised when they emptied her dirty laundry out on the floor; she could have been arrested bringing in a dead otter. Greenpeace and the press got it all on film, and we can watch it on the five o'clock news. What happened in here?"

I told him and added, "Exxon was embarrassed at these meetings by not being able to answer some important local questions. I'll bet this is the last press conference."

We left, and I started looking for a phone booth not being used by reporters calling in their stories. When I got through to Billy Choate in Homer, I told him his truck (my home) was doing fine. "Has anything been done there about the spill?" I asked.

"Not much," he answered. "Last night we had a meeting to discuss how it could affect our salmon season."

"The oil's coming your way," I warned. "I've studied the currents, and if the southeast winds continue to blow in the Gulf of Alaska, it could wash up on the Homer Spit within a month."

"What's happening over there?" Billy asked.

"Nothing to stop the oil!" I almost shouted. "Listen, if enough floating crude escapes Prince William Sound, it could follow the north gulf coast and enter both Cook Inlet and Kachemak Bay. What isn't sucked into our front yard could foul Kodiak and keep going out the Aleutian Island chain. Hell, even Bristol Bay isn't safe. The oil could then ride the currents out into the Gulf of Alaska, make a big circle to the south, and hit the coast of Canada in British Columbia. If enough of this black plague was still floating, it could drift up through southeast Alaska and return to Prince William Sound. This spill is so big it could affect every fishery in the state."

Later that evening, Doug, Steve, Kurt, and I met for dinner. While discussing the day's events, we struck up a conversation with a group of friendly women at the next table. After introductions, Steve asked if they were in town because of the spill.

"No, we live here," answered one woman, whose name was Wendy.

"Do you work for one of the oil companies?" I asked, knowing that most of the residents of Valdez had oil-related jobs.

Wendy bristled. "No, we haven't sold our souls to oil. Everyone I know, including many who work for Alyeska, are very upset about the spill. They built this town with oil dollars, but we're Alaskans too."

I backed off fast.

"I apologize for getting upset," she added. "Some reporters make everyone living in Valdez sound like a bunch of uncaring oil executives. I just needed to let off some steam."

The pressure was off, and we all talked for a while. "Where are you staying?" Wendy asked when we were ready to leave.

"In our cars," we answered in unison.

"Why don't you stay at my house?" Wendy said after she stopped laughing. "I have lots of room in the basement, and you can use the shower and cook in the kitchen."

We didn't hesitate in accepting her gracious invitation, and that night we slept off the streets in the home of a new friend.

I woke up on day nine wishing the oil spill was just a bad April Fool's joke, but no such luck; even the long lines for cleanup work were humorless.

The big event of the day was a press conference held by Governor Steve Cowper. On entering the civic center for the meeting, I noticed two bulletins tacked to the wall. The first, a Coast Guard update, stated that a large oil slick had escaped the sound and entered the Gulf of Alaska. The second notice came from Exxon and said: "Press Conference—Sunday, April 2, 4:00 P.M., Press Only."

Both my predictions had come true, but neither made me happy.

Governor Cowper began his talk by stating that Alyeska had not contacted him since the first day of the spill, and if he didn't see a drastic improvement in its effort to clean up the oil, he would shut down the pipeline. We cheered and gave him a standing ovation. Maybe his ultimatum would light a fire under the oil companies!

During the question session, someone asked the governor why the state didn't take over control of the spill, and he answered, "Alaska has $10 billion in our Permanent Fund savings account, but we don't have the organization in place to take over. The state and Coast Guard will monitor the cleanup, but Exxon is the best qualified to get the job done."

Governor Cowper assured us that the state was reviewing oil company tax breaks and proposed future drilling in Bristol Bay and the Arctic National Wildlife Refuge (ANWR). He also stated that Alaskans, not Texans, would be hired to clean up the spill. His hard stand with the powerful oil companies made me feel better about the current crisis and the environmental future of our state.

After the press conference, I needed to get some fresh air, so I walked down to the boat harbor. While admiring an old wooden boat, I started talking to its captain. It didn't take long before we were discussing the spill. "That damn captain of the *Exxon Valdez* should be hanged," he barked.

"I'm not defending Hazelwood—he made a big mistake—but now he's become the scapegoat for the whole catastrophe. He's not the only one responsible for the spill," I pointed out.

I must have sparked his interest because he said, "I'm listening."

"Alyeska and Exxon are obviously at fault for failing to prevent and contain the spill," I continued. "The United States Coast Guard is also responsible. It's their job to monitor and enforce the rules governing tanker traffic, and they didn't do it. In 1984, against local protest, they downgraded their radar to save money. As a result, the *Exxon Valdez* was off their radar screens at the time of the accident. In the original contingency plan, all tankers were to stay in the designated shipping lanes and slow down if they encountered icebergs. A marine pilot was also required to remain on the ship until it left Prince William Sound. On March twenty-fourth, the Coast Guard gave the *Exxon Valdez* permission to leave the shipping lanes after they sighted floating ice, but the ship didn't slow down. The pilot also got off before Bligh Reef. The Coast Guard does a great job saving lives at sea, but on this spill they failed by not monitoring the tanker."

I paused while the fisherman packed his lip with Copenhagen. "The third major party at fault is the Alaska Department of Environmental Conservation. Granted, its funds had been cut and it was operating with too few personnel, but DEC was still responsible for overseeing Alyeska's oil-spill response. They did warn the state of the oil companies' inability to prevent and contain a spill, but they still approved their contingency plan. They were paper tigers with no teeth to enforce the rules."

"So you're saying we should also hang the oil companies, Coast Guard, and the state?" the fisherman asked.

"If we did string up everyone responsible, we would need a lot of rope," I answered. "Ultimately, the blame for this spill can also be traced to the end user of nonrenewable resources, and that's all of us. We contributed to the spill by overconsuming. Too many of us demanded cheap, plentiful energy so we could continue to enjoy one of the highest standards of living in the world. In Alaska, oil dollars created many jobs, paid our taxes, and created our $10 billion Permanent Fund. Now we must pay for those benefits."

"I'm just as guilty as anyone," I added. "I've enjoyed the wilderness of Alaska for seventeen years but have done little to protect it."

"Sounds like you blame everyone for the spill," the fisherman replied.

"I do, but some less than others," I said. "In the sound, you fishermen and the environmental groups fought a long, hard battle to prevent what has happened. I admire your efforts and only wish others would have given you more support. If we had, this spill could have been prevented. The whole system failed, so we all should hang if captain Hazelwood must."

"You should write down what you just told me and send it to a newspaper," said the fisherman through his smile.

"It will be in the book I've been writing for the past two years," I said. "It's time for me to help protect Mother Earth and start repaying what she's given me."

I spent most of day ten trying to get a press pass for the 4:00 P.M. Exxon meeting. What I got was the old runaround and instructions to get a pass at the press conference just before it began.

The guard at the door refused to let me enter, but he did let me talk to the man in charge—a young, clean-cut, Exxon executive dressed in a yellow sweater, creased slacks, and polished loafers. "I'm writing a book about the spill," I said after introducing myself. "At your headquarters they told me to get my press pass here at the meeting."

"Do you work for a publisher?" he asked.

"Better than that—I own the company," I replied while handing him my R&P Publishing business license.

He looked at my beard, wrinkled wool shirt, faded jeans, and logging boots and said, "Sorry, I can't let you in."

I gave it one last try. "Listen, I live in the Bush, but I'm not anti-oil. I use gas in my boat and drove a car to Valdez."

"Give the guy a break," chipped in Pat, the San Francisco writer, who was standing behind me with several other press people. "He can't write about your press conference by listening to it on the radio."

The official hesitated, turned to the policeman, and said, "Okay, I'll take a chance—let him in."

As I thanked the Exxon official, Pat and the reporters applauded.

I took a seat in the back of the room next to where the Valdez public radio station, KCHU, was set up to broadcast. They had done a great job covering the press conferences and airing a rumor hot line. When gossip, such as merchants doubling their prices, spread through town, they had investigated and reported the facts. I gave the announcer the thumbs-up sign, and he acknowledged me with a nod as he began broadcasting the meeting.

Exxon's Iarossi began by announcing that the oil now extended into the Gulf of Alaska. A hundred vessels with 760 workers were employed on the spill, and the Soviets had offered to send a giant skimmer ship to help in the cleanup. The damaged *Exxon Valdez* would finish unloading its remaining cargo of oil the next day and then be refloated off Bligh Reef and towed to a safe moorage for repairs. Tanker traffic would resume transporting crude oil to the Lower 48 once the crippled ship was secure. At the wildlife hospitals, 150 birds and 30 sea otters had been brought in from the sound. Seventeen otters remained alive, and 5 cleaned, healthy birds were released back into the wild.

The press conference ran smoothly without Alaskans in the audience to ask questions, but I much preferred the emotion and concern the local citizens had added.

During dinner that evening, I sat with a tired but excited Steve. "After we finished the employment sign-ups, I spent the day helping out at the animal hospital, and it sure felt good to do something useful. The volunteers working there are giving new meaning to the words dedication and caring. They work under wet, stinking, crowded, noisy, frantic conditions surrounded by pain, suffering, and death. After building and cleaning cages, washing sticky oil from feathers and fur, feeding sick survivors, and tagging and freezing the dead, my senses are numbed out."

"I plan on working at the hospital tomorrow," I said. "What do I need to take?"

"Rain gear, if you have it, but there's also some there," he answered. "Today, I talked to a guy who works for Alyeska, but he came in on his own to see the treatment facilities. He felt real bad about the spill, and when he saw volunteers standing in water wearing tennis shoes with plastic garbage bags for rain coats, he left and brought back thirty full sets of rain gear and rubber boots."

Steve paused, then added, "You know, Keith, the big oil companies may only be concerned about profits, but many of their employees are good, caring people."

The next day I went to the animal hospital and was put to work cleaning otters. After sedating an animal, we placed it on a scrubbing table with two people on each side and one holding its head. It took about three hours of repeated washings and rinsings to clean the oil from its sleek fur. As we worked, I could see the fear in the eyes of these gentle creatures, who in the wild shy away from contact with humans. Many volunteers had deep gashes on their hands—bites of desperation from those they tried to help.

I helped clean two otters; a third died on the scrub table. Before returning to Wendy's house and going to bed, I went into the hospital's makeshift cafeteria to get something to eat. As I sat there alone, a woman came in and asked me if I would take care of a three-week-old otter for the next eight hours. I followed her to get instructions on how to care for the orphaned, female pup whose mother had died in the spill.

When I picked up the foot-long, fuzzy fur-ball, I experienced what can only be described as a maternal instinct. I shook off my fatigue, swallowed the lump in my throat, and began feeding the helpless, squealing, baby otter a blended formula of clams and milk. I fed her every two hours, then took her temperature. If the thermometer read above 100°F, I cooled her down by rubbing snow on her back flippers. When she got too cold, I'd hold her close to my body for warmth. Toward the end of my shift, I looked up with the sleeping pup in my arms to see Nancy, my Sadie Cove neighbor, watching me.

With a tear running down her cheek, she asked, "Keith, what are you doing here?"

"Playing mom," I answered.

The next day, VECO still wasn't hiring workers to clean the beaches, but they were contracting any boat afloat. While in the Valdez harbor I met Gary Gray, the friend who had helped me put the roof on my sauna back in 1974. I asked him if he was looking for a job on the spill.

"Just got one," he answered. "I'm the captain of the *Lady June,* that 80-footer tied to the cannery dock. We came to the sound as a tender for the herring run, but it doesn't look like we'll be harvesting anything but oil. VECO just hired my boat for $5,000 a day plus fuel and groceries."

"Do you need any more crew?" I asked.

"Sorry, Keith, I don't," he said. "Gotta run—we're leaving in two hours."

VECO required every oil-spill worker to complete a health and safety class; so like hundreds of other job hopefuls, I signed up for the three-hour course. The industrial hygienist lectured on the normal hazards of working on boats: seasickness, hypothermia, and drowning. He also covered the special problems involved in the cleanup effort. Crude oil contains toxins, such as benzene, which could cause skin cancer, leukemia, respiratory ailments, blurred vision, rashes, and nausea. Hazardous waste would add another dimension to the dangers of working on Alaskan waters.

On April 5, at 1:00 P.M., the *Exxon Valdez* was refloated on the high tide and towed twenty-five miles west to a protected bay on oil-stained Naked Island. That night, at Wendy's house, I met Cindy. She and her husband, Jim, fished for a living and were year-round residents of Virgin Bay on Ellemar Island, four miles from Bligh Reef. I asked if they saw the *Exxon Valdez* after it ran aground, and she told me her story.

"We were up early on March twenty-fourth," Cindy recalled, "and heard on the marine radio about a wreck on the reef. It was still dark, but with the calm water we decided to take our skiff and see if we could help. We got there just at dawn, and I'll never forget what we saw. As we got closer, the huge hull of the tanker towered above us. Toward the bow we noticed something big moving in the water. When we realized what it was, I almost got sick. Seven hours after the ship hit Bligh Reef, the crude oil was still gushing out of the underwater gashes in the hull and boiling up four feet above the surface of the sea. Nobody could have stopped that oil."

Those geysers of oil spread over the waters of Prince William Sound and affected far more than the wildlife that lived there. Fishermen had their herring harvest canceled and waited to see if the salmon season would open. Local businesses were desperate for help as their employees succumbed to the allure of VECO's $16.69-per-hour wages for cleanup crews. Most tourist-related businesses were experiencing a rash of cancellations, and coastal residents worried about contamination of their subsistence foods.

The effects of the spill extended far beyond Alaska, too. In the Lower 48, people were concerned and angry about rising fuel costs, but many Americans also wanted to help with the cleanup effort. Michael Neece saw the need for a reliable communication system and talked the state into funding an information center. He recruited my help, and I joined several others on the first day the telephones were hooked up. In a bare, two-room office, we sat on the floor and answered phone calls. A German newspaperman telephoned for information on the spill, and a woman in Florida inquired about sending money for bird rehabilitation; but most of the callers wanted to come to Valdez as volunteers. With no places in town for them to stay, we discouraged their coming but promised to call them back when things were better organized.

My second day at the information office, Michael offered me a full-time, paid position. I declined his offer because I wanted to be out in the field cleaning up the oil. Eventually, they would have to start hiring workers to clean the beaches.

That night I ran into John Wolfe, just back from fighting to keep the oil out of Sawmill Bay.

"How goes the battle?" I asked in greeting.

"A long way from over, but so far we've saved the hatchery," he answered.

"Who are you working for?" I inquired.

"VRCA," he answered. "It's a small environmental-services company owned by the Arctic Slope Regional Corporation. We're working with the state's Division of Emergency Services, Department of Environmental Conservation, and the Cordova District Fishermen United to protect the salmon hatcheries. Found a job yet?"

"Not yet, but I'm on every list in town," I answered, trying to sound optimistic.

"Hang in there," John advised. "I'll let you know if I hear about any openings."

Day fifteen began as usual with the sign-up at the state employment office. I was leaving the building when Steve ran up and said, "John Wolfe is looking for you."

When I found John, he said, "I've got you a job. Our boom man at the Esther Island salmon hatchery was evacuated this morning with pneumonia, and you'll be taking his place. Can you be ready in an hour?"

"I've been ready for two weeks," I answered.

John led me to a small office where he introduced me to Larry Safford, the vice-president of VRCA. Larry had a phone to each ear, but he still managed to shake my hand. When he finished his conversations, he said, "John told me about your lodge and life in the Bush, so we know you can handle this job. We're sending you out as a site expediter to work with the hatchery manager and Cordova fishermen to finish setting up the protective boom. Keep us informed of your progress and the location of oil in your area."

Larry answered his telephone, and John and I drove to the airport.

We flew out through Valdez Narrows, banked west over spruce-covered fjords, and looked down on the Columbia Glacier as it slowly crept out of the snow-covered Chugach Mountains into the sea. At its base, blue-green icebergs floated lazily in the calm water. The tranquil beauty almost made me forget the reason for the flight.

Suddenly, I realized that I hadn't seen any oil and looked harder. A few minutes later, I saw a dark cloud floating just below the surface of the water. I poked John, pointed down, and yelled over the roar of the engine, "Oil?"

He shook his head and hollered back, "No, a school of spawning herring. The oil's about ten miles south, but the wind could blow it up here at any time."

I had his attention and shouted, "Larry gave me a general idea of my job, but could you go into a little more detail?"

"Most of the boom is already in place, but it needs constant maintenance because of the tides and waves," he answered. "Your job is to protect the hatchery by keeping that boom up."

His job description still seemed vague, but I figured the VRCA foreman at the hatchery could fill me in. "Who's my boss?" I asked.

"You don't have one," John answered. "The man you're replacing was the site foreman, and Lance, your boss, flew out this morning to Sawmill Bay. I doubt he'll be back."

"Great!" I shouted. "Just like Sadie Cove: learn by doing. Sure glad I watched your video on the Cook Inlet spill."

John smiled and gave me a thumbs up as we flew into the hatchery.

Protecting the Salmon Hatchery

As we circled Lake Bay, I looked down at six rows of bright yellow boom set up to protect Esther Island salmon hatchery. After landing next to the floating fish pens at the head of the bay, John introduced me to Jeff Olsen, the tall, blond, hatchery manager. The plane took off, and Jeff skiffed me out to meet the Cordova fishermen hired to defend the hatchery from the oil spill.

Three fishing boats were rafted together on the calm water, and as we approached, the ten stern men and women on board eyed me suspiciously. I didn't blame them: for all they knew, I was another oil man come to make excuses for the spill that threatened their livelihoods and lifestyles.

I climbed on board and cringed as Jeff introduced me as the new boom expert. No one stepped forward to shake my hand, so I took a deep breath to control my anger and said, "I'm no expert, and don't trust anyone who says they are. The experts said they could prevent or contain any spill in Prince William Sound. I live in Kachemak Bay, and there's a damn good chance this oil will hit the beach in front of my home in Sadie Cove. Nobody wants to clean up this mess more than I do!"

Tom, captain of the *Kioki*, stepped up, held out his hand, and said, "Glad to have your help, Keith."

After shaking everyone's hand, I said, "I've lived on the water in Alaska for sixteen years, but you'll need to fill me in on local tides, currents, and winds."

Tom, Jeff, and I then took a skiff and toured the three plastic booms defending the entrance of the bay and an additional three surrounding the fish bins in front of the hatchery. The 24-inch, primary boom stretched 2,000 feet across the mouth of the fjord and was tied to each shore with heavy line. A 2-foot, weighted curtain hung underwater to keep oil from washing underneath. The smaller inner booms were evenly spaced along the mile-long bay. On the beach in front of the hatchery a small mountain of extra equipment was stacked for future use.

The booms looked good floating on the calm bay, but could they combat strong tidal currents and southeast winds and still protect the hatchery from the oil? Right now, nature was on our side, and her chilly, northern breath blew the oil south.

As my first day at Esther Island ended, I crawled into bed feeling tired but good about finally leaving Valdez and helping protect the biggest salmon hatchery in the world from the greatest oil spill in U.S. history.

It was still dark the next morning when we met to assign the day's work. Jim and his crew on the *Mirage* would unload absorbent boom from a supply boat just in from Valdez. Bob with the *Parks 19* planned to adjust and reset boom anchors, and Tom's *Kioki* would head south to patrol for oil. Cynthia, a spirited young woman hired by the hatchery to monitor the spill, took me out on the first of four daily boom inspections.

Dawn's first light sparkled off the snow-blanketed mountaintops as our skiff clattered through the thin layer of ice covering the inner bay. The cold wind numbed our noses, but the struggle to get through the booms without untying them from shore soon warmed us.

On arriving at the outer boom we found it damaged from rubbing against the rocky shore. "This harbor boom wasn't made for these unprotected waters where waves and tides can tear it up," I said as Cynthia used her radio to call for help.

"The hatchery has ordered heavy-duty, ocean boom, and it should get here next week," she remarked. "We'll all feel better when it's in place."

The *Kioki* helped us repair the boom before leaving on its oil patrol, and then Cynthia and I skiffed out into Wells Passage to take the daily water sample. She would later run tests at the hatchery to measure hydrocarbons. During the end of March her tests showed 1.5 parts per million of oil in the water, but now her readings were zero. I hoped it stayed that way.

The rest of the day we kept busy inspecting and repairing our defenses, installing battery-powered blinker lights on the outer boom, and unloading groceries and fuel for the fishing boats from a tender sent from Valdez. The *Kioki* returned just before dark and reported the closest oil was ten miles south.

For the next week we put in twelve- to sixteen-hour days, and I came to respect the hard-working fishermen and hatchery crews. Both groups had separate jobs, but their goals were the same—protecting the young salmon. The threat of oil contributed to an underlying tension that increased when the wind started blowing from the southeast.

When I left Valdez for the hatchery, Larry Safford told me to check in regularly with his office. Easier said than done—Esther Island was isolated, even by Alaska standards. Our only outside communication was over the VHF radio, and with 400 oil-spill boats in the sound trying to call out through one marine operator channel, it took me a frustrating week to contact Valdez. I finally reached Larry and gave him my update. "Let me talk to your boss, Lance," he said after I'd finished.

"Never met the man," I answered. "He left for Sawmill Bay before I arrived. I'm the only VRCA employee at the hatchery."

"You're promoted to site foreman," he said after a slight pause. "Keep up the good work."

The oil-spill operation was like a war, and I'd just received a battlefield commission.

As we continued talking, I expressed my concern. "Larry, this moderate southeast wind has blown the oil within five miles of the hatchery. Do you have the latest forecast?"

"It's supposed to blow like hell out of the southeast," he answered. "Keep me informed. If the oil gets within three miles of you, we'll send out skimmers."

After signing off, I contacted Jeff and the fishing boat crews for a meeting to discuss our battle plans. Nature had turned from friend to foe. As predicted, the southeast winds increased and pushed the oil steadily toward the hatchery. Jeff put in an emergency call and learned that the sea boom would arrive in two days. The question was—could we get it set up in time?

While we awaited its arrival, we kept busy repairing our existing booms and doing everything possible to strengthen our fortifications. The fishing boats increased their patrols, and each night one of them anchored outside the booms. We stockpiled extra supplies in a bay to the east, so if we were hit by oil and couldn't open the booms, we could still move personnel and material outside our primary defenses.

A Super-cub on floats, contracted by the hatchery, increased its flights and twice a day flew Cynthia out to film the enemy with her video camera. Each night we watched her latest pictures of the advancing oil.

We knew from the Battle of Sawmill Bay that the plastic containment boom we had in place could not stop wind-driven oil. However, we could deflect it. So we angled our number-three boom to channel the oil into Seal Cove, a shallow, rocky area on the east side of Lake Bay. If the oil overran our first and second booms, Seal Cove was expendable.

If oil hit our outer, primary boom on an incoming tide, the strong currents could suck it beneath the 2-foot-deep, underwater skirt. So we strung 6-inch absorbent boom in double rows behind the plastic containment boom. If oil got past these defenses, we would use our skiffs and bigger fishing boats to skim it off the water. Three booms around the floating fish pens were our last line of protection for the millions of baby salmon that swam in ever-changing dark swirls inside their temporary, saltwater home.

Oil was three miles out when the 40-foot fishing boats *Cape Kumlick* from Valdez and *Cape Countess* from Cordova arrived as reinforcements. Six skimmers began attacking the leading edge of the oil, and at night we could see their lights slowly drifting between Perry and Culross islands.

The navy sea boom reached our defenses aboard the 80-foot *Max* as the oil moved to within a mile of Esther Island. With it came the *Malagos* and Coast Guard cutter *Sweetbriar*. As our small fleet of fishing boats powered out to join them, the first light of day painted the low clouds blood red. Charley, captain of the *Cape Countess*, had fished the sound for fifty years. "Red sky at morning, sailors take warning," he said like a prayer. We both knew the danger wasn't from the weather.

On board the *Max* we met Dave, an oil-spill consultant sent to teach us how to set up the heavy-duty boom. He was one of the few experts I'd met who impressed me. After instructing us on technique, he rolled up his sleeves and demonstrated the procedure. "At the Battle of Sawmill Bay, I learned a good lesson—show fishermen what to do and then get the hell out of their way," he said as we began assembling the boom.

We used an air compressor to inflate the steel-reinforced sections of boom and bolted them together with heavy metal plates and chain. One by one they went over the side and joined the growing black sea serpent trailing from our stern. As the fishing boats towed off the completed sections, the Coast Guard cutter set four 2,000-pound anchors to hold our boom in place. The new boom made our old defenses look like a toy designed to contain rubber duckies in a bathtub. When we finished our installation, the inch-thick mousse was only a half-mile away.

We had worked hard to safeguard the hatchery, but in the end our defenses were never tested—the wind mercifully shifted and pushed the oil south.

With the threat of oil diminished, the bigger boats left to continue the battle in other areas, and several of our crew flew into Cordova for a day off. When the captain of the *Kioki* returned, I met him on the dock. "In town they're calling us Exxon whores!" Tom shouted in anger.

What he said also made me mad, but after considering the crises and those who had made the remark, I knew we didn't have to defend our actions. "There are two kinds of people in this world: doers and complainers," I said. "Complainers are jealous jerks who sit on their butts and bad-mouth the doers. It doesn't matter what Exxon's paying us; we're out here trying to save the sound. Don't let them get to you, Tom. You're doing a great job."

During my two weeks at Esther Island, I kept informed of spill events outside our isolated area through nightly television broadcasts and three-day-old newspapers. Oil continued to spread outside the sound and threatened Kodiak Island and Cook Inlet. The giant, 425-foot Soviet skimmer *Vaydaghubsky* worked the waters near Seward, while in Homer and Seldovia local people frantically constructed booms out of logs, plywood, and plastic. All available commercial boom was being shipped to the sound, so other communities in the path of the spill had to make do with the materials they had on hand.

In Prince William Sound the battle continued on many different fronts. With the hatcheries protected, workers began setting up booms on natural salmon streams, and VECO crews finally started cleaning up heavy concentrations of crude from the beaches. Large numbers of dead and dying birds and otters flooded the critter hospitals while a few Cordova fishermen collected floating oil in plastic buckets and received a bounty of $5 a gallon. Environmental groups called for criminal charges against executives of Exxon and Alyeska, and politicians toured the spill and demanded tougher pollution laws.

A cloud of doom hung over the state's commercial fishing industry. No one knew how oil would affect the outgoing baby salmon or returning adults. Would the national and foreign markets buy Alaska fish? While state agencies debated closing commercial salmon fishing in all affected areas, Exxon hired a disaster psychologist from Kansas, for $600 a day, to help coastal Alaskans mentally cope with the spill's aftermath.

Through this black cloud of anger, frustration, and unanswered questions, the fishermen saw a ray of hope—the hatcheries. They had saved the fishing industry in the sound once before, and they could do it again.

The epicenter of Alaska's 1964 earthquake was in the northwest corner of Prince William Sound, almost directly under Esther Island. The land and water bucked and rolled so violently that when the last tremors faded, parts of Montague Island in the southern reaches of the sound had risen more than thirty-eight feet. This upheaval affected the coastal streams and nearly destroyed the commercial salmon fishing in the area. To save the sound's suffering salmon industry, far-sighted fishermen formed the Cordova District Fishermen United (CDFU). In 1975, they received state funding and established the Prince William Sound Aquaculture Corporation (PWSAC). This private, nonprofit, regional association started its first hatchery in 1977 at Port San Juan (site of the Battle of Sawmill Bay) and then expanded to Esther Island and Cannery Creek. This unique organization helped rebuild Prince William Sound's commercial salmon industry to a $100 million-a-year business. By increasing the salmon runs, they also improved sport and subsistence fishing.

When the *Exxon Valdez* hit Bligh Reef and its cargo of crude oil began poisoning the waters of Prince William Sound, PWSAC and CDFU immediately swung into action to defend their hatcheries. They hired oil-spill consultants, bought boom, and used local fishermen to protect what they had built up over the years. It was still too early to know if their efforts would be successful in saving the salmon, but they had my admiration for a job well done before and during the spill crisis.

With the oil a safe distance to the south, I asked for a hatchery tour. Jodi was my friendly guide. "The hatchery is in the fish ranching business," she began. "We breed, raise, and release the young salmon and harvest returning adults. At Esther Island we rear all five types of Pacific salmon, but we have the best luck with pinks and chums."

I asked if there were any variations in how they raise the different species, and she answered, "The biggest difference is in how long we keep the young salmon. We have separate, long-term rearing areas for kings, silvers, and reds."

We walked outside to an empty, concrete spillway, where Jodi said, "I like to begin my tours with the returning adult salmon. At maturity, the fish raised at our hatchery migrate back from the open ocean to Prince William Sound. Those not caught by commercial, sport, or subsistence fishermen swim to Lake Bay. When they are ready to spawn, we open these manmade fish ladders and the salmon swim up into the hatchery."

"Do you pump salt water into the fish ladders?" I asked.

"No, we use fresh water from the lake above the hatchery," she answered. "We also use that water to provide hydroelectric power for most of our energy needs."

I was amazed by the efficiency of their system—they produced a renewable resource using alternative energy.

Jodi led me back inside, where we both walked through a shallow tub of disinfectant to protect the baby salmon from any viruses that might be hitch-hiking a ride on our boots. Standing in the butchering room, she explained how the salmon were quickly killed, the ripe eggs and sperm extracted, and the carcasses sent down a long pipe into a waiting tender, which took them to a fishmeal processor. "Is that how the hatchery makes the money to continue operating?" I inquired.

"One of the ways," she answered. "PWSAC also gets a 2 percent assessment tax on all commercially caught salmon in the sound, and when the hatchery has taken all the eggs needed, we contract fishermen to harvest the remaining fish in Lake Bay."

We walked into a large adjoining room, where Jodi continued. "This is where we fertilize the eggs with the sperm and care for the eggs until they hatch. After hatching, the baby salmon migrate through these waterways into the next room, where they grow into the fry stage."

As we entered the huge incubation room with its shallow water troughs stacked to the ceiling, I raised my voice to be heard over the sound of running water. "Do many of these baby salmon die?" I asked.

"In nature, about 1 percent of the fry survive the winter," Jodi answered. "At our hatchery we have a 97 percent survival rate."

In the next room, two workers sat hunched over their benches tagging the inch-long fry. Jodi described the detailed process and added, "This is a monotonous but important job. Each spring we tag 300,000 pinks and 100,000 silvers by implanting a tiny metal wire in each salmon's head. When these fish return as adults, they provide us with valuable information that helps determine the success of our operation."

Next, we walked outside and followed the salmon as they swam down a long, plastic waterway into the floating fish pens. "The fingerlings are automatically counted on leaving the hatchery, and we put about 10 million salmon in each pen. Until they're released, we feed them every half-hour."

"What happens after they're set free?" I asked.

"They stay in Prince William Sound and feed on plankton for about two weeks," she answered. "Then they swim out to sea. When the salmon reach maturity, they return to where they were born and the cycle begins again. This year our hatchery will release 170 million pinks, 90 million chums, and smaller amounts of kings, silvers, and reds."

"How many survive to spawn?" I inquired.

"Between 7 percent and 9 percent," she answered. "If we release 300 million fish, about 25 million return."

It was hard comprehending such big numbers, but easy to admire what PWSAC and their hatchery crews had accomplished. Five years earlier, there were no salmon runs in the Esther Island area.

That night after dinner, I joined Jeff, the hatchery manager, at the floating fish pens and watched as 25 million fry were released. "This makes all the hard work worthwhile," he said with a smile. "I've worked at these hatcheries for eight years, and my favorite time is when we lower the nets and give the fry their freedom. We've done everything we can to get them to this point. Now it's up to them."

Jeff didn't say anything about the oil in the sound through which the young salmon must swim, but I knew it was on his mind. In a way, these released fish were his kids, and after raising and defending his brood he was concerned about their future. No one knew how many salmon would survive the natural and manmade hazards on their waterway to maturity, but Jeff and the PWSAC hatcheries would be waiting to continue their fish ranching roundup.

With the hatchery no longer threatened, it was time for me to go. However, the storm that blew the oil south also grounded all aircraft in our area; so I was surprised to see a low-flying helicopter ride gale-force winds into Lake Bay. When it landed, the pilot said he had room to take me back to Valdez, but first we were flying to Naked Island so that an ABC camera crew could film the *Exxon Valdez*.

Gusty winds bounced our helicopter all over the sky as we approached Naked Island. After passing the northwest headland, we saw what one newspaper called the "tanker from hell." As the cameraman took pictures of the silent ship, I realized the *Exxon Valdez* was just a huge hunk of floating metal with some holes in its bottom. People, not the tanker, had created the hell.

We landed on the beach so that the camera crew could film our pilot while he poked a stick into a 2-foot-deep puddle of crude oil for the evening news. While on Esther Island, I never saw the oil up close. After walking along a shore that was smothered by the stinking black sludge, I only had one question—how could anyone clean up the mess?

Upon landing in Valdez, I went to the VRCA office to get my next assignment. The oil had spread west along the gulf coast, so Larry Safford had gone to Kodiak and John Wolfe to Homer. I told the man in charge that I was returning to Kachemak Bay to fight the oil in my own front yard. Driving out of Valdez, I wondered what I'd find back home.

Windy Bay's Black Beaches

My long drive from Valdez to Homer made me road-weary, but I forgot my sore rump when I saw Kachemak Bay and the far mountains that surround my home in Sadie Cove. With my fingers crossed, I drove out onto the spit to see if the oil had arrived before me.

The waves that crashed onto the shore looked clean, but along the high-tide mark I found several black, oily globs about the size of a squashed orange. Were these the advance scouts for a whole army of floating tar balls, or would these waters be spared the nightmare experienced by Prince William Sound? With the threat of oil lurking on the horizon, the local folks had been desperately preparing their defenses. When they learned that all available commercial oil boom was being shipped to the sound, they made do with what they had and built their own boom out of logs, plywood, and sheets of plastic. Most of the 30,000 feet of boom constructed by communities around the bay were already protecting priority areas.

After walking the beach, I returned Billy's pickup truck and drove my car to the post office, where I ran into my neighbor Nancy. She had just crossed the bay and, to my great relief, reported that Sadie Cove was still untouched by oil.

While sorting mail I said hello to Barbara, a long-time woman friend, and told her about my job defending the Esther Island salmon hatchery. "So you're one of those Exxon spillionaires!" she said with a scowl.

I didn't know what to say. Instead of explaining my position and defending my actions, I grabbed my mail and left. While sitting in my car, I tried to understand her verbal attack. At first I was mad, but then I saw the reason for her reaction. In Valdez, during the first days of the spill, I, too, was angry with anyone working for the oil companies. Although the oil had started contaminating Prince William Sound more than a month earlier, it was just starting to wash up on Homer's beaches, and now I was working for those who created the catastrophe. I understood the anger, frustration, and fear, but I had no desire to stay in town and get caught up in the emotional and political battles. As in Valdez, I wanted to be out in the field, but now the front lines were in my own front yard.

At the Exxon spill headquarters I asked to see John Wolfe. I was told he was on Pearl Island setting up a field command center to start cleanup efforts in the Gulf of Alaska. When I called him on the radio phone, he said, "I need you out here right now—catch the next chopper to Pearl Island."

I threw some gear into a pack and arrived at the airport just as the ten-seat helicopter started warming up. The only other passenger introduced himself as Bubba Grant, a member of Exxon's national oil-spill response team. We struggled into bright orange flight suits, fastened our seat belts, and with the engine roaring were sucked into the sky.

Our 40-mile flight took us south across Kachemak Bay and past the entrance to Sadie Cove. By squinting my eyes, I could barely make out my home in the distance. Two minutes later we were bouncing through turbulence in the Rocky River Pass and encountered heavy fog over the area where I'd guided lodge guests for silver salmon. Our pilot gained altitude to avoid the low clouds, and we soared into a dazzling world where mountaintops floated on a sea of white fluff. For a moment my mind blocked out the noise and vibration from our helicopter, and I smiled at the beauty that surrounded me.

Bubba broke the spell when he tapped me on the shoulder and pointed down at a large oil slick on the now visible Gulf of Alaska. A few minutes later we landed on Pearl Island next to the rented resort that now served as Exxon's field command center.

When we walked in, John doused his cigarette in an overflowing ashtray, left his seat in front of a long table full of communications equipment, and handed me a cup of coffee while introducing me to the other people in the room. "Keith, I think you know Laurie from Homer, our radio operator and cook. The man in uniform is Tom, a member of the Coast Guard's Pacific oil-spill strike team."

The strong coffee tasted good, but I had time for only one sip. As Laurie and Tom answered calls on the VHF radio, John motioned for me to follow him outside. "We're just getting geared up in this area," he said. "Bubba and I are in charge of the coastal area from Nuka Island to Kachemak Bay, and tomorrow morning I want you to start overseeing the work in Windy Bay. Its beaches were heavily impacted, and we have a boom and beach crew there now."

"Will I be an expediter or a foreman?" I asked.

"Neither," he answered. "We both still work for VRCA, but they've contracted us out. You've been promoted to an Exxon field supervisor. Now, before you thank me, I want you to know this position is a hot seat. You'll be answering to this command center, our Exxon bosses in Homer, the Coast Guard, and both federal and state agencies while taking care of your crew's problems in the field."

We walked back inside to go over details of the cleanup effort; I knew I'd just accepted the hardest job of my life.

Early the next morning while coffee perked on a woodburning stove, someone broadcast over the radio, "Good morning, Vietnam!" No one said anything at the command center, but I think everyone realized the similarities.

During breakfast a helicopter landed, and its two passengers came inside to talk to John and Bubba. I sensed tension between the men and walked into the kitchen for more coffee. "What's going on?" I asked Laurie.

"They're from DEC," she answered in an angry but hushed voice. "When oil first arrived in this area, we immediately started setting up this command center to direct our skimming operations. DEC shut us down and kept us off the island for ten days because the resort's toilets and drinking water didn't pass their inspection. John and Bubba were forced to fly out of Homer, and because of marginal weather in the Rocky River Pass, they weren't always able to fly out to the gulf. They could have picked up more oil if we had been on the island. DEC didn't know its priorities—they hampered the cleanup effort in this area because of a couple of stinking toilets!"

A few minutes later, John and I boarded a chopper for our flight to Windy Bay. We flew northeast for ten minutes, crossed over a spruce-covered ridge, and descended into a bay about half the size of Sadie Cove. From the air, the sixteen boats looked like toys. We passed over the boom-protected salmon streams at the head of the bay and a crew of thirty men working on one of many oil-fouled beaches. When we landed, Rich from the *Malamute Kid* skiffed over to pick me up. Before flying off, John reminded me to call in my nightly report to Pearl Island, and Rich and I powered out to meet the rest of the boom team. Like Rich, Larry with the *Modona* and Bob on the *Murlett* were fishermen from Homer.

"Our first priority is safety," I said after giving the crews an update on the cleanup plans. "You already know the hazards of working on the water, but don't underestimate the risks of handling oil. The salmon streams are protected by the booms you set up, so when more floating crude reaches this area we'll all concentrate on skimming it off the water. Since it won't take all three of your boats to maintain the booms, you'll also help clean the beaches."

"We don't have to tell you how worried we are about how this spill could affect our lives," said Rich. "We'll do anything to get it cleaned up."

The boom boats took off to inspect the streams, and Rich skiffed me over to meet the beach crew. On the way in, he said, "Keith, we're all glad they put someone local in charge of Windy Bay."

Pat Norman, the VECO beach foreman, met me on the shore. He and his men were all from the nearby native villages of Port Graham, English Bay, and Port Chatham, and they had arrived a week earlier on their fishing boats.

Pat introduced me to the oil-smeared group. "I'm the Exxon field supervisor for Windy Bay, but I live in Sadie Cove, not Houston, Texas," I began.

Before I could continue, one of the men asked, "Can we get some gloves and those white paper suits I saw in Homer?"

"For the last month I've been working on Prince William Sound. During the first days of the spill we were also short on supplies," I answered. "Now we're on the front lines, and it will take a while for the equipment we need to get here. We'll have to do the best we can with what we have."

Pat mentioned that we were just about out of the plastic bags used to carry out the oil, and I made a note to tell Pearl Island. If we ran out of plastic bags, it would shut down the job.

"Why can't we bring in heavy equipment to pick up this mess?" asked a worker sitting on an oily rock. "These shovels are too slow. We work all day on this small beach, and after the tide comes in, we have to start all over again."

"Right now we're doing phase-one cleanup, which means collecting only heavy concentrations of oil," I replied. "I understand Exxon is trying to get permits to use equipment, but for now all oil removal on the beaches will be nonmechanical."

"You can't tell us how to clean up this bay. This is our land!" shouted one of the men.

I took a deep breath and said, "I know this is your land, but these orders cover the whole spill and are agreed upon by a committee made up of state, federal, and Exxon personnel. If you or I don't follow them, we'll be replaced by someone who will. I don't understand or agree with all the orders they give me, but my priority is to clean up this damn oil, and that is what we are going to do."

"Can we eat the clams and mussels around here?" asked another worker.

"All the seafood in this area will be tested for hydrocarbons, but for now don't eat anything out of this bay," I answered. "A supply boat is due in tomorrow with food and fuel."

My response caused more complaints, and I didn't blame them. They, like myself, took much of what they ate out of the sea, and now that source of food was in jeopardy.

Pat sent the crew back to shoveling oil and then joined me as I walked over to inspect the boom on the nearby stream. As we waded along the smelly, black beach, he said, "It's good you're here. We need someone in charge. Every day, four or five helicopters land, and the guys who arrive on them all give us different orders. Most of the time I don't even know who they are. It causes a lot of confusion."

"I'll solve that problem right now," I replied. "From now on, all your orders come through me."

At the stream, Pat and I watched hundreds of salmon fry swim out under the oil-stained boom. When he skiffed me out to the tug and barge anchored in the bay, I asked him to call me later with the number of bags of oil his crew collected that day so that I could call in the information to Pearl Island.

The tug, *Uncle Sam*, was tied to a rusty barge loaded with eight large garbage dumpsters. While the captain gave me a tour of his operation, a skiff loaded with bags of oil came alongside, and the crew threw their cargo into the dumpsters. He told me that it would take two weeks to fill the barge. While checking over his supplies, I saw several barrels of liquid detergent and asked him to set up a cleaning station so that all the crews could clean up after work.

As we stood on deck, the landing craft *Rama Lee* tied up to our barge with a load of boom, plastic bags, and other much needed supplies from Homer. While we unloaded, two more fishing vessels steamed into Windy Bay. The *Endeavor* and *Peggy J* each brought three skiffs and their operators. Dick, a boat-building neighbor of mine from Dunnings Lagoon in Kachemak Bay, was one of those on board, and I informed him that he and his boat, *Flying Fish,* were now my command skiff.

When the boom boats returned, Rich invited me to stay on the *Malamute Kid.* As we ate dinner the wind began blowing from the southeast, and by the time I called Pearl Island, whitecaps covered the bay. I gave John my report, requested a long list of supplies, and asked more than a few questions. "How's your weather?" he asked when I finished.

"The wind and waves are building," I answered. "The tug and barge plus three fishing boats are staying here, and the rest of us are pulling anchor and heading for a more protected moorage."

"Now you know why they call it Windy Bay," John replied.

In the fading light, we had a 5-mile roller-coaster ride through Rocky Bay to the calm waters of Picnic Harbor.

During the night the storm blew itself out, and early the next morning we started back to Windy Bay. Halfway through Rocky Bay we ran into a huge patch of floating oil. I called Pearl Island on the marine radio, but Bubba answered from his helicopter. "John and I are flying three miles south of your position. That slick you just encountered was blown in by last night's storm and extends five miles out into the gulf. We've notified Homer, and more boats are on the way. With this calm weather you'll be able to skim it off the water before it gets to the beaches."

I called all the boats in my task force and told them to meet us at the entrance of Windy Bay with all the extra boom they could carry. It took a little more than an hour to establish our skimming operation. Each team of two boats slowly towed a 300-foot section of boom through the spill. This technique funneled the oil to the back, where it could be collected by a skiff. The fishing boats worked the open water while our skiffs maneuvered closer to shore.

Our method of collection worked well, but we had trouble getting the oil out of the water. We tried everything from fishing nets to buckets, but finally resorted to hauling it aboard the skiffs by hand. The *Malamute Kid* and *Modona* had trapped a mass of oiled seaweed, tar balls, and mousse, and their skiff man, John, was working alone to haul it into his boat. I put on rain gear and gloves and jumped down to help. When we finished, John, the skiff, and I were covered with black slime, and I had a big glob of the goo in my eye. When I could see again, I added a case of goggles to my supply list.

Boats built specifically for skimming oil hadn't arrived in our area, so the fishing boats had to do the job. Others had had our problem of hauling oil out of the water, and they had invented a tight-meshed dip net. Several of these new spill tools were made in Seldovia and flown out to us in the field. A helicopter dropped them on a nearby island, and I skiffed over to pick them up.

The oil-covered rocks made me concentrate on each step. A frantic, high-pitched scream startled me when I reached the pile of nets. Twenty feet away, an otter struggled to stay afloat as she swam on her back through a heavy concentration of oil—a dead pup clutched to her chest. As I watched, she made one last feeble effort to break free and sank. Two more casualties of the spill would never be counted.

At midday, the 80-foot tender *Westward* joined our skimming operation. Its captain, Jim Simpson, powered up to each of our boom-towing boats and used a large fish pump to suck the crude into his hold. For several hours our system worked well, but then the wind came up and made it impossible to keep the oil in the booms. What we missed blew onto the beaches of Rocky Bay.

It was now almost seven weeks since the *Exxon Valdez* had run aground on Bligh Reef, more than 200 miles northeast of Windy Bay, and my tenth day on the gulf coast. The floating oil had either washed up on beaches or moved past our area. With no more skimming and only one fishing boat needed for boom patrol, crews from the *Malamute Kid, Modona,* and *Endeavor* had a new job. Exxon command called them the fast-response team, and their job involved flying by helicopter to clean up heavily contaminated beaches unreachable by boat.

One morning I skiffed six members of the team to the chopper pad. "How's it going at Rocky Point?" I asked Larry, the captain of the *Modona.*

"It's the worst I've seen," he answered. "The oil's so deep it goes over the tops of our rubber boots. We're shoveling pure crude and could work that beach for two more weeks, but this is our last day. Tomorrow's the deadline set by state biologists to be off all areas where seals have their pups. If we were still cleaning up that beach, maybe the seals would go somewhere else to give birth. But what do I know!"

Later that day, I skiffed over to see the beach crew in Windy Bay. It was hot, with not a whisper of wind, and the strong stench of oil fumes made me wrinkle my nose. Pat, the foreman, nodded toward several workers sitting on the beach and said, "They don't feel so good."

"How many of you are sick?" I asked.

The eleven men who raised their hands said they were dizzy, light-headed, and most of them felt nauseous. "This job is shut down," I shouted so everyone could hear me. "I want everyone off this beach—right now! Go to your boats, where there's fresh air."

I called Pearl Island, explained my situation, and was told to stand by. A few minutes later, the fast-response team returned from bagging oil at Rocky Point. "It's hotter than hell out there," Larry said as I met them on the beach. "Some of us got too much sun. I feel like shit!"

Pearl Island called back, and John said, "Bubba and I are flying to the medical boat in Port Chatham to pick up an EMT and will be in Windy Bay within a half-hour. We're going to evacuate anyone who's still sick, so get them assembled at the chopper pad."

After calling all the boats, eleven men joined me to wait for the helicopter. When it landed, John took me off to the side while Bubba and the EMT spoke with the men. "You did the right thing stopping the work," he said in a concerned voice. "It's too late to fly everyone who's sick to Homer, so we're transporting them to a medical boat six miles away in Port Chatham for examination and treatment."

As the first five boarded the chopper, John asked, "Were any of the fast-response team sick?"

I called the *Endeavor*, and whoever answered said all the men were okay. I knew fishermen were proud and independent and were hardened to pain and suffering, but this situation was different. I called back and said, "Listen up! The medic just reminded me of the facts. Today, the conditions were perfect for the release of hydrocarbons from the oil. Benzene, toluene, xylene, and hydrogen sulfide are toxic, and overexposure to these poisons can increase your risk of leukemia, pneumonia, or heart attack. If you feel the slightest bit sick, get your butt to the beach."

They got the essence of my communication—Larry and three other men came ashore.

The next morning an industrial hygienist flew to Windy Bay with testing equipment and a case of respirators. In the afternoon, all those who had been evacuated returned to work, and we held a long safety meeting. That night the command center on Pearl Island called to say a medical boat was on its way from Homer and would be permanently assigned to our area.

Every day new boats came to join our small fleet. Among the vessels sent out to collect wildlife victims of the spill was the *Kittywake II*, skippered by my friend John Rogers. When they dropped anchor in Windy Bay, I visited the grim-faced crew. "In the past two days we've recovered 170 dead birds: mostly ducks, a surprising number of loons, and one eagle," John said as he handed me a cup of coffee. "The few we caught alive were flown to the Homer animal hospital for treatment."

"Did you find any sea otters?" I asked.

"Yes, we did, but we turned them over to an otter boat," John answered. "Darn depressing work, but we haven't seen the worst of it. Drew and his crew found almost 700 birds on the beach at Gore Point. They built a fire out of oiled beach logs and videoed each bird as they threw it on the funeral pyre. He was fired when they got back to town."

"What the hell for?" I asked.

"Because we're supposed to bring them in for analysis," he answered.

"Like it's hard figuring out what killed them," blurted out one of his crew.

"Drew was rehired after he showed them the video and proved he did his job by getting them out of the food chain," John continued. "Other animals, like eagle, bear, and coyote, feed on the oily carcasses and then they're also contaminated."

Most of the birds in Windy Bay were dead, but five miles away there existed a sanctuary. The unpolluted waters of the Rocky River flowed into a tidal marsh before emptying into the sea through a narrow channel. The boom boat *Starisky Star*, with Doug and his crew, had the near impossible job of keeping the oil out. I inspected their area on an incoming tide and watched as strong currents broke the three booms they had stretched across the entrance to the flats. They couldn't make repairs until slack tide, so we took a skiff into the quiet waters of the marsh and found it alive with many hundreds of different waterfowl, including a flock of Canadian geese. "This oasis isn't safe even though we don't have much oil on the water," I said to Doug as we toured the refuge. "The next storm may refloat the crude off fouled beaches, and it could be sucked into this marsh if you can't find a way to keep the boom in place."

"I think we can solve the problem by using metal cable instead of line to hold the boom," Doug came back. "Don't worry, Keith, we'll figure it out. I plan on bringing my kids to this area for silver salmon fishing next summer."

Doug and his crew fished the outer coast in the summers and were welders in Homer during the winter. If anyone could save the Rocky River sanctuary, they could.

Back in Windy Bay, the tug *San Carlos* came in with an empty barge. As the captain and I watched the *Uncle Sam* head for Homer with a full cargo, I asked, "Do you know what happens to the oiled waste we collect from the beaches?"

"It depends on what kind of oiled material you pick up," he answered. "The crude skimmed off the water is recycled, oil mixed with seaweed and wood is burned in incinerators in Valdez, and oiled gravel is shipped to toxic-waste dumps in Oregon and Washington. Someone should invent a machine to separate oil from gravel so that we wouldn't have to ship our beaches to the Lower 48."

As we continued talking, I received a call on my hand-held radio to prepare the barge for a helicopter drop. Exxon had rented a huge chopper—rumored to cost $4,000 an hour—to haul out the bags of oil collected by the fast-response team at Rocky Point. Everyone in Windy Bay watched as the jumbo helicopter hovered over an empty garbage dumpster and released the contents of its dangling cargo net. In five trips, not one bag landed outside the bins.

Never before had Windy Bay seen so much activity. Our small armada included fishing boats to house the beach and boom crews, medics, and DEC and Coast Guard overseers; a tug and barge; critter-collection vessels; a scow with shower and laundry facilities; and a boat to clean the boats. Skiffs zipped from ship to shore while tenders, helicopters, and floatplanes brought in people and supplies.

Everything was running smoothly when Pearl Island called to say Exxon had plans to reorganize the fleet. During the first hectic days of the spill on the gulf coast, local fishing boats were contracted to fight the oil. They filled an important need and did a great job, but now bigger ships were being hired to house the crews and store supplies. Exxon told me to cancel the contracts with the Port Graham fishing boats as soon as the floating hotel arrived in Windy Bay.

The next morning, I watched the expected 80-foot *Widgeon II* tow the 100-foot housing vessel *Marin I* past the entrance to Windy Bay and head for Picnic Harbor. This wasn't part of the plan, so I radioed the change to command headquarters and skiffed over to talk to the captain.

Will met me on the *Widgeon's* deck, and I said, "I understood you were coming to Windy Bay. Why the change?"

"It's unsafe," he answered. "The *Marin* has no power, so if I anchor in Windy and a storm blows in from the southeast, I'm going to have one hell of a time towing it to a safe moorage. It wouldn't be safe for my boats or our crews. Better to stay in Picnic Harbor and skiff your workers the five miles to the beaches."

He had fished these waters for many years, and I agreed with his reasoning. However, when Bubba arrived by chopper, he canceled the *Widgeon's* contract for not following orders. After the helicopter left, I went to the bridge to talk to Will. "The *Marin* is still on contract, and it's ready to house a beach crew," he said. "I'll stand by until another escort vessel takes my place. Whoever they get, I hope they aren't stupid enough to take her to Windy. Your bosses have no idea how dangerous these waters are." He paused, slammed his fist on the desk, and barked, "Damn, Keith! We should take over this spill cleanup."

I thought for a minute and answered, "Will, we couldn't do it. I don't like working for the company who created the spill any more than you do, but even though we're the ones with the boats and muscle to get this mess cleaned up, we don't have the organization and money to get the job done."

The *Widgeon* and *Marin* remained anchored in Picnic Harbor, and I returned to Windy Bay, where two days later, the *Optimus Prime*, a 185-foot catcher/processor, arrived as our new housing vessel. I told the Port Graham fishing boats to return to their home port and went on board to meet the captain. Tabb gave me a tour of his ship, assigned me a room, and took me up to the large, modern bridge to meet Rex, the VECO field supervisor for our area. As we inspected the ship's computer, Fax machine, $10-per-minute satellite telephone, and a variety of radios, Rex said, "VECO has hired two new beach crews, so it's going to get real busy out here."

The next morning we were invaded by the three task forces assigned to our area. Helicopters flew in an all-woman replacement crew from Port Graham to work the beaches in Windy Bay while living aboard the *Optimus Prime*. Two large charter boats steamed into Picnic Harbor from Homer and unloaded the Rocky Bay team on the *Marin*. A small convoy of fishing vessels arrived from Seldovia with the Chugach Bay task force. Since this team would work more exposed beaches, they lived on their boats wherever they could find a safe moorage. The cleanup effort on the gulf coast had finally shifted into high gear.

Seventy beach workers bagging oil created a production problem. However, instead of shutting down the job because of a full barge, DEC gave us permission to set up beach storage pits. We worked together locating suitable areas above the high-tide line and built them to DEC specifications. The temporary shore caches also made it safer to skiff the 50-pound bags to the barge—now we could wait for calm weather.

Dealing with oil wasn't our only waste problem. DEC and the Coast Guard sent out a bulletin stating they would fine anyone caught pissing on the beach, so the workers had to go to their boats to relieve themselves. This inconvenience was eliminated when a landing craft chugged in with plastic, portable outhouses. We located the Rent-A-Cans on shore, much to the relief of the crews, and they would be serviced, hopefully on a regular basis, by a honey-bucket boat from Homer.

Our cleanup was running smoothly when the marine weather forecast announced a storm warning for our area. I didn't have to alert the boats to the danger of 50-knot easterly winds and 25-foot seas; they were already pulling anchor and heading for the protected waters of Picnic Harbor. As the heavy chain clanked aboard the *Optimus Prime*, the captain told me he wanted more sea room, so our destination was Port Dick, fifteen nautical miles east. To get there, we would be traveling through open water into the teeth of the oncoming storm. As our bow cut through the white, crested waves, and the wind whistled around our bridge, I thought of Will and was glad we had the power to get out of harm's way.

We sat in Tacoma Cove, tucked behind Gore Point, and although we were only a half-mile from land, the offshore, 90-mile-an-hour gusts caused us to drag anchor. The forty-eight boats seeking refuge in Picnic Harbor had the same problem. They, like us, were safe from the angry seas, but the williwaws screaming down the mountain spun them around and threatened their crowded moorage.

After two days of catching up on sleep, watching video movies, playing cribbage, and reading, the storm blew itself out, and we rode a moderate swell back to the black beaches of Windy Bay.

Upon our return, it didn't take long for trouble to find me. I'd just sat down to lunch when Bryson, of DEC, came into the galley and said, "I want to talk to you on the bridge. Right now!"

I took a deep breath, pushed back my plate, and led the way up the two flights of stairs. Bryson pulled out a tape recorder, turned it on, and said, "I'm citing you for oil-spill violations, and anything you say can and will be used against you."

After taking another deep breath, I reminded myself this was part of my job. When I didn't say anything, he continued. "We just found several bags of oil floating in the water, and one of the portable toilets blew over. You have fifteen days to answer these charges."

Instead of saying what I had on my mind, I replied, "I'll respond right now. For the record, these violations were caused by the storm we just went through. We overlooked a few details because we were in a hurry to get our boats and crews to a safe moorage."

Bryson turned off the recorder and said, "Keith, I know as an Alaskan you are out here to clean up the oil, but these tickets will force Exxon to give you better support."

"Then give me all the citations you want," I said.

When I started the nightly meeting on the *Optimus Prime*, my mind felt like a bowl of cold oatmeal. After drinking a cup of strong coffee, I walked into the crowded, smoky room and reintroduced the different members of our cleanup teams. Among them were the newly arrived bear monitors. These trained men would patrol the beaches, armed with Mace and foghorns, to protect our crews.

Next, I asked each of the three VECO task-force bosses to give me their daily production reports. After they read off their bag counts, Randy from the Rocky Bay team said, "Today we had three different helicopters land on the beach we were working, and each group gave us different orders on what we could and couldn't do. We need an Exxon boss in the field to eliminate this hassle."

"Those same choppers landed on my beach," added Roy from the Chugach Bay team. "Keith, you're the field supervisor for the Windy Bay crew, but why can't you also be in charge of our teams?"

"I'll talk to Pearl Island," I answered.

"This afternoon, I received the following instructions from Exxon command in Homer," I continued. "Anyone caught with drugs, alcohol, or firearms will be immediately terminated."

A boat captain said, "I understand the reasoning behind the first two, but why no guns? Every fisherman I know carries a rifle on board."

"I don't know why, but if you've got 'em, get rid of 'em," I answered. "I won't start inspecting boats for two days, so you can fly them out on a floatplane charter."

"Now, if you didn't like that bulletin, you're going to love this next set of orders," I continued. "No more digging oily gravel from the beaches, and you're not allowed to use those chainsaws you received last week."

"What the hell is going on?" Roy blurted. "They change that gravel-digging order every two days, and why did they give us chainsaws but not let us use them?"

"All I know is that it's our job to clean up the oil," I answered. "So this is how I read today's instructions. Scoop, don't dig, the oily gravel. If oily logs or limbs create a danger to your crews, use the chainsaws to eliminate the hazard."

Tabb, captain of the *Optimus Prime*, changed the subject by informing everyone that his ship would begin rationing water since the supply tender wouldn't arrive for three more days. Although the *Optimus Prime* could make fresh water from salt water, Tabb chose not to because of the oil in the bay. A fisherman told Tabb he had been drinking from Windy Bay streams for as long as he could remember, and why didn't he run a hose to shore and fill his tanks. This idea was immediately rejected by DEC because of the possibility of people getting beaver fever from the untreated water.

The next to speak was Dale, captain of the landing barge *Bradley River*. "My boat is full of oily waste, and Homer has a three day waiting line to be unloaded. We'll stay here if you give us a beach to clean."

"Great!" I replied. "Tomorrow you can start on Black Lagoon."

"Where the hell is that?" Dale asked as he looked at the nautical map hung on the wall.

"You won't find it on any of the local charts, because it's an oil-spill name," I answered. "Black Lagoon is only a mile west of Grungy Cove."

At the end of each meeting I tried to dispel the rumors that added to our organized chaos. We found white particles floating in the water, and some said they were from the dispersants Exxon was dropping on the oil. We took samples and sent them to be tested. On hearing that Clint Eastwood was flying out to inspect our cleanup effort, I laughed while the women in Windy Bay tried to comb the oil out of their hair. I didn't laugh when a chopper pilot told me he saw a giant oil slick entering Sadie Cove.

The meeting ended three hours after it began, and I went up to the bridge to call in my report. While talking to Pearl Island, I volunteered to take charge of the other two task forces until they could get more Exxon field supervisors to our area. When they said, "Go for it," I took command of fifty boats and 150 oil-spill workers.

Later in the week, the captain of a supply boat told me about a deck-loaded, vacuum truck that was sitting idle in Port Dick. I had heard the suction trucks were originally designed for oil spills on land, so I called Pearl Island and asked if the unused rig could be sent to Windy Bay to help clean our beaches. The next morning, the 60-foot fishing vessel *Tarisa Marie* arrived with a 25-foot truck parked on its aft deck.

When I went on board, the captain explained why they were so glad to have come. "We have a $50,000-per-month contract, but so far we haven't sucked up one drop of oil. After four weeks on the water, we are all dying a slow death from the boredom. Glad you can put us to work."

I described my plan. "Several oiled beaches on Windy are next to deep water, and maybe we can combine our operations and do some good."

After I showed them the beaches, the truck operator said, "No problem. All we need is 100 feet of 6-inch hose, two skiffs to stretch it to shore, and we can suck those beaches clean. This super-sucker can pick up a cement block at full power."

Everyone was excited about the plan except Pearl Island. When I called to order the hose, they said no to my idea because we were in the nonmechanical phase of the cleanup. Even after explaining the procedure and pointing out that the truck would never set a tire on the beach, they still shot down my proposal.

Exxon command on Pearl Island were only following orders passed down to them. Out in the field, we were trying to clean up an 11-million-gallon oil spill with orders that tied our hands behind our backs. I wanted to ask what incompetent desk jockeys were making the decisions, but I didn't.

John Wolfe and I worked for VRCA, so we received no scheduled time off, but all Exxon personnel worked three weeks on and three weeks off. Out in the field, Leon replaced Bubba, and then John Webb took charge of all seven task forces operating on the outer gulf coast.

I liked this big, friendly man from Texas. Webb passed on the orders he received from his bosses, but he also cared about what the oil had done to our state. He didn't play power and control games, wasn't afraid to get his feet wet, and was generally liked by the men in the field. When his time came to rotate out, he said, "You're going to be real happy to see me back."

I didn't know what he meant until I met his replacement, Aubrey, better known as Brownie. He was very effective at getting the job done, but his method of operation reinforced why I had worked for myself for the past seventeen years. The first time I met the new fleet commander, he said, "I know you live in this area; but to work for me, I want you biased Exxon, not biased Alaska. Can you do that?"

Exxon couldn't buy my loyalty with their big bucks, but if I told the truth I would no longer be working on the spill. My job as an Exxon field supervisor put me in a unique position: I could clean up more oil than their imported supervisors from the Lower 48 by bending my orders. I still had to cover my ass to keep my job, but I didn't have a career and retirement program to protect. I looked the fleet commander straight in the eye and said, "I can do that."

Toward the end of May, I and the other Exxon field supervisors were helicoptered into town for a meeting at Homer command. After a pep talk by the regional boss and a discussion of power struggles with DEC, the Coast Guard, VECO, and the local Multiple Agency Committee (MAC), we got down to the real reason for our gathering. Exxon was paying $450,000 per day for oil-spill boats contracted out of Homer. To lower this expense, each field supervisor was ordered to cut three boats a day until that figure dropped to $150,000 per day. Locally, we had been fighting the spill for only one month, and already they were cutting back on the cleanup effort.

Before closing the meeting, one of the Homer bosses looked at me and said, "Morale in Windy Bay must be pretty good. Yesterday we flew over your area and fifty workers were lined up on the beach doing the can-can."

"Actually, morale isn't good," I answered. "The beach workers have the hardest job on this spill. Seven days a week, twelve hours a day, in all kinds of weather, they dig, scrape, and wipe oil, and after work they're confined aboard crowded boats. We've got orders not to let them ashore during their time off, but why don't we give each crew a barbecue on one of the clean beaches?"

The Homer bosses said they would consider the idea.

After the meeting, the regional director called me into his office and informed me that although I was doing a good job, Exxon had a policy of having only their own personnel as field supervisors. I would be replaced when they could bring in someone from one of their offices in the Lower 48.

May spilled into June, and I continued cutting boats according to my orders. While trying to decide between firing a medical charter or a supply ship, John Wolfe called to inform me that Exxon was closing down Pearl Island and moving the field command center to the *Optimus Prime* on Windy Bay. Exxon was sending him to the Homer office to consult on the Cook Inlet cleanup and moving me to Picnic Harbor, where I would continue supervising the Rocky Bay and Chugach Bay crews. After signing off, I let out a big sigh of relief—I still had my job.

On my last night aboard the *Optimus Prime,* I started the nightly meeting by turning the Windy Bay crew over to Tiny, an Exxon supervisor from Louisiana. After calling in my report, I asked for and received three days off before moving to Picnic Harbor. I'd been out on the gulf coast for thirty-five days with only one day off, when I'd flown into Homer to have a painful tooth pulled.

The next morning, I packed my gear and went up to the bridge to say good-bye. "Don't destroy Homer on your time off," joked Tiny.

I laughed and said, "I'm not going to town. The chopper's dropping me off in Sadie Cove—I haven't been home since the first day of the spill."

Picnic Harbor's Burn Team

I expected the worst on the fifteen-minute helicopter ride from the oil-soaked beaches of the Gulf of Alaska to my home in Sadie Cove. Several pilots flying out from Homer had told me they'd seen what looked like large slicks entering my cove, so I figured my three days off would be spent cleaning up my beach with supplies I'd brought from the *Optimus Prime*.

The chopper dropped me off in front of my home, and I ran down the beach looking for oil. The only thing I found was one small tar ball, and as I sat on the clean gravel, a flood of relief washed over me. I glanced up and saw a mountain goat on a nearby cliff with her week-old kid peeking out from under her legs. The joy in me grew as I fought to hold back the tears. When a loon sent its lonely call across the water, I started laughing and crying at the same time. So far, Sadie Cove had been saved from the spill.

At that time, Slim and Brunhilda, his wife of two years, were the only neighbors in Sadie, and they had been busy building log booms to protect their shoreline. During a visit, Slim solved the mystery of the pilots' reports of oil in the cove—the rust-colored spruce pollen looked a lot like oil when it settled on the water.

My other neighbors, John and Nancy Hillstrand, were both gone. Nancy ran the otter recovery center for the Homer area, and John, a commercial fisherman, waited in Homer for state officials to open the salmon season. A policy of zero tolerance closed all fishing in any area polluted by oil. So far, no harvesting of salmon had been allowed in lower Cook Inlet or along the outer gulf coast.

I hiked in the mountains and took long saunas, but my thoughts kept returning to the black beaches. Even in sleep I couldn't escape the spill—I kept having nightmares about drowning in a sea of oil. After three days at home, I was ready to get back to work and finish the job.

Jim Simpson, captain of the *Westward*, picked me up in his skiff after my helicopter ride to Picnic Harbor. During the short ride to his boat, Jim said, "The *Marin* doesn't have any empty beds, so my deckhands built you a bunk in a vacant, walk-in, bait freezer in the bow of my boat. You'll have the quietest, best-insulated room in the fleet."

When we stepped on board I wrinkled my nose at the strong smell. Jim noticed my reaction and said, "All my fish holds are full of oily waste."

"You mean you're still full of the oil you sucked out of our skimming booms more than a month ago?" I asked in amazement.

"That and several tons of contaminated beach gravel," he answered. "Until they figure out a safe way to unload my ship, I'm contracted to stand by the *Marin* as her tow boat."

When the crews finished work, the two VECO supervisors and I took a boat to Windy Bay for our nightly meeting on the *Optimus Prime*. Brownie started off by announcing that all Exxon field supervisors must stay on the beach with their crews. I pointed out that I had two crews and couldn't be in both places simultaneously. The fleet commander told me not to worry about it—the Chugach Bay task force was leaving the next day for Cook Inlet to dip-net tar balls in the tide rips. I didn't mind losing one of my teams, but if Exxon continued taking workers off the beaches, we'd never get the oil cleaned up before winter.

After the meeting, Brownie told me to cancel the contracts for all the boats in my Rocky Bay task force except for the four skiffs we needed to take the crew to the beaches. We had three 30-foot fishing vessels and thirteen skiffs to take care of our thirty-worker beach crew. I agreed with terminating most of the skiffs, especially those on $1,200-per-day contracts, but fought to keep the bigger fishing boats. During my verbal battle with the fleet commander, Brownie asked if I was biased Alaska and I knew my job was on the line. I wanted to tell him that he and his bosses in Homer had no idea what kind of boats we needed to do the job. They flew around in helicopters that landed on the beaches instead of skiffing through the surf, and they could escape a fast-moving storm instead of running through heavy seas. I also wanted to say Exxon's plan to cut down operating costs was creating big problems in the field. Instead, I said, "I'm biased about the safety of my crew. We need bigger fishing boats to transport the workers to the outer beaches and skiffs to get them to shore. If we do it all with skiffs, someone will get hurt or killed!"

In the end, I kept two fishing boats and four skiffs.

My new command skiff, *Chenik*, was operated by my best friend, Kevin Sidelinger. He came to Picnic Harbor after he'd blown an outboard motor while skimming oil up the coast, and he wasn't the only one with this problem. We were blowing up a skiff motor every two weeks, and no one could figure out the reason for the high mortality rate until we received the test results for the water sample we sent in during our first days in Windy Bay. The white specks we had found in the salt water weren't dispersants, as we had feared, but paraffin from the North Slope crude spilled in Prince William Sound. Paraffin, a natural component of petroleum, was clogging up the outboards' cooling systems, so they overheated and blew up. We solved the problem by regularly flushing the motors with the steam cleaner we used to clean the crews coming off the beaches.

The Rocky Bay task force spent most of its time working on Grungy and Badger coves. Both presented their own problems; both were the heaviest-oiled beaches in our area.

Grungy Cove, about the size of a football field, would have been the perfect location to study the different effects of oil on a beach. It had everything: oily sand, gravel, and rocks; a small stream with salmon fry; an archaeological site; oiled seaweed and logs; mousse, tar balls, and puddles of oil on the surface; and oil soaked two feet into the beach. Because of its narrow entrance and somewhat protected location, we could contain the oil with booms and work it in all but the worst weather.

No such luck with Badger Cove. Its four beaches faced south, and except for Chugach Island four miles off the coast, the sea was unbroken from the cove all the way to Antarctica. Any winds or swells from the south or east made it impossible to go ashore, so Badger became our priority beach during calm weather. To determine which area we'd work the next day, every night at six o'clock we tuned in 4 megahertz on our single-side-band radio to listen to Peggy Dyson give her marine weather forecast from Kodiak. She talked to boats all along the gulf coast and broadcast local conditions as well as general weather patterns. No one knows how many lives Peggy has saved through her accurate forecasting, but I do know she saved our butts more than once.

The wreck of the *Kathy Joanne* reminded us of what could happen if we didn't watch the weather. A storm washed the fishing boat ashore at Badger Cove, and waves ripped the 70-foot steel hull in half. The boat's motor, transmission, and drive shaft were scattered among the rocks, and the pilot house was so crammed full of driftwood my crew couldn't have done a better job.

When John Wolfe and I landed on the Badger beaches in early May, oil covered the shore. When we started cleaning it up in mid-June, most of it was buried under two to three feet of gravel. We were permitted to remove only heavily oiled gravel, so my crew became oil miners and scooped out the veins of black goo with their hands. After weeks of work, most of the heavy concentrations were removed from the upper beaches. Then one day during a very low tide, we struck it rich. Where the gravel met bedrock, we found a layer of oil 6 to 12 inches deep, 20 feet wide, and 700 feet long. We were going to be on Badger Cove beaches for a long, long time.

During the last week of June, the winds died and temperatures rose as we worked Badger Cove. The mornings were cool and tolerable, but by lunch time the oil-slicked beaches shimmered in 90°F heat. To make matters worse, Exxon and VECO required everyone to wear hard hats, rubber boots and gloves, and a protective full-body Tyvec suit. Add goggles and a respirator, and each worker had his or her own sauna.

Mark, our medic, cautioned me about heat stroke, and his warning gave me an idea. I called a safety meeting on a clean stretch of beach just before the crew took their lunch break. Mark talked about how to prevent getting sick from the heat while I had two of our skiffs drop anchor fifty feet off shore. "What's the number-one way to stop heat stroke?" I asked.

"Cool the body with lots of water," Mark answered.

"Okay!" I said with a smile. "For the safety of this crew, we're all going swimming."

I waited for the cheering to die down before continuing. "Please don't take advantage of the situation—no nudity or marathon swimming."

With skiffs off the beach and an EMT on shore, I figured I'd covered my ass if a chopper full of VIPs flew over our location. One of the crew had a video camera, and he filmed the human wave of thirty workers as they ran screaming into the water. Even Charlett, our Coast Guard monitor, took a frigid dip. Like everyone else who went swimming, after diving in, she screamed and scrambled back to the beach. Later that day, I thought I saw some smiling eyes peeking out from behind the crew's respirators.

In mid-July, the *Optimus Prime* called to tell me a new Exxon field supervisor had arrived from Texas, and they wanted him to work with me for a few days before he took over command of the Chugach Bay task force, which had just returned from Cook Inlet. Frank seemed eager to learn but had no experience on the sea. The next morning, after listening to the marine weather forecast, I called the *Optimus Prime* and said our crews wouldn't be going out until the ocean swells came down. Frank glanced out a porthole on the *Marin*, observed the still waters of our protected moorage in Picnic Harbor, and said, "It looks calm to me."

"Why don't you and Frank take a skiff and see what the waves are doing out in Rocky Bay," I said to Randy, the VECO beach supervisor.

As they sped out toward open water, I chuckled to myself, knowing what would happen. Randy and I had gone out to check the weather several times in the past. He was a commercial fisherman in Cook Inlet and only knew one speed—full out fast. On leaving Picnic Harbor, the swells would slowly build until the flat-bottom skiff came clear out of the water before slamming into the next wave with tongue-biting, bone-jarring force. Randy said he wanted his passengers to ride in the bow to spread out the weight, but I think he just liked to watch them squirm. It took all your strength to hold on and not get thrown out of the skiff, and Randy would keep the throttle wide open until you screamed, "Enough!"

They returned ten minutes later with Randy wearing a shit-eating grin and Frank a little shaky in the knees. As they took off their dripping rain gear, the new Exxon field supervisor said, "I see what you mean."

I could have explained the reason we weren't going out to work, but by giving Frank a big water baptism, maybe he would realize how little he knew about our Alaskan waters and listen to the fishing-boat captains in his new task force.

At our next meeting on the *Optimus Prime*, I met Willard, Tiny's replacement for the Windy Bay crew. After getting my day's bag count, he said, "Keith, Exxon has just received a state permit for a test burn of oiled logs in Grungy Cove. Your crew will be in charge of the fire, and if everything goes well, we'll be able to burn on the beaches from Prince William Sound to Kodiak Island. The spill contaminated millions of pounds of logs, so this trial burn is very important."

Willard handed me five pages of permit regulations and continued. "You have only one day to get everything ready, but Ignacio from Homer command said he would make sure you have all the equipment you need to comply with the permit rules."

Early the next morning I took my crew to Grungy Cove to pick the best fire site, bring over a Rent-A-Can, cut clean and oiled wood, and split dry kindling to begin the blaze. About noon, a skiff pulled up with an assortment of used equipment. We set up the rusty fire-fighting pumps for a test run and found they didn't work. I called Marina, the radio operator on the *Optimus Prime*, and said, "Call Ignacio in Homer and tell him the Viking is hot. If he doesn't send me the gear he promised, there won't be a test burn tomorrow."

Four hours later a helicopter landed, and out jumped Mr. Ignacio wearing a T-shirt that read "Don't Mess with Texas." As we unloaded the equipment he started giving everyone orders on how to operate the pumps, and his arrogance started the whole crew grumbling. However, his superior attitude faded when we couldn't get the expensive gear to work because of missing parts and hose fittings that didn't match. At that point he boarded the chopper and flew off before I could ask him why the machinery hadn't been tested in town.

That night I held a meeting for my crew on the *Marin*. "Tomorrow's test is all set to go—we scavenged parts and fittings from the *Westward*, so the pumps are operating," I began. "To make sure this test burn is a success, you will take orders from only one person—me. If you're asked to do anything by the Homer Exxon office people or any member of the attending agencies, politely tell them to talk to me. Nobody outside this crew is going to screw up this burn. This test is a great opportunity to contribute to the cleanup effort. If we are successful, we can burn the oily logs on the beaches instead of shipping them to the Valdez incinerator, so let's show them the best test they've ever seen."

Very early the next morning, we skiffed to Grungy Cove, and each member of the crew took care of his or her assigned task. As the tide receded, we set out booms to contain any possible waste, retested the pumps, and checked the toilet paper supply in the plastic outhouse.

At 9:00 A.M. the helicopters started arriving, and one of my crew passed out hard hats and safety goggles to men and women from DEC, Department of Natural Resources, Fish and Game, State Parks, Exxon, VECO, the Environmental Protection Agency, and the Coast Guard. When my boss, John Webb, arrived by skiff from the *Optimus Prime*, I informed him of my instructions to the crew about taking orders only from me. He didn't reply, but his smile told me he thought it was a good idea.

After the last helicopter landed, I doused the mountain of wood with lighter fluid and lit the fire with a propane weed-burner while members of my crew started two portable, high-speed fans. As the 40-foot flames licked at the sky, a park ranger asked me if I'd taken any steps to prevent the blaze from getting out of control. I showed him three separate teams with pumps and fire hoses and then spoke into my hand-held radio—the ten men I had stationed in the woods held up their shovels and wet burlap sacks.

Thirty minutes later we started adding oiled logs. The fire gave off no black smoke, and although DEC had no instruments to measure for air pollution, they seemed pleased with the results. In four hours we burned five cords of contaminated wood and melted the sand under our test burn.

"Tell your men they did a great job," John Webb said after the last helicopter took off.

"Does that mean we'll be able to burn on other beaches?" I asked.

"That's up to the different agencies," he answered. "We'll have to wait for their decision."

With the test burn completed, we went back to cleaning beaches. My new orders from Exxon command didn't allow the removal of any oiled gravel, so we spent a lot of time polishing fouled rocks while waiting for permission to begin the mechanical cleanup.

When Brownie returned from his three weeks off, he flew all the field supervisors into Homer for a meeting. On entering the office, I met Rich and Larry from the fast-response team. They had just finished building and testing a machine to wash oiled gravel and were waiting for Exxon's approval so they could put it into operation on the beaches. I congratulated them and went off to talk to Brownie before the meeting started.

I found the fleet commander and said, "I wrote a report on the test-burn procedure, so other crews can use what we learned."

"We don't need your report," he answered.

I took a deep breath to control my anger and asked, "Is there any word on when we can start burning?"

"Not yet," he replied. "One of the agencies is questioning why there wasn't any air-pollution measuring equipment used on the test."

The meeting began with Brownie announcing that the Coast Guard and DEC had approved beaches in Windy and Tonsina bays for mechanical cleaning and that operation would begin as soon as the equipment arrived. He then handed out a confidential report containing Exxon's estimates of how many days it would take to complete mechanical cleanup for each task force. When I saw they planned to spend only six days in Rocky Bay, I raised my hand to protest, but Brownie ignored me and asked an oil-removal expert to comment on his recent inspection of the beaches. The expert said he thought the estimates were too high. When he used Rocky Bay as an example and stated it would take only two days to mechanically clean my area, I lost control and blurted, "Bullshit!"

Brownie gave me a wicked look, and I bit my tongue to keep from saying more.

The first thing I did on returning to Picnic Harbor was to contact the field supervisor for DEC. I showed him the report and said, "Exxon will stop the entire cleanup effort when the mechanical phase is completed. If they use the timetable in this report, they will be gone within a month. We both know those beaches are a long way from clean. I hope you and the other agencies are strong enough to keep them working."

Exxon's estimates on how long it would take to finish the mechanical cleanup proved to be wrong. The Windy Bay crew received used equipment and after two weeks still couldn't get their steam cleaners to work properly. In Grungy Cove, we finally received permission to start flushing our beaches, but when I asked when we could get the equipment they didn't have an answer.

One night after work I expressed my frustration to the captain of the *Westward*. "Maybe you can use the gear Exxon gave us during the first days of the spill," he replied. "We used it a few times to clean up, but I forgot we still have it on board."

Out on deck we found a high-pressure, steam-cleaning machine buried under a pile of absorbent boom. When I called the *Optimus Prime* and asked if we could use it on our beaches, they said, "Go for it." That night we tested the unit and the next morning loaded it onto a skiff for Grungy Cove.

I picked the worst part of the beach for our first trial run. We used the two high-pressure hoses from the gas-driven machine to wash the blackened gravel with 170°F steam, and then we flushed the loosened oil down the beach with a cold-water pump. The oil floated on the incoming tide, and my crew used absorbent pads to mop it up. We also strung three rows of boom around our work area to make sure none escaped. Our mechanical method sure beat hand-polishing rocks.

On August first, Gerry, a new Exxon field supervisor from Baton Rouge, Louisiana, flew into Picnic Harbor. He came to work with me before taking over my crew. It looked like my days on the oil spill would soon be over.

Gerry and I worked in Grungy Cove on my last day with the Rocky Bay task force. "You're getting a great crew," I said as we ate lunch. "Behind those oily faces are dog mushers, gold miners, loggers, fishermen, cowboys, farmers, housewives, and business people. Some are Vietnam vets, most are dedicated, and all have done one hell of a fine job cleaning up this mess."

"Their morale seems to be good," Gerry commented.

"It is," I replied. "Last week, Exxon gave everyone a day off for a barbecue. We played football and volleyball and then feasted on steaks, crab, and corn-on-the-cob. The only thing missing was a keg of beer, but everyone had a good time."

"What will you do now?" Gerry asked.

"I'll find out at tonight's meeting," I answered.

When I stepped on board the *Optimus Prime* I had mixed emotions. Part of me felt relieved that I might be fired, but another side of me would be very disappointed that I couldn't see the job through to the end. Brownie started the meeting with an announcement. "The burn permits have been okayed. Keith, you will supervise all the beach burns in our area. Tomorrow, you and your crew will leave on the *Ushagat* for Petrof Point."

I couldn't keep the smile off my face.

The next morning, Mike, the skipper of the *Ushagat*, and I had a meeting to go over details for our new assignment. He needed the whole day to get his boat supplied with food, water, and fuel, so we set 9:00 P.M. as our departure time for the five-hour trip to our first burn site. My crew of thirteen would be housed in a hastily constructed plywood shack built on the back deck of the 60-foot fishing boat. I stored my personal gear on board and went off to take care of a long list of details.

Because of a last-minute meeting I couldn't make our departure time, so I told Mike to leave without me. Another boat was going to Tonsina Bay later that night, and I could meet him there. The 90-foot luxury yacht *Scorpius* was transporting only two men. They were approaching each boat in the fleet to transfer their spill contracts from Exxon to VECO—for the purpose of saving money.

After living in a walk-in freezer for eight weeks, I found it hard getting used to the large bathrooms, wall-to-wall carpeting, and private staterooms. I talked to the captain on his spacious bridge and then went out on deck. At midnight we rounded Gore Point with a full moon shimmering overhead and sparkling moonbeams dancing on the calm sea. For a moment I thought back on how Lila and I had planned to spend our honeymoon on its beach—three years before it had been tarred by the spill and feathered by hundreds of bird carcasses. An hour later we made our rendezvous with the *Ushagat*. I rolled out my sleeping bag on a plywood bunk and went to sleep to a chorus of nine snoring men.

The next morning we skiffed into the beach at Petrof Point, where we found eleven large stacks of oiled logs and Jeff, the Kachemak Bay State Park ranger. As we started the fire, George, our bear monitor, walked into the woods to protect us from bruins and the forest from possible sparks. When the fog lifted, an army of bugs came out to keep us company while we tended the blaze.

That day eight different helicopters landed to inspect our work. Among them was a group of Exxon bosses from Homer who dressed and talked like they were attending a high-society picnic. I wanted to give them all hard hats, goggles, and gloves, stuff them into Tyvec suits, and put them to work. The experience might have dulled their superiority complex.

While my Exxon bosses were on the beach, the park ranger spent an hour talking them into allowing us to take oil-soaked logs out of a nearby stream and adding them to the fire. Why did we need their permission to clean up the contamination their company created?

That night, Larry, the crew's VECO supervisor, and I kept watch over a small mountain of red-hot coals. By morning our team had finished burning fifteen cords of oiled logs, so we boarded the *Ushagat* and headed for our next scheduled fire.

On the second day of our burn at Tonsina Bay, two helicopters landed on a raid for drugs and alcohol. Exxon sent out Alaska state troopers to make the search legal, but all they found was a bottle of whiskey and a six-pack of beer stashed in the hold of the crew ship. After confiscating several fishing knives and firing a man who refused to let them search his personal gear, they flew back to Homer without making any arrests.

During my last days at Picnic Harbor, VECO gave urine tests to their entire crew of forty-five workers, and only 5 percent tested positive.

It took ten days to complete the burn at Tonsina Bay, and as the *Ushagat* rounded Gore Point on our way back to Windy Bay, we crossed paths with the fast-response team. I called Rich on the *Malamute Kid* and asked, "How goes the battle?"

"You're now talking to the bioremediation team," he answered. "We're treating the fouled beaches with a fertilizer that's supposed to help microorganisms break down the oil."

"What happened to the gravel-washing machine?" I inquired.

"Exxon said no," Rich said. "It cleaned 400 pounds of gravel an hour, but it cost $20,000 to build, weighed four tons, and measured twenty-four feet long. It's in storage, but the concept of washing oiled gravel isn't dead. Bill Day from Homer built a portable unit, and an all-volunteer crew is using it to clean the beach at Mars Cove in Port Dick."

"I just heard of their operation," I remarked. "Exxon informed all its supervisors not to give them any help."

I signed off, and we continued on to our next burn site at Black Lagoon on Windy Bay.

As summer eased toward fall, the silver salmon returned. We watched their numbers increase until the bay was alive with jumpers. Every night, anyone who had a fishing rod was out in a skiff trying to catch one for dinner or land the monster that would win our Windy Bay derby. I could almost forget about the oily beaches with a 15-pound salmon testing the limits of my light tackle.

We finished burning at Black Lagoon, and on August 21, my crew left for our next fire at Rocky Point. I stayed behind for a short meeting on the *Optimus Prime* and then caught a ride with Kevin to join my team. The weather was clear and calm as we skiffed the seven miles to my next assignment. Kevin and I talked about our lives back in Kachemak Bay, and we both regretted not being able to go on our annual moose hunt. The oil spill had drastically disrupted many lives in Alaska, but for this year it would soon be over. Fall storms would shut down Exxon's cleanup effort on the gulf coast.

At Rocky Point we threaded our way through narrow rock passages and around floating islands of kelp before reaching a beach where my crew unloaded our equipment. Kevin headed back to Windy Bay, and I started looking for a good burn site. No one had worked this area since mid-May, when it was shut down by the state as a seal pupping site. During low tide we bagged tar balls and then cut oiled logs as the tide came in.

In the afternoon, John Webb and John Wolfe landed in their helicopter a quarter-mile down the beach from my crew. As we inspected the area, the blazing sun made the oily rocks slippery and dangerous. Soon after they took off, another chopper landed with DEC inspectors, and again I toured the beaches. By the time the DEC people flew out, the tide had come in, and moderate-size waves were crashing against the cliffs, cutting off the beach route back to my crew. While climbing the oil-slick cliff, I looked down at the white, swirling water and reminded myself to be careful. On top, instead of tracking oil through the woods, I tried to jump over a large crevice, slipped, and fell backward into the pounding surf.

The sea was a blessing and a curse—it broke my fall but then tried to drown me. I bounced off the cliff on my way down and regained consciousness twenty feet from land. While treading water, I coughed up the salt water I'd swallowed, swam back to the base of the cliff, and tried to hold on to the oily rocks. The next wave picked me up, broke my grip, and sucked me back into the sea. I tried yelling for help, but knew the crew was too far away to hear me. The only way out was up the cliff, and I would have to do it on my own.

Again and again I struggled to claw my way up, but each time the waves broke my hold. I was in the cold, salty water for what seemed hours, and I could feel my strength leaving me. The next time I reached the rock face, I jammed my upper body into a large vertical crack. The following wave didn't yank me loose, so I slowly shimmied up the rock chimney to the top. After catching my breath I started whistling. I don't know how long I lay there shivering and slipping in and out of consciousness, but finally I looked up to see good old George, the bear monitor, coming out of the woods.

George called for help, kept me still while he checked for broken bones, and asked questions to keep me talking. When the crew got to me, they carefully cut off my wet shirt and pants. I remember looking up and seeing one of the men standing there stark-ass naked; he had given me his dry clothes. An evacuation helicopter landed as they finished cutting a trail through the woods. The medic gave me a quick inspection, strapped me to a rigid board, stuck an IV needle in my arm, and helped haul me to the waiting chopper. The *Optimus Prime* had sent Kevin and his skiff with an EMT from Windy Bay. I caught a glimpse of my friend and wanted to tell him I was okay, but the oxygen mask over my mouth kept me from speaking.

I was too numb to feel much pain on the helicopter ride to the Homer hospital. When we landed, they wheeled me into the emergency room, where nurses wrapped me in warm blankets, took X-rays, and cleaned my cuts. As my shivering subsided, the doctor told me my body temperature was down to 94°F, but I had no broken bones. He wanted to keep me under observation for the next several days, so the friendly nurses took me to my room, where I immediately fell asleep.

An early-morning phone call startled me awake, and I winced at the soreness in my body. "How are you feeling?" asked Marina, the radio operator on the *Optimus Prime*.

"Not bad after going through Mother Nature's wash and rinse cycle," I answered. "There must be a few places that aren't bruised, but I haven't found them yet."

"I'm coming to town, so I can bring in your personal gear," she replied. "Your crew sends their best, and there are several people here on the *Optimus Prime* who want to say hi."

Those I talked to didn't give me any sympathy. Mostly, they gave me a hard time about taking the day off. I appreciated their caring and realized what a great bunch of people I'd been working with all summer. After hanging up, it took a while to get rid of the lump in my throat.

John Wolfe came in later to check my condition and help fill out the accident report for VRCA. When he asked how it happened, I had already given the question much thought. "There are three reasons why I fell," I said. "First, there was oil on the rocks. Second, I was worn out from working 500 hours a month. Third, shit happens."

He chuckled and asked if I needed anything. "You can get me some clothes," I answered. "I haven't told the doctor, but I'm getting out of here today."

As he left, I said, "John, thanks for giving me the chance to help clean up the spill."

Marina came, helped me check out of the hospital, and drove me to the Exxon command center, where they asked when I wanted to go back to work. "It's over for me this year," I answered. "I'm going home to Sadie Cove to recharge my mental batteries and heal my body. Will Exxon be back next spring?"

They couldn't answer my question.

Reflections

I had an oil-spill hangover! Although my part in the cleanup effort was over and I had returned to Sadie Cove to get my home ready for winter, I couldn't get the spill out of my mind. So, rather than try to block it out, I reflected on the experience.

The best way to evaluate the spill was to look at how much oil was recovered. In the Homer district alone, we shipped out 9 million pounds of contaminated material during the summer of 1989. But how much of that was oil? Experts say that on an average spill only 10 percent to 15 percent can be collected. I remembered what Exxon's Iarossi had said during a press conference in Valdez: "Prince William Sound will be as clean as before the spill." The recovery rate on the Alaska spill may be as low as 5 percent.

So are there any positive aspects of the *Exxon Valdez* oil spill? We must recognize and thank those who worked on the water and beaches to clean up the mess: coastal fishermen who used their boats and knowledge to protect the salmon hatcheries; workers who set up booms, shoveled gravel, polished rocks, and flushed the beaches; those who collected and cared for the oil-covered critters; Coast Guard and DEC personnel monitoring the work; all those who kept the fleets supplied; decision makers, who did their best; news media, who kept the public informed; environmental groups; and local volunteers.

Exxon must also receive some credit. They did eventually organize the work forces and spent more than $2 billion in the process. However, they were forced to clean up the spill and paid for most of their operation with increased gasoline prices.

After the *Exxon Valdez* hit Bligh Reef, its spilled oil affected 1,300 miles of Alaskan coastline, involved 1,300 boats and aircraft, employed 11,000 workers, and killed 100,000 birds and 1,000 sea otters. Keep in mind that these wildlife statistics reflect only those critters collected. It was the most studied oil spill in history, but will we use that knowledge to protect our environment? Only the future will give us the answer, but now we have no excuses.

I'm no expert, but after working on the Exxon disaster for five months, I gained some insights into doing a better job on future spills. First, communication is the key to better prevention, response, containment, and cleanup. Government agencies, private corporations, environmental groups, and consumers must learn how to join forces and fight pollution problems instead of each other. We are all captains of our own ships, but we sail the same sea.

Never, ever let the company guilty of creating the pollution be in charge of its cleanup, but do hold that company financially responsible.

Target high-risk areas such as Prince William Sound and establish, train, and equip local fast-response teams. Like a volunteer fire department, these teams could have other jobs, but they would be ready to react when an emergency happened.

More research and development are needed to lessen our dependency on fossil fuels and to find better ways to prevent, contain, and clean up oil spills. By perfecting the use of alternative and renewable resources, such as wind, water, tides, and the sun, we can reduce the consumption of petroleum products—the number-one cause of our pollution problems. By building safer oil tankers, developing better boom, and constructing efficient, portable gravel washers, we can help protect our environment. Polishing rocks and bagging up a beach is not the best way to save it.

How do we raise the money needed to protect and save our planet? Those who pollute must pay—both corporations and consumers. We can start by adding a $1-per-gallon state tax on gasoline.

In the fall of 1990, I sat on my deck in Sadie Cove and reflected on what had happened during the past summer. Exxon did return, but with a smaller work force. Helping with the continued cleanup effort was Joseph Hazelwood, former captain of the *Exxon Valdez*, after he was sentenced to 1,000 hours of labor on the oiled beaches. The Alaska Oil Spill Commission published its findings and recommendations while legislators passed stronger pollution laws. The environmental catastrophe was the subject of much writing, including Art Davidson's book *In the Wake of the Exxon Valdez*. Ten million pink salmon returned to the Esther Island fish hatchery, but many coastal natives were still afraid to eat traditional seafoods such as clams and mussels.

Those involved with the *Exxon Valdez* oil spill will never forget it, but it may become only a footnote in history books. Internationally, the Alaska spill was small compared to the 88-million-gallon spill created when two tankers collided off the coast of Trinidad in 1979. Further, future decision makers will continue to focus on the threat of nuclear war as one of the most critical factors to our survival, but hopefully they will understand that the fight to save our environment is also a war, and the Alaskan spill one battle in that conflict. Both wars have the same stakes: the survival of our planet and life as we know it.

During the past several million years of the earth's history, many different plants and animals have inhabited this planet, and some, like the dinosaurs, have ceased to exist because of acts of nature. Humans evolved to dominate the world and in the process have caused more extinctions. The way we are polluting our planet, we may as well place ourselves on the endangered species list. We are in the ironic position of creating the very conditions that could lead to our own extinction.

What is the solution? If enough people want change, it will happen; each individual has the power to change governments, corporations, and themselves. Each citizen can use his or her vote to elect politicians who can balance economic and environmental issues. Corporations can be pressured by their stockholders and customers into realizing that an anti-pollution policy is good business. Each individual must also analyze his or her life to reduce pollution and overconsumption.

Corporations will be the hardest to change because their operational policy is set by profit-and-loss statements. If they don't adopt environmental standards, we can apply external pressure in the form of government fines and consumer boycotts of their goods or services. Internal pressure can be applied by educating corporate employees and stockholders that quality of life extends beyond pay raises and company profits.

During the first summer of the Alaska oil spill, a friend of mine had a conversation with an Exxon employee brought up from Texas to work in the Homer command center. This person stated that in Texas the people expected and accepted the fact that they couldn't walk along their seashore without stepping on a tar ball. In Alaska, or anywhere else in the world, we don't have to lower our quality of life by accepting contamination of our environment. This Exxon employee didn't have to accept it either.

As the war on pollution continues, more pressure can be brought to bear on companies by their own concerned employees. Any man or woman who believes in protecting the planet from pollution can climb the corporate ladder to a position of authority and then use his or her power to change company policy.

After my part in the cleanup effort was over, I had a deep conversation with Rick, a long-time friend from Homer, about another casualty of the oil spill—the Alaska spirit. He and his family had moved north in the early 1960s, when people living in small towns and homesteads bartered for many of their needs, helped each other survive, and lived in harmony with the land. Rick lived through the 1964 Good Friday earthquake, and he and his Alaskan neighbors voluntarily helped each other rebuild their state.

During the late sixties to mid-seventies, a different kind of spirit settled in Alaska—greed. Oil was discovered on the North Slope, and construction began on a pipeline. Twenty-six thousand workers were needed for the largest private construction project in the world, and many people moved north for these well-paying jobs. As billions of dollars were pumped into the state, barter and subsistence living became less important.

When the *Exxon Valdez* crashed into Bligh Reef, the Alaska spirit blazed back. Cheechakos and sourdoughs alike volunteered to fight the effects of this human-made disaster. However, as Exxon spent millions of dollars to clean up the spill, their big bucks made volunteering almost impossible, and again greed set neighbor against neighbor.

Will the Alaska spirit ever be like it was before the pipeline? Maybe it will when all the oil wells have dried up and Alaskans return to a life tied closer to the land.

Afterword

Chapter
20

In 1972, I left the city and went on a Viking adventure to search for what I wanted to do with my life. I found where I wanted to live in Sadie Cove, Alaska, but my quest wasn't over. While learning to survive with nature and building my home where the mountains met the sea, I continued looking for a way to make a living. After fifteen years of selling moose manure and seven years creating and running a wilderness lodge, I started writing my book.

I began the project to promote Sadie Cove Wilderness Lodge, but now my reasons have changed. The resort is no longer in operation due to injuries I received during the Exxon oil-spill cleanup—my right shoulder doesn't work the way it did before I fell off that oily cliff into the Gulf of Alaska. And, as my book evolved, I developed a love/hate relationship with writing. I hated sitting on my butt for long stretches of time, but loved the creativity, concentration, challenge, and cathartic effect of reliving my life by writing my autobiography.

My method of scribbling the manuscript also changed. For the first two years I hand-wrote my thoughts, but then I began keyboarding the text on a Macintosh computer at home in Sadie Cove. I'm sure this modern miracle saved a whole forest of trees from being made into the paper I would have used to rewrite the book.

The computer operates on power created by the small hydroelectric system I finally built for myself on the stream. After sixteen years of Coleman lanterns, my new Pelton wheel produces more energy than I can use and allows me to live even more self-sufficiently.

This alternative energy system has another function—fire safety. The high pressure developed to operate my Pelton wheel can be diverted into a fire hose that produces a 90-foot jet of water. Now my worry isn't putting out a cabin fire, but knocking the building down. If I had had this fire-fighting capability in 1988, I could have saved the Studio from its flaming destruction.

My path hasn't always been an easy one, and I have struggled down the muddy side of life. I've shared my road with several fine women, but most of my time in Sadie has been spent alone. As an optimistic realist and a romantic, I still believe in finding that special lady, but if she never rows up to my beach, I know I can still be happy by sharing this life I have created with family and friends.

On May 18, 1980, Mount St. Helens erupted in the state of Washington. One of those who died in the explosion was Harry Truman, the man I met as a boy while attending a camp on Spirit Lake. Harry had lived in the shadow of the mountain for more than fifty years, and although he was warned about a possible eruption, he chose to stay with the life he had built rather than be evacuated. I can understand his decision—Sadie Cove will always be my home.

Living in Alaska's wilderness for the past twenty years has taught me the pleasures of hard work and to enjoy the process as well as the end result. I found personal fulfillment by building my home and lodge in Sadie Cove, selling Mooseltoe in the cities, helping clean up the *Exxon Valdez* oil spill, and writing my autobiography. Now it's time for another Viking adventure—self-publishing and promoting this book. Again all I can do is try.

Robert Frost best summed up how I feel in the last five lines of his poem "The Road Not Taken":

I shall be telling this with a sigh
Somewhere ages and ages hence:
Two roads diverged in a wood, and I—
I took the one less traveled by,
And that has made all the difference.

Index

Alaska Viking

Sponsors
of
Operation Viking

If you're interested in television advertising, we suggest you seek professional help.

Location and studio production.

Multi-format editing:

One-inch, Betacam SP, 3/4, VHS

Sophisticated effects and layering.

Video paint system.

Complete production services from script to final master.

Award winning editors.

Creative, comfortable environment.

Quality video duplication.

The Videoplex
3700 Woodland Drive, Suite 700
Anchorage, AK 99517
907 • 248-9999

907 • 235-8406

HOMER SAW

FACTORY SALES & SERVICE
Stihl • Husqvarna
Moniter • Polaris

Mikel Bensend
R. E. Bob Schmutzler
Claire Waxman

1529 Ocean Drive
Homer, Alaska
99603

FOOD FOR PEOPLE AND THE PLANET

235-7571
1316 Ocean Drive
Homer, Alaska 99603

Ishmalof Lodge

P. O. Box 6430
Halibut Cove, Alaska 99603

907 • 296-2217
(year around)

907 • 235-3888
(summer home)

907 • 296-2200
(FAX)

Beluga Lake Float Plane Service Air Charters

Jon M. Berryman

P. O. Box 2072
Homer, Alaska 99603
907 • 235-8256

SAIL PATRONILLA
An American Classic

Capt. Joe Bennett

1220 Rosecrans • Suite 251
San Diego, CA 92106
619 • 291-7122

LINDA GUNNARSON
Editor ❧ Publishing Consultant

66 Alida Street
Ashland, OR 97520
503 • 482-4971

Homer Ocean Charters, Inc.
235-6212 or 563-4188

ALASKA'S BEST FISHING
1986 Halibut Derby Winners

DAY CHARTERS
FISHING SAFARIS

Sea Witch
Sourdough

P. O. Box 91268 • Anchorage, Alaska • 99509

Homer Secretarial Services

Loretta Marx
Pat Springer

1213 Ocean Drive
P. O. Box 1613
Homer, Alaska 99603
907 • 235-7766

- Court Reporting
- Résumés
- Word Processing
- Answering service
- Courier Service
- Copies
- Mail Pick-up/Forwarding

Back Country Gallery
Bed & Breakfast

Kirk Nelson
907 • 235-6952

SUNSET RIDGE INN

HC 67 Box 918
Anchor Point, AK 99556

Beachcombers Restaurant

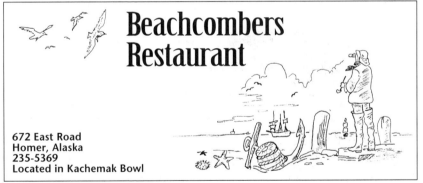

672 East Road
Homer, Alaska
235-5369
Located in Kachemak Bowl

Quality Outdoor/Clothing & Equipment

Quiet Sports

SALES & RENTALS

Dan Delmissier
Owner/Manager

144 W. Pioneer • Homer, Alaska 99603 • 907/235-8620

MUGS and JUGS

Original
Handpainted Ceramics

Created by
Alaskan Artists

Linda Feiler

Box 148
Anchor Point
Alaska 99556
907 • 235-8457

We Ship Anywhere

Milepost 156 Sterling Highway

**Homer Spit
Alaska**

SALTY DAWG

235-9990

SALOON

Long 151°25"10' W
Lat 59°36"9' N

**DOCKSIDE
HOMER, ALASKA**

4460 Homer Spit Road

"Overlooking Homer Harbor"

907 • 235-8337

HALIBUT CHARTERS

GULL ISLAND CRUISES

GIFT SHOP

DELI

D O C K S I D E

Laundry • Showers • Dry Cleaning

Russ & Vicki Blaine

Homer Cleaning Center

3684 Main Street
Homer, Alaska 99603
235-5152

In Memory of
Carl E. Wynn
December 1895 — February 1988

He was born in a log cabin at Rolla, Missouri. His philantrophic activities were many. Carl pursued a lifelong interest in nature, wildlife and the preservation of endangered species. He built a multi-million dollar worldwide business as a supplier of automotive parts and accessories, petrochemical speciality products and builders' hardware supplies.

Carl enthusiastically supported me and my book. He will be missed.

Rest in peace.

Hal Gage
Gage Photo Graphics

Commercial Photography
Graphic Design

2008 E. Northern Lights Boulevard
Anchorage, Alaska 99508-4101

907 • 272-4356

Shannon Weiss
Illusions Too

Graphic Design
Macintosh Training
& Consulting

3305 Oregon Drive
Anchorage, Alaska 99517
907 • 276-8590

Sadie Cove General Store

R & P Publishing
P. O. Box 2265-A
Homer, Alaska 99603
907 • 235-2350

Please send me the following items:

Description	Price	Quantity	Total
Alaska Viking	$13.95 each		
Mooseltoe*	$5.00 each		
Alaskan Moose Manure*	$3.00 each		
*Product description next page	**Shipping**		
	Total		

- Send check or money order (no cash or C.O.D.) payable to R & P Publishing
- Please add $1.50 for each item to cover shipping and handling.
- Canadian orders: Please adjust total with current exchange rate.
- Any item may be returned for a full refund if not completely satisfied.

Name _____

Address_____

City/State/Zip _____

Allow 4–6 weeks for delivery.
This offer is subject to withdrawal without notice.

Pg 18
37 - 6 16. herring

MOOSELTOE

Mooscience has proved beyond question that wherever Mooseltoe hangs, romance blooms. Charm a chandelier, decorate a doorway, enrich any room with your Mooseltoe; then Be Prepared. Expect not merely more kisses but moosier kisses. (If you've ever been kisses by a moose, you know what we mean.) Love will be lovelier, indeed.

ALASKAN MOOSE MANURE (POOP FOR PLANTS)

Treat all your plants with our clean, odorless, 100% organic fertilizer. More than just a darn good manure. A humorous descriptive booklet included. Guaranteed to be a conversation piece at cocktail parties, smokers, Bar Mitzvahs, county fairs, and goat ropings.